Interactive Learning

The Art and Science of Teaching

Norman W. Steinaker and Lorraine S. Leavitt

National University

KENDALL/HUNT PUBLISHING COMPANY
4050 Westmark Drive   Dubuque, Iowa 52002

Photo Credits:

Section Openers:
Close-up of girl's face: Image © Carlos Caetano, 2008. Used under license from Shutterstock, Inc.
Male teacher: Image © 2008 JupiterImages Corporation.
Girl at drawing board: Image © Lisa F. Young, 2008. Used under license from Shutterstock, Inc.
Boy at computer: Image © Thomas M. Perkins, 2008. Used under license from Shutterstock, Inc.
Woman at desk: Image © 2008 JupiterImages Corporation.
Girl using microscope: Image © Laurence Gough, 2008. Used under license from Shutterstock, Inc.
Teacher at student's desk: Image © 2008 JupiterImages Corporation.
Classroom: Image © Lisa F. Young, 2008. Used under license from Shutterstock, Inc.

Chapter Openers:
Male teacher: Image © 2008 JupiterImages Corporation.
Woman at desk: Image © 2008 JupiterImages Corporation.
Classroom: Image © Lisa F. Young, 2008. Used under license from Shutterstock, Inc.

Contents:
Page iii: Image © 2008 JupiterImages Corporation.
Page iv: Image © Thomas M. Perkins, 2008. Used under license from Shutterstock, Inc.
Page v: Image © Lisa F. Young, 2008. Used under license from Shutterstock, Inc.
Page vi: Image © 2008 JupiterImages Corporation.
Page vii: Image © Lisa F. Young, 2008. Used under license from Shutterstock, Inc.
Page viii: Image © 2008 JupiterImages Corporation.

Interior:
Pages 21, 32, 43, 67: Image © PhotoCreate, 2008. Used under license from Shutterstock, Inc.
Page 58: Image © Lorraine Swanson, 2008. Used under license from Shutterstock, Inc.
Pages 77, 115, 191: Image © Andresr, 2008. Used under license from Shutterstock, Inc.
Page 170: Image © WizData, inc, 2008. Used under license from Shutterstock, Inc.

Cover Images:
Girl with Teacher: Image © Bobby Deal/Real Deal Photo, 2007. Used under license from Shutterstock, Inc.
Boy: Image © artproem, 2007. Used under license from Shutterstock, Inc.
Girl at desk: Image © iofoto, 2007. Used under license from Shutterstock, Inc.
Two students with laptop: Image © Cryptos, 2007. Used under license from Shutterstock, Inc.
Four students: Image © iofoto, 2007. Used under license from Shutterstock, Inc.
Background letters: Image © Milan Ljubisavljevic, 2007. Used under license from Shutterstock, Inc.

Contents

 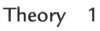 **Theory   1**

section 2   Organization   85

Instruction   121

Preface

A century ago when asked what is an effective teacher the answer would be "A good teacher is a good person" or "An upstanding citizen who keeps children in line." As our society has become more complex, so has the effective role teachers need to take. Although the traditional ideal is still somewhat relevant, it is a fraction of how we define and what we need effective teachers to be. Today we have a more complex understanding of who students are and how they learn. An effective teacher must be a multifaceted and equally talented educator. Hence, we need teachers to embrace interactive learning as the art and science of teaching flourish.

The study of teaching is not a dispassionate process. The contention between the art and science of teaching is a fundamental debate we often require novice instructors to analyze. This book is poised to become a seminal work in the field of education. It captures the fusion of the art and science of teaching and explains how to accomplish this successfully in one's own classroom.

Interactive learning is one of the most influential concepts to have emerged from research on teaching and learning in the last two decades. New understandings have raised questions in regard to the traditional customs of transmitting knowledge. It is widely accepted among educators that teaching and learning are two different and distinct functions. If the teaching and learning processes are to work effectively, a unique kind of connection must exist between the two. In addition, educators and researchers increasingly recognize the role students play in productive learning environments. Inquiry, discovery, exploration, and connecting to peers are of keen importance in the instructional process.

The book originates in the real day-to-day world of the practice of teaching. It represents the distillation of a lifetime of teaching in many learning environments. As opposed to a memoir of war stories in the classroom, it is intended as a reference for educators who seek ways to stimulate their learning environments in a systematic way. It moves readers to strive beyond the perfunctory task of transmitting knowledge in a manner that forms learners into passive receptors. Readers come to understand the components and synergy created when teachers engage in transformative instruction.

This is an excellent book written for beginning teachers who are considering how to achieve a variety of learning outcomes. In each of the chapters the theoretical framework and rationale of interactive learning is discussed. Theory is then carried through to a tangible plan of action, thus removing abstract impediments. The book is also a superb reference for more experienced educators because it embodies a powerful educational philosophy. Experienced educators may find either reassurance or guidance by reading this volume. The teaching practices explained in this book can easily be extended from private to public schools, to urban school settings and others such as rural or suburban schools.

For some readers this volume could change their understanding of what teaching means as interactive learning offers a broader, deeper perspective on teaching and learning in the classroom. Conversely, the quality of student learning is fundamentally dependent on the action taken. Interactive learning is a call to action.

Valerie Amber, Ed.D.
Assistant Professor
Teacher Education
National University

Acknowledgments

We want, first of all, to acknowledge the scholars, practitioners, and researchers in education whose work has inspired and informed us and has guided us as we developed this book. We want to thank Marvin Holm, Cathy Booth and Garrick Le for their ideas, insights and contributions to the work. Particular thanks to Marvin who helped implement the ideas in this work, to Cathy who reviewed the work and encouraged us to look for wider audiences and to Garrick who was a strong help for any technology issues we faced. We especially want to thank our colleagues at National University including Valerie Amber, Terry Bustillos, Marilyn Koeller, and James Mbuva for their encouragement and friendship. They made suggestions, gave ideas, and were with us throughout the process of preparing this manuscript.

On a personal note we want to thank our spouses and our families. We first want to thank Blanche and Ned who were so supportive, thoughtful, and caring through the writing process. Their patience and their love have meant so much to us. We could not have done it without their love and constancy. We also want honor Lorraine's parents Alex and Blanche Schulman for their encouragement.

Introduction

Teaching is both an art and a science. The art is the interactive component of the teaching–learning act. It could be said that good teaching is good human relating. This definition summarizes the art of teaching. The science of teaching is the analysis of how teaching and learning is done and the process by which it is accomplished. The how of teaching and learning is a result of a joint effort by both the teacher and the students. In this work our purpose is to explore and analyze both the "how" and "why" of teaching. We further believe teachers can analyze any lesson. We have identified seventeen components of teaching and learning and demonstrate how they can be used for analysis of any specified lesson. We feel it is incumbent on every teacher and those in charge of training in any profession to understand the teaching–learning process and to be able to analyze the process. They need to know that the task is to value students, value the area of study, and help the student to change the intangible to the tangible. This can be done by recognizing interaction as symbolic of the art of teaching and being able to study the "how" and "why" of teaching and learning through the format for analysis presented in these seventeen strands of teaching and learning as they are illustrated through the five categories of interactive learning.

This work is divided into three sections, each with its own introductory statements. The first part concerns theory and is presented in chapters 1 through 6. In these chapters we first provide an overview; then all the strands are discussed in terms of each category of the interactive taxonomy. In the second part of the work we focus on organization. We discuss learning activities in chapter 8 and group structures in chapter 9. The third part focuses on Instruction. We have defined five teaching–learning strategies for each category of the taxonomy. The final chapter on implementation is added so that you can ponder how you could implement the taxonomy in your own classroom. In that chapter we share some of the ways that the taxonomy has been implemented. It is important to understand the theory, learn how to organize your classroom for interactive learning, and then provide you with teaching–learning strategies that you can implement and use in your classes.

In this work we focus on interactive learning as a methodological sequence of learning. We review the process of teaching and learning through the five categories of interactive learning. Then we present teaching activities at each level of the taxonomy and identify seventeen group formats and organizations. We continue with chapters on planning and change, and close with a chapter on implementation of the taxonomy. For us, interactive learning is the *modus operandi* of teaching and the *modus vivendi* for learning. Interactive learning is a necessary beginning to the process of learning and must be central to student achievement. Interactive learning can be understood as the reader recognizes and follows the seventeen strands of interaction present in every lesson. In sum, we present, in this work, an analysis of the teaching–learning process that can help teachers not only understand the process, but become active participants within it. We provide a format for analysis of interactive learning in seventeen ways. This analysis of the teaching–learning act is unique in that we define and discuss each of the seventeen strands of interactive learning through all categories of this taxonomy. These strands of interactive learning are cognition, experience, teacher roles, student roles, evaluation, motivation, discourse, creativity, critical thinking, problem solving, writing, thinking, learning, teaching, and leadership. Each of these strands is discussed as they relate to each of the five categories of interactive learning. We ourselves have developed several of the strands. The experiential, critical thinking, creativity, and problem-solving strands were first published by Steinaker and Bell in 1979. They also developed the teacher and student roles and the evaluation roles. The writing taxonomy was developed by Steinaker and Bustillos (2007). For this work we have developed the strands of motivation, discourse, thinking, learning, teaching, and leadership roles for teachers and students. We also conceived and developed the interactive learning taxonomy. The cognitive taxonomy was developed by Bloom, Englehart, Furst, Hill, and Krathwohl (1956). We did not include their affective and psychomotor taxonomies because they are implicit within other strands.

We discuss thinking, learning, and teaching in a way that is different from usual discussions of cognition, teacher roles, and student roles. For us, these three are identifiable strands for which there needs to be a specific focus. We have provided that focus and have shown how they are demonstrated at each category of the taxonomy of interactive learning.

This work is a guidebook on the *art of teaching* which is expressively presented through the interactive activities and group work at every category of the taxonomy. In addition we present, through what we term the *science of teaching*, sequences on how teaching and learning are achieved and how they are demonstrated. You will find in the activities listed at the end of each chapter problems, questions, and issues that you can be involved with to help you analyze what teaching and learning are all about. These activities, for the most part, focus on the science of teaching. When you have finished this work and have completed the suggested activities, you will understand both the art of teaching and the science of teaching.

At this point we need to illustrate our system. The table provided illustrates the strands of learning we have used for analysis of the teaching–learning process. The taxonomy on which we have organized the work is the interactive learning strand.

We have taken each of these instructional strands and keyed them to the interactive learning taxonomy. In the first five chapters of this work we have traced how they fit into each category of the taxonomy of interactive learning. As you read this work you can see how these strands fit together during the instructional process. We have used them in discussion groups, teaching–learning activities, and teaching–learning strategies.

Interactive learning, as we have defined it, is a strong and viable way to not only to engage the students, but also to augment their learning. Well planned and carefully implemented, interactive learning can be an outstanding structure and organization for helping students learn. It can motivate students to learn, ensure their involvement in learning, and help them participate in learning. They not only participate in planning and developing the learning process, but they also can work with the teacher in evaluating their learning. Interactive learning can be implemented at any grade level from kindergarten through graduate school. We believe that learning is a process of active involvement, shared understanding, and implementing and using learning in a variety of settings and contexts, and interactive learning can be carefully sequenced and planned, ensuring that the students are creatively involved in the process. Teachers need to know how to ensure that this occurs. They also need to know how to use these strands for instructional analysis and for personal lesson planning. Through these analyses, teachers can come to a clearer understanding of the process through which learning takes place.

Interactive learning is a sequential development through the process of learning as it progresses within the five categories of what we have termed the taxonomy of interactive learning. These five categories are invitation, involvement, investigation, insight, and implementation. Concomitant with these categories of learning are categories or taxonomies describing teacher roles, student roles, evaluator roles, motivation, discourse, critical thinking, creativity, problem solving, and writing. Further, we use the experiential taxonomy developed by Steinaker and Bell (1979). The levels of experiential taxonomy are exposure, participation, identification, internalization,

Taxonomies Used for Instructional Analysis

Interactive Learning	Cognition	Teacher Role	Student Role	Evaluation
Invitation	Memory	Motivator	Attender	Observer
Involvement	Translation	Catalyst	Explorer	Questioner
Investigation	Interpretation	Moderator	Experimenter	Assessor
Insight	Application	Sustainer	Extender	Measurer
Implementation	Analysis	Critiquor	Influencer	Determiner
	Synthesis			
	Evaluation			

Motivation	Discourse	Creativity	Critical Thinking	Writing
Readiness	Condition	Need	Recognizing Variable	Define
Relationships	Challenge	Visualizing	Defining Variable	Describe
Rapport	Connection	Experimenting	Organizing	Detail
Respect	Communication	Completing	Generalizing	Discuss
Responsibility	Consideration	Showing	Using Variable	Determine
	Change			

Problem Solving	Thinking	Learning	Teaching	Experience
Problem Identification	Sensing	Responding	Engaging	Exposure
Exploring Data	Apprehending	Personalizing	Particularizing	Participation
Trying Options	Accepting	Interacting	Functionalizing	Identification
Selecting Solution	Modification	Contextualizing	Verifying	Internalization
Implementing	Extending	Expressing	Sharing	Dissemination

Teacher/Leadership	Student/Leadership
Preparer	Participant
Coordinator	Cooperator
Resolver	Investigator
Adviser	Creator
Consultant	Disseminator

and dissemination. For each category of the taxonomy of learning, these roles work together. Finally, we also consider cognitive taxonomy. Developed by Bloom and his colleagues (1956), Anderson and Krathwohl (2001) revised the taxonomy again with six categories. Forehand (2005) further commented on their work. This taxonomy of cognition has been the identified standard for processing and learning information. We have used a later interpretation, where there are seven levels of cognition (Sanders 1961; Giffi and Dean 1974). These are memory, translation, interpretation, application, analysis, synthesis, and evaluation. We will identify them within the five levels of the taxonomy of interactive learning. We have not included, however, psychomotor or affective taxonomies.

Through a carefully sequenced and well-planned series of learning activities, each of these roles is explained and developed. We feel all these roles are closely linked in the development of lessons toward ensuring optimum learning. We also believe that a single lesson can encompass some or all of the levels of the taxonomy of interactive learning. For us, every lesson requires interaction between teacher and students, among students, and among students with resources. Learning is done in a community where students and teacher learn from each other and where there is an interactive and positive climate for learning. This is what we are about in this work. We want to share this vision of interactive learning and help you learn how you can begin to use this exciting concept of interactive learning in your instructional assignment.

In this work, we develop the idea of interaction by discussing each category of the taxonomy of interactive learning and the concomitant roles described earlier. In chapter 1 we define the taxonomy of interactive learning, and identify and discuss the roles and strands that correlate with the taxonomy. We also provide an overview of interactive learning, because it is important for teacher use and for student learning that there is a clear overview of the process of learning. Here we begin reviewing both the art and science of teaching.

In chapter 2 we define and describe the initial level of the taxonomy of interactive learning, which is invitation. It is important to prepare students to become engaged in the learning experience. How students can experience active engagement in the learning process is the major focus of this chapter. In terms of lesson analysis, the teacher role is that of a presenter. The student role is as an attender. In terms of evaluation, the role is that of an observer. For motivation, the role is readiness both on the part of the teacher and the student. Condition is the first category for discourse. In terms of creativity, the students come to a condition of wanting to create a product. Critical thinking involves recognizing. The problem-solving role is the identification of the problem. When students write, their role is defining. For the process of thinking, the initial level is sensory. Learning begins with responding, while the invitation level for teaching is engaging. In cognition, the levels are memory and translation. Each role will be presented fully and carefully developed so you can understand how invitation to learning is professionally accomplished, and is achieved and understood by students.

In chapter 3, the second category in the taxonomy of interactive learning is presented, which is involvement. Involvement is a unique and interesting category. Here students become actively involved with the lessons. They begin to work together to accomplish various kinds of learning in which they have decided to become involved. Here the teacher role is catalyst, a term that describes what the teacher does during this important step in the instructional process. The student role is that of an explorer. The role of questioner defines the work of the evaluator. The role for motivation is developing working relationships. The discourse roles are making a connection through challenge. For creativity, the role at this level of the taxonomy of interactive learning is visualization. Problem solving brings the student to the role of discovery. The role for critical thinking at this level is interrogating. When writing, at this level, the role is to describe. The thinking level here is apprehension. Learning at this level involves responding. In terms of teaching at this level, the category is particularizing. In terms of the levels of cognition, translation correlates with this level of interactive learning. Each of these roles is fully explicated and linked together as the learning sequence moves through the involvement level of the taxonomy.

The third level of the taxonomy is discussed in chapter 4. Learning level three in this taxonomy is investigation. The other roles correlate smoothly with this defined level of interactive learning. The teacher role moves from catalyst during the involvement level to that of a moderator during the investigation level of learning. The student role is that of an explorer, which coincides well within this level of learning. Evaluation is shown through the role of assessor while in motivation students are building rapport. Change involves communication here and critical thinking is developed through organizing. Creativity is noted as doing the activities visualized in level two of the taxonomy. Problem solving engages the learner in discovery. Writing at this level brings out detail. The term in the thinking sequence at this category of the taxonomy that best describes what is happening is acceptance. This level of learning is personalizing and in terms of teaching the level is interactive, which correlates directly to this category of the taxonomy. Cognition is demonstrated through application. Interactive learning at this level in the total context is active and investigative for the learner. The roles, strategies, and components of this category of interactive learning are fully explained here.

Insight is the fourth level in the taxonomy of learning and is the focus of chapter 5. It is here that the students begin to internalize what they have learned and use their learning in a variety of contexts. The teacher role as sustainer exemplifies this. The student role is that of an extender, where the learning is transferred to additional contexts. The evaluation role at the insight level is that of a measurer. Motivation at this category is described by the term respect. For change the term is consideration. Critical thinking is observed as generalizing while creativity is completing. In the role of selecting a solution, problem solving is demonstrated. In terms of writing, the learner is involved in discussing the topic. Thinking is represented at this level as modification. Learning has been noted to be contextualizing. Teaching at this level of the taxonomy is functionalizing. It is at this level of the taxonomy of learning that students internalize the skills or attitudes encompassed within the learning experience. Cognition is represented by application and synthesis. These strands of interactive learning are discussed in full here.

The final level in the taxonomy of interactive learning is implementation, which is discussed in chapter 6. This category of interactive learning is sometimes overlooked by teachers and students, but it is an essential component of the total learning experience. Here all the roles represent the dissemination level of experience—thus the name implementation. In this category, which encompasses the use and sharing of what has been learned, the roles change from intrinsic to extrinsic. For the teacher at this level, the role is that of a critiquor. This role encompasses both a critique of the experience and of the movement toward new learning experiences. The student role at this level is that of an influencer, which also exemplifies implementation and sharing. In terms of evaluation, the final level is that of a determiner, who evaluates the totality of the experience. Motivation is shown by students demonstrating responsibility for their achievement and the sharing of what they have learned. Change is implemented at this level of learning. This kind of change is what is implemented to form a new context for the topic. Critical thinking is finalized with the term of utilizing. Creativity involves sharing and showing at this level of learning. Problem solving is demonstrated through implementing the chosen solution. In the writing process, the level is demonstrated through determining. Thinking culminates here as extension. Learning is expressed in this final category as expressing and teaching is finalized as sharing. Finally, cognition is represented by evaluation. Each of these strands in the learning process comes together at this final level of the taxonomy of learning. These initial chapters involve a discussion of each category of the taxonomy of interactive learning.

In chapter 7, a series of classroom activities is presented. These activities are correlated with the levels of the learning experience noted earlier. They include a variety of instructional activities usually done in groups. All of the activities can be implemented in classrooms from elementary through graduate school. The use of these activities at all categories of the taxonomy demonstrates the power of interactive learning. A rationale for their use in interactive learning is included.

In chapter 8 we present interactive group structures. In all, we present seventeen group formats and structures. These are cooperative groups, focus groups, pairs, triads, dialectic groups, jigsaw groups, roving groups, two kinds of numbered groups, flexible groups, problem-solving groups, exploratory groups, single-task groups, panel discussions, critiquor groups, and whole-class groups. They are specifically defined and linked to the categories of the taxonomy of interactive learning. We recommend the use of these group structures and group strategies in all classrooms. We include a variety of group structures at every category of interaction. Many can be used at all school levels. Some are specific to particular grade levels.

In chapters 9 through 13, teaching strategies for each category of the taxonomy are presented. For each category of the taxonomy, there are five teaching strategies. In all, twenty-five strategies are included. At the invitation category they are incentive exposition, data presentation, demonstration, directed observation, and interactive data review. For involvement, the strategies are linking, reviewing data, unstructured role-playing, participatory hands-on activities, and ordering. At investigation, the teaching–learning strategies are field activities/making connections, applying data, interacting/showing/conferencing, hypothesizing, and testing. For insight, the strategies are skill reinforcement, re-creation, simulation/role playing, comparative contrastive analysis, and summarization. At implementation the strategies are reporting, oral and visual presentations, dramatization, group dynamics, and seminar. Each teaching–learning strategy is specifically defined. Its use in the classroom and how it can be implemented are discussed. Strategies are linked to group activities and to group formats and structures.

In chapter 14 a format for lesson planning through the taxonomy of interactive learning is presented. After demonstrating the structure for lesson planning at each category of the taxonomy, we include a lesson-planning format. This lesson-planning format is one that can be used at all grade levels. It is simple to use, yet professional in its structure and organization.

The change process is presented and discussed in chapter 15. We felt that we needed to expand on the change process as described in chapters 2 through 6 because, for us, change is the very essence of teaching and learning. It was important to do this and show how it worked with cognition, problem solving, critical thinking, and creativity. We also included some comments on critical pedagogy and how it works with our system of lesson analysis. Further, we provided our own interpretation of critical pedagogy that summarizes our view of the change process through critical pedagogy. In this chapter the teacher is provided with a view of change from our perspective. Finally, chapter 16 shows how to implement the taxonomy both from a historical perspective and from current practice. The book concludes with a brief end note. Also included are references and three appendices. They are: Appendix A: Interactive Lesson Planner, pages 197–198; Appendix B: Completing the Interactive Lesson Planner, pages 199–201; and Appendix C: SDAIE Strategies, pages 203–204.

Every chapter includes activities for students using this text. These activities are at the end of the chapter. They are designed to be completed in small groups. Appropriate time should be provided for students to complete the assigned activities. The activities are broad based and require the use of this text as a resource and reference. Students are encouraged to use any additional resources that may be available to them. We felt it was important that students be engaged in activities that will cause them to ponder, to review, to prepare reports, and to really get into the theory, the organization, and the instructional processes presented in this work. The use of the activities will add a necessary dimension to understanding interactive learning and toward a professional understanding of the totality of the teaching–learning process.

As can be seen from the content of this work, we firmly believe interactive learning is a responsible and effective way to organize the classroom and to develop learning sequences that have meaning and substance for both students and teachers. Interactive learning encompasses both the art of teaching and the science of teaching. For us it is the touchstone to learning and an approach that is needed in all classrooms from preschool through graduate school. This is what teachers must do to provide an environment and learning climate that will result in augmented student learning. The classroom is a community where students and teacher learn together and communicate ideas and information to each other in a collegial setting. Thus far, the foundations for interactive learning have been established and the whole process has been outlined. In the following pages this interactive learning process will be developed, discussed, explained, and explicated.

There are two ways of reading this work. The first is to read through each category of the taxonomy of interactive learning and find out how all the components of interaction work together at each category. Through this approach you can see the whole structure of the learning experience at each category of the taxonomy of interaction. This way you can understand how learning takes place and the interactive structure in which it happens. Once you understand this, you can then turn to the foundations sections and the material on simulation, motivation, and lifelong learning to gain the full picture of this analysis of interactive learning. In this first method, you can gain insight into the science of teaching and see how the teaching–learning act can be analyzed in terms of teaching the elements we have identified.

The second way is to go through each of the chapters dealing with the categories of the taxonomy by following each component. Through this kind of reading you can sense the art of teaching and how each component plus the interactive opportunities is linked together to provide a positive perspective into the artistic mosaic of teaching and learning. You could, for example, read the sections on the role of the teacher in each of the chapters. Then you could go to another strand and follow that through until you have completed the reading. After this, you could go to the foundations chapters and the ones on simulation, motivation, and lifelong learning to complete your study of the taxonomy of interactive learning. Each approach is valid, and serves as an instructional tool for teachers to become more effective in delivering the lessons and working closely and effectively with students in an interactive lively learning setting.

Finally, we suggest, this work is an impetus to research into teaching and learning. Not only can teachers use it, but also researchers. Every one of the seventeen strands can be studied. This, in effect, is a basic work on teaching and learning. It provides a professional base for understanding the teaching–learning act and a way to do qualitative or quantitative research on classroom interaction. The work provides theory, organization, and instruction. In this sense this work is unique because it provides a theoretical base and then a way to organize your class and define ways you can engage students in a strong learning environment. Use the book as you assess and analyze your own teaching, as you organize your class for interactive learning, and as you develop strategies for a vibrant instructional program. Through its use we feel you can learn about how you teach and why you teach, helping you become a more effective professional.

Costa Mesa, CA
January 2008

Theory

First it is important to share with you the theoretical base for interactive learning. Theory is the groundwork of teaching and learning. Theory causes us to ruminate on why we are teaching, how we are teaching, and what the purpose of our teaching might be. Every teacher needs to have a firm grounding in theory to become the best teacher possible. Students need to understand what they are learning and why. Theory is about knowing, but it is also about valuing and implementing those understandings and values. Theory tells us why. Organization tells us how. Instruction tells us what and how. We know that theory without organization and instruction is not viable. We know that organization and instruction are not significant without theory. This is why we focus on these three as a *gestalt* approach to the teaching–learning act.

Our theory is organized around the taxonomy of interactive learning with the five categories of invitation, involvement, investigation, insight, and implementation. These categories of interactive learning provide the framework around which is built a sequence (you can call it a taxonomy) of five levels for the sixteen other strands: cognition, teacher roles, student roles, evaluation, motivation, discourse, creativity, critical thinking, writing, problem solving, thinking, learning, teaching, experience, teacher leadership, and student leadership. As mentioned in the introduction, cognition was developed by Bloom and his colleagues (1956). Teacher roles, student roles, evaluation, creativity, critical thinking, problem solving, and experience were developed and published by Steinaker and Bell (1979). We have worked on motivation for several years. We worked with Marvin Holm, and James Mbuva worked with us in developing some ideas on motivation; we are grateful for their contributions. We created the taxonomy of motivation in our strands. Discourse, thinking, learning, teaching, teacher leadership, and student leadership we developed ourselves. The writing strand was prepared by Steinaker and Bustillos (2007). In all, we used seventeen strands for our theory base and for our format for lesson analysis.

In this section the theory is organized into six chapters. In the first chapter we have provided an overview of the total process of interactive learning with a brief discussion of each of the seventeen strands. It is important that you review chapter 1 carefully because it is there you are introduced to the frame of reference and to each of the strands. Each strand is important for you to learn as you focus on becoming an effective teacher. In chapters 2 through 6 we show how each of the strands is identified and used at each of the five categories of the taxonomy of interactive learning. We do this in some detail so you will have an operant perspective on how each strand is used at each category of the taxonomy. We want you to study these descriptions and perspectives and think about how you could recognize a particular strand at that particular category of interactive learning. It is important that you discuss each strand and how it relates to other strands. Learn the meaning of each strand and how you can trace that thread through all five categories.

We suggest that there are two ways of reading through this theory section. Read chapter 1 thoroughly and discuss it in your small groups. Once you have understood how the work is organized and know the categories and the strands, you can choose how you want to read the rest of the theory chapters. You may, as many have done, want to read and discuss each category, including all the strands. In this way you could really understand how instruction is delivered and understood at invitation first and then move to involvement, investigation, insight, and finally implementation. A second way to read this work is to take one strand and read about it at each category of the taxonomy. After you finish with one strand, you can move on to another until you finish with all the strands.

Regardless of how you decide to read this section, we want you to thoroughly understand the theory and how it is represented at each category of interactive learning. This is very important because we want you to know the taxonomy and all its strands before you move on to other sections of the book.

We close this introduction to the theory section by suggesting that you do lesson analyses of your own teaching or observe another teacher working with students. Perhaps you may want to do research using this theory. You could do research on a single strand, several strands, or the lesson as a whole. Whatever you do, use the theory, follow the organizational suggestions, and develop instruction based on the teaching–learning strategies, group structures, and suggested teaching–learning activities. Remember the theory, organize carefully, and instruct strongly.

Interactive Learning

Interactive learning is a dynamic interactive discourse between the teacher and the students, between students and resources, and among students. Interactive learning encompasses all content areas and all dimensions of learning. Interactive learning is good human relating. Positive relationships are essential to interactive learning. Interactive learning can be used at any age level from infancy, to maturity, and throughout life. Human beings learn most effectively through interactive contexts. We learn best in settings where we can relate to one another and to the resources available to us. We need verbal interaction and written communication to process ideas and perspectives. Interactive learning helps provide these kinds of learning communities. The art of good human relating is intrinsic to internalized learning. Teaching and learning is also a science. Interactive learning involves curriculum, planning, the use of teaching–learning strategies, developing learning sequences, and the use of teaching models. Interactive learning involves an understanding of cognition (Bloom et al. 1956), the learning process, the experiential taxonomy, and the sequence of the learning process (Steinaker and Bell 1979). Through discourse, the process of change is demonstrated. Not only is the process of change demonstrated, but the development of the skills and abilities needed to implement change are learned (Steinaker 2003b). Motivation can be identified and is in place in every category of interactive learning. Motivation is a key element to the learning process. Motivation is a process, initiated by the teacher and demonstrated by the students. The teacher roles and the student roles in motivation change from category to category. In the implementation category, the change results in the students assuming responsibility for their learning. Motivation correlates closely with the levels of interactive teaching and learning.

In addition to including the cognitive taxonomy in our work, we want to introduce three other taxonomic sequences that bring new constructs to the teaching–learning process. We have identified them as thinking, learning, and teaching (Steinaker 2002). Thinking is the process of associating stimuli and information to experience. This is a different way of analyzing and assessing thinking that broadens cognition. Learning is the process that relates thinking to actions, feelings, and skills. Teaching is the process of valuing actions, feelings, and skills (Steinaker 2002). Before we begin to analyze the strands of the instructional process through the first level of the taxonomy, we should introduce the steps in the sequences of thinking, learning, and teaching so there is a clear understanding of

> *Interactive learning is a dynamic interactive discourse between the teacher and the students, between students and resources, and among students.*

the steps in these processes. There is a sequence to each of these processes. Thinking involves the following steps or tasks:

Sensory: The learner senses or receives stimuli through visual, aural, kinesthetic, or olfactory means or any combination of the senses. This level of thinking is used in the invitation level of the taxonomy.

Apprehension: The learner focuses on the stimuli and orders or arranges the stimuli into a reactive framework. This is most evident in the involvement level of interactive learning.

Acceptance: The learner identifies an association in terms of past experience. At this point the association has limited or no meaning or value as an action or behavior. Investigation is the level at which this level of thinking is most apparent.

Modification: The learner relates the association to past experience, which results in a modified perspective or point of view. Modification is apparent at the insight level of interactive learning.

Extension: The association is extended to another point of view, a new focus, a skill, or a new action or behavior. Extension is evidenced at the involvement level of interactive learning (Steinaker 2002:2–3).

Learning is also represented through a series of activities represented by a five-level sequence. It should be noted that these levels of learning correspond to the taxonomy sequentially. These levels of learning are as follows:

Responding: The learner tests the thought and thinking processes in terms of feelings and actions and expands the feelings or actions within a larger purview of experience. The learner visualizes or conceptualizes a direction, an attitude, a response, or a value.

Personalizing: Verbalizing or trying out the feelings, actions, or skills in terms of personal meaning. Gathering additional information and projecting a value.

Interacting: Communicating, sharing, discussing, interpreting, and interacting with the feelings, actions, or skills either personally or in the context of a socializing or group association. Identifying a value.

Contextualizing: The step in the process when learning becomes a valued behavior, skill, attitude, or action within the learner's experience. Accepting and acting on a value for the behavior, skill, action, or attitude.

Expressing: The dissemination or use of the action, skill, concept, feeling, or behavior within a personal value construct and expressing it with others (Steinaker 2002:3).

Teaching, too, involves a sequence of actions that encompasses a learning experience and interaction with students. The steps in this sequence are as follows:

Engaging: The teacher posits a value or values in a context of positive or expected outcomes and provides background, data, and stimuli for the students.

Particularizing: The teacher focuses the students on the process of achieving the valued outcomes.

Functionalizing: The teacher works with the student in a walk-through or tryout of the feeling, action, skill, concept, or behavior. The student is able to perform the action or demonstrate or describe the skill, behavior, concept, or feeling.

Verifying: The teacher supports the student in progressing toward internalization, analysis, synthesis, and evaluation of the feeling, action, skill, concept, or behavior and it becomes a part of the student's living and learning contexts.

Sharing: The teacher helps the student transfer the learned action, feeling, skill, concept, or behavior to a new context or to disseminate what has been learned to others (Steinaker 2002:5–6).

These three sequences that involve thinking, learning, and teaching are important as they relate to how people learn. In the levels of the taxonomy of learning they are included in order to touch on all phases of interactive learning and to add to the total understanding of the dimensions of interactive learning. Interactive learning involves these three sequences and they are fully explicated in the chapters dealing with each category of the taxonomy of interactive learning.

Interactive learning is a process similar to reciprocal teaching. Reciprocal teaching was initially noted, by its developers, as "a problem-solving process engaged in by inquiring groups" (Joyce, Weil, and Calhoun 2004:15). The content focus for reciprocal teaching was on reading comprehension (Joyce et al. 2004). It was, however, applicable to other content areas. Brown and Palinscar (1989) proposed four comprehension or interactive techniques. These comprehension techniques were akin to the construct of interactive learning. These were developing questions, summarizing, clarifying, and making predictions. "The teacher models the use of [these] four comprehension techniques. . . . Then, the students take turns leading the group to the next paragraph or section" (Joyce et al. 2004:15). The authors further noted that the teacher's role is modulated as the students become more proficient and are able to monitor their own use of the strategies. Here again there is a link to interactive learning, with the student becoming more and more responsible for the learning process. "The self-monitoring, based on the development of metacognitive control of the strategies, is a very important part of the teaching technique. The teacher provides the support needed, but diminishes his or her role as the students master the strategies" (Joyce et al. 2004:15–16). The roles of the teacher and the students change as reciprocal teaching leads the students more deeply into the learning experience. Through this perspective, reciprocal teaching can be seen as encompassing a process with differing levels of cognition and learning.

It can thus be seen that any consideration of reciprocal teaching also requires an understanding of changing teacher roles and changing student roles. This construct of developing and changing teacher and student roles is intrinsic to the taxonomy of interactive learning, where they are specifically defined and discussed. Along with these roles there needs to be a clear understanding of the role of evaluation on the part of the teacher and the students as well as an understanding of the processes of creativity, critical thinking, and problem solving. These roles and processes were identified, defined, and discussed by Steinaker and Bell (1979). Interactive learning includes all these processes and they, in this inclusive context, become a *gestalt* professional instructional exercise for the teacher and a total learning experience for the students. Interactive learning can be used at any grade level and in every content area. Interactive learning is a definable process. This interactive process is neither esoteric nor obscure. It is straightforward and easy to understand, to learn, and to use. The interactive process has five steps. These steps, or levels, we call the taxonomy of interactive learning. The categories within the taxonomy are invitation, involvement, investigation, insight, and implementation. Each of these categories of the taxonomy will be defined and explained in this work. Each of the sixteen strands of instruction will be correlated to every category of the taxonomy as they are demonstrated at each category.

Before defining and explaining the steps in the interactive learning process, we need to note the congruent roles that become evident through interactive teaching and learning. Those roles are teacher roles, student roles, evaluator roles, steps in motivation, discourse, critical thinking, creativity, and problem solving, as well as the sequence of writing. Each of these instructional strands has a sequence of five steps correlated to the taxonomy of interactive learning. In essence, they, too, are taxonomies. Also included are sequences and the process of thinking, learning, and teaching. All these sequences or taxonomies will be discussed at each defined level of interactive learning with emphasis on how they correlate to the process. The five-step roles of the teacher are motivator, catalyst, moderator, sustainer, and critiquor. The roles of the student are attender, explorer, experimenter, extender, and influencer. In terms of evaluation the roles are observer, questioner, assessor, measurer, and determiner. Each of these roles in the evaluation process is followed by both the teacher and the students. Motivation consists of these steps: readiness, relationships, rapport, respect, and responsibility. Marvin Holm (2002), in implementing the motivation process, included seven words that will be discussed at the appropriate categories of the taxonomy. These are purpose, partnership, planning, priorities, principles, passion, and perseverance. The process of change through discourse has been noted with these steps: condition, challenge (connection), communication, consideration, and change. Critical thinking is summarized with these steps: recognizing, interrogating, organizing, generalizing, and utilizing. Creativity emerges in five steps that include motivation, visualization, doing, completing, and sharing/showing. Problem solving involves identification, discovery, trying options, selecting solution, and implementing solution. Finally, writing is also a five-step process. Those steps are to define, describe, detail, discuss, and determine. Each of these congruent processes will be discussed at every level of interaction because they are closely correlated with them. In addition, with each component of reciprocal teaching—questioning, summarizing, clarifying, and predicting—the relationship to interactive learning will be correlated and discussed. It should be noted that before any of these four techniques or any levels of interactive learning can be effectively used, there needs to be another technique in place. We call this technique "preparation" and it must be in place with students for learning to be successful. Preparation for interactive learning and indeed reciprocal teaching takes careful and thoughtful planning. Students must be ready to begin the interactive learning process. The teacher must prepare for the lesson or the learning experience. Preparation is essential to successful learning. When planning is involved, there also needs to be a linkage with past experience and past learning. Students need to know vocabulary and have some ideas; they also need an introduction to the content and how their past experiences relate to the content expectations of the new learning topic. That initial linkage is known as the "anticipatory set" (Hunter 1980) or as "incentive conditioning" (Steinaker and Bell 1979). Preparation also takes careful planning on the part of the teacher. The teacher needs to have a vision of the outcomes and the objectives of the learning experience as well as a deep and clear understanding of the process involved and the long-range goals of the experience. In terms of planning, the teacher can use any lesson plan model or can set up the lesson sequence using the five steps in the interactive learning process. What format used is less important than careful and thorough planning. The Madeline Hunter seven-step lesson plan is one that is frequently used (Hunter and Russell 1981). An online lesson planner can also be used. This is the *Heuristic Electronic Lesson Planner*, available at http://helplp.com as a subscription program (Steinaker 2007). Lesson planning using the five-step interactive lesson planner (ILP) format can be found in Appendix A.

Brown and Palinscar (1989) did careful evaluations of their construct of reciprocal teaching. They implemented the program "for about 20 days of instruction with small groups of elementary and middle school students who have problems comprehending text" (Joyce et al. 2004:16). Coupling this instruction with periodic maintenance sessions, they found students more than doubled their comprehension of reading and maintained this when tested "several weeks later" (16). Alfasi (1998) extended the study to high school students, finding the same general effects as noted by Brown and Palinscar (1989) and others. We posit that a consistent use of reciprocal teaching along with a defined linkage to interactive learning can result in strongly augmented learning. Interactive learning, as an ongoing intervention or teaching model, can be used at all grade levels and in every content area. With the five-step process of invitation, involvement, investigation, insight, and implementation, along with careful planning and preparation, much learning can be accomplished. In this context of interactive learning, reciprocal teaching becomes intrinsic to the process. Every step in the process involves interaction and reciprocity. Each of the components noted will be discussed at each of these five levels.

It should be mentioned as we close this chapter that we are doing a complete analysis of the teaching–learning act. This analysis is valid for a single lesson or for a series of lessons, a unit of study, or a thematic sequence. This complete analysis is designed to help the teacher really understand and use the totality of the teaching–learning act, and thus be able to provide effective and substantive learning experiences for their students.

To know the "how" of teaching and apply it to the teaching–learning act is to develop professionally and to be able to translate that professionalism to the learning experiences of the students. This is a need that must be addressed by teachers and others in education everywhere. It is essential that the teacher frame the lesson plans within the context of interactive learning and to embed that perspective into each lesson. Lesson planning and instructional delivery are processes, and knowing the "how" of teaching and being able to deliver instruction that will result in optimum student learning.

The taxonomy of interactive learning is a dynamic and a gestalt approach to student learning and academic achievement. The teacher must have a clear understanding of the process as a prelude for planning and delivery of instruction. The purpose of interactive learning is to develop success in a learning sequence through providing interaction, extensive group work, and dialogue. Careful planning is essential to augmented learning. Although the teacher does the initial planning, students need to participate in the planning process and at the final level of the taxonomy take responsibility for complete planning. Through developing the process of interactive learning, this will become apparent and the role of the students coming to being responsible will be fully explicated. Interactive learning means that there is frequent and continuing dialogue within the lesson. The dialogue is between teacher and students and among the students. It is focused on the topic and process of the learning experience. It is through this active and dynamic dialogue that students can develop and demonstrate optimum learning.

Activities

Listed in this section are some activities to be used once this chapter has been read. These activities are designed to be done in a group setting. They can, however, be done individually. They are meant to be shared with peers, but they could also be written and turned in to the instructor. We have listed only a few activities. Students and the instructor may come up with additional activities on their own. We recommend the group process wherever possible. Every student should select activity 7 and follow it through for each category of the taxonomy. The purpose of the activities for the first six chapters is to understand the theory and to be able to clearly and thoroughly analyze a lesson through all strands of the taxonomy of interactive learning.

1. Define good human relating as it pertains to teaching. Do this in your small groups and share your definition with other groups. How are the definitions similar and different?

2. Select one of these sequences: thinking, learning, and teaching. Discuss it in your group. React to the sequence and share your reaction with your class. If there are three or more groups, assign each of the sequences to one or more groups.

3. Reflect on the changing roles of the teacher. Discuss what these roles mean to you and to your group and share your reflections with your peers.

4. What does interactive learning mean to you and your group? Develop your meaning from how it is presented in the chapter.

5. Explain "preparation" as it pertains to reciprocal teaching and interactive learning. How would you use "preparation" in your planning process?

6. "The taxonomy of interactive learning is a dynamic and gestalt approach to student learning" (p. 9). Discuss this statement in your group and make a presentation about it.

7. Identify a particular strand of interactive learning that you want to follow through all five categories of the taxonomy. Keep a log of how the strand is used at each category. Write a definitional statement here, and then, as you study each chapter, write in additional information and detail about how it is used during each category. Each member of your group should take a different strand. You will be expected to discuss your strand with your group at the end of each of the next five chapters.

Invitation

An invitation to learning "poses example after example of the process [and] *engages the participation of the student in the process*" (Schwab 1965:47). Schwab (1965) was concerned with the teaching model of scientific inquiry with a focus on biological sciences. His ideas, however, are pertinent to this level of interactive teaching and learning. Invitation is the first category in the interactive learning process. This is a critical step in the process because the students need to become engaged with the learning sequence, express interest in the material, and feel a need to continue with the process. This is the step in the learning sequence where students become actively engaged in the learning sequence. This step in the teaching–learning process needs to be very carefully planned and even somewhat scripted. Short-term goals and objectives need to be in place and long-range outcomes planned.

The teacher can also use curriculum mapping if the long-term outcomes are part of a theme or of a longer unit of study. Invitation is the first time students become aware of the topic and the focus of the lesson or study. At this step students are exposed to the learning experience. There needs to be a cognitive link through memory and translation. The teacher needs to provide these links interactively to ensure student interest and willingness to continue the learning experience. Each of the components of interactive teaching and learning need to be in place during this step in the teaching–learning process. This initial level of invitation is critical to the ultimate success of the lesson, theme, or unit.

Each lesson and the sequence of lessons within a unit or theme need to be framed. Framing the lessons is an essential component of planning. *Framing* means to provide context, to set parameters, and to develop strategies for interactive learning that will ensure students' interest and help them accept the invitation to learn. Framing involves planning and structuring the lesson to include interactive dialogue and the establishment of readiness. The framing process continues throughout all lessons at this category. Reframing occurs in each succeeding level in the taxonomy of interactive learning. Instruction and learning are framed and reframed as components of each category are identified and become a part of the instructional process. We shall now look at each of the components or strands embedded in the total construct of interactive learning that were established in the introduction to this work: cognition, experiential activity, the teacher role, the student role, evaluation, motivation, discourse, critical thinking, problem solving, creativity, the process of thinking, the initial process in learning, and the construct of learning and writing. Each of these strands is intrinsic and evident within the invitation level of learning.

Invitation is the first time students become aware of the topic and the focus of the lesson or study.

KWL

What we **k**now
What we **w**ant to know
What we have **l**earned

COGNITION

The levels of cognitive thinking most apparent at this level of interactive learning are memory and translation. Using these two levels of cognition helps provide a link from previous learning or experiences to the new lessons or area of study. Memory includes the need for the student to understand the link between the new learning experience and the past lessons and experiences in the student's life. This can be accomplished interactively as the teacher and the students focus on the new learning and discuss how it relates to what has already been experienced. Students can do this in small groups or as a class. Linkage occurs when the earlier learning is translated to the new setting. The linkages must be made so that there is cognitive understanding within the student about how the new learning fits with the previous learning or experiences in the student's life.

Interaction is essential at the invitation level. Interaction is an important aspect for English learners and teachers need to use specifically designed activites in English (SDAIE) strategies. Among these SDAIE strategies is one called KWL, which stands for what we *know*, what we *want* to know, and finally what we have *learned*. Interaction is a key component to this strategy and to other SDAIE strategies. See Appendix C for descriptors of sixteen SDAIE strategies. For a review of SDAIE strategies, see *Kaleidoscope* (2002). Discussions of bilingual education can be found in Lessow-Hurley (2005) and Ovando, Combs, and Collier (2006). It is one of the keys to interaction at this invitation level of learning. When groups are used, each can develop specific ideas about what needs to be learned. Groups can come together in a whole-class discussion to finalize a list of needs. This should be done for individual students as well as for the whole group. In these kinds of interactive exercises, students use both memory and translation as they begin to project what they know and what they want to know. It is through cognitive thinking that they develop a sense of curiosity or wonder about what has been, what is, and what is to come. Cognition plays an important role during the invitation category of interactive learning.

Memory is "remembering previously learned material, recalling facts or whole theories [and] bringing to mind" (Steinaker 2007:21). Some terms that describe objectives or questioning strategies are "defines, identifies, describes, lists, names, [and] remembers" (Steinaker 2007:21–22). For translation, the learner "changes information to a new context [and] uses different symbolic form or language" (Steinaker 2007:22). Using symbolic language means simply that students use terminology and vocabulary introduced to them by the teacher, who has presented information about the new study to them. Terms used to describe translation are "matches, grasps meaning, tells, understands" (Steinaker 2007:22). As we review these definitions and terms, we can see how discussion, small group structures, and an interrogative organization can fit into the cognitive dimension of interactive learning well. The use of small interactive groups generates engagement and interest and helps focus students on the nature of the learning experience, what it can mean to them, and what the process of learning will be. They are remembering how previous learning has linkages to this area of study. They are also using translation for engaging themselves within the learning experience. The active use of these two levels of cognitive thinking can make the invitation to learn a positive experience for the students.

EXPERIENTIAL

At invitation, the experiential category is exposure. It is through exposure activities that students become engaged in the new learning setting and develop a specific focus on material and resources. This is a new learning experience even though cognitively there have been linkages past experiences. Experientially there should be a link to previous learning. This link is developed through a teaching strategy called "incentive conditioning" or "goal setting." This strategy literally requires establishing the linkage and providing motivational incentives for engaging the learning experience.

It is defined as "establishing relationship to previous learning. Introducing the lesson. Establishing set and objective" (Steinaker 2007:30). It is concomitant with set and objective in the Hunter and Russell (1981) lesson plan sequence. Exposure level of experiences could well be done interactively in small groups, generating dialogue about materials, discussion among students and teachers. There are four other teaching strategies at the exposure level: data presentation, demonstration, directed observation, and data exploration. Each of these teaching–learning strategies can be used interactively. There are descriptors for each of the teaching–learning strategies. Data presentation is "providing information, establishing stimuli, identifying resources, using media" (Steinaker 2007:30). We can see, when using these strategies, that there can be an interactive dialogue between teacher and students and among students. Both students and teachers can raise questions to clarify and define issues and terms. Demonstration is another strategy. The term describes it use. The teacher, along with the students, is "demonstrating ideas and choices. Showing how to do/processing. Using realia or modeling" (Steinaker 2007:30). This strategy can foster interaction. Students use realia or materials and develop questions about them. Students work in small groups or as a total class groups. The fourth teaching–learning strategy of the five in this category of interactive learning is directed observation, defined as "focusing on particular or selected stimuli, establishing lesson parameters, [and] identifying what to look for" (Steinaker 2007:31). In this strategy, the focus is narrowed, parameters are established, and the uses of information, realia, and resources are established with the expectation that students will understand these elements clearly and will be able to make some determinations about what it is that they have undertaken. Interactive dialogue needs to take place. Students can either decide to become involved in the learning experience or can decide that it is of little or no interest to them. Interaction through discussion and group work can help them make a positive decision. The final teaching strategy at the invitation category of interactive learning is data exploration. This strategy is defined as "student and teacher interacting with the data. Identifying how to find information. Checking for understanding and readiness for next steps in the lesson. Often done interrogatively" (Steinaker 2007:31). The descriptor itself defines this strategy as interactive. To move on through the experience of learning, this strategy should be in place and there should be an interrogative setting where discussion and some initial decision making needs to be made to prepare for the next level in the taxonomy of interactive learning. This strategy can be very important to the teacher and to the students. Of all the strategies at this experiential level and for this invitation category of interactive learning, this is one that should be used. You do not have to use all the strategies identified here, however. You may use a few, or if there is a need for a thorough exposure to the material, all can be used.

TEACHER ROLE

The teacher roles at the invitation level of interactive learning are those of a motivator and presenter. The teacher as motivator is the presenter and prepares the students for the experience. Cognitively the teacher helps the students remember previously learned material, assists in recall, helps students bring to mind links to past learning and events, and helps them translate their focus to the new unit of learning. At the translation level of cognition, the teacher helps them correlate the old with the new, as well as ensures that the students grasp meaning and are able to relate and share their ideas. The students can demonstrate understanding of the new learning. In terms of cognition, the teacher focuses the dialogue on such terms as *defines*, *identifies*, *names*, *describes*, *lists*, and *remembers*. Teaching strategies could include goal setting, data presentation, demonstration, directed observation, and data exploration as noted earlier.

Teaching models that could be used include direct instruction, mnemonics, the picture word inductive model, inquiry, a variety of group structures, including role-playing both structured and unstructured, and advance organizers (Joyce et al., 2004).

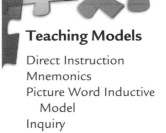

Teaching Models

Direct Instruction
Mnemonics
Picture Word Inductive
   Model
Inquiry
Role-Playing
Advance Organizers

Source: Joyce et al., 2004.

The instructional role for the teacher is informational. The teacher provides information and materials to the students and responds to questions from students. In this informational role, the teacher also observes the students at work and adjusts information according to their needs.

In addition, the teacher's role is for planning the instructional process. The teacher plans the arrangement of the environment, provides media and materials for the students, and develops a variety of stimuli for the students. We cannot stress enough how important it is for the teacher to frame the lessons through an arranged environment and in a form the students will not only understand, but will be challenged and become engaged in. Group structures, resources, realia, and teaching–learning strategies need to be included in the planning. Opportunities for dialogue and interaction need to be identified and a proposed sequence must be put in place. The teacher in the invitation category must know the sequence of motivation, critical thinking, creativity, problem solving, thinking, learning, and teaching. In addition the teacher should be consciously aware of discourse, and the expectations needed for writing. The teacher must value student dialogue and react positively to what the students ask, question, or say. At the same time, the teacher must keep the students focused on this new adventure in learning. As this level of interactive learning continues, the teacher must check for understanding and make sure that the readiness level of motivation is in place. Of all the levels of interactive learning, this is the most critical because the engagement of the students in the process must be ensured. The teacher's invitation to learning must be accepted by the students so that continuing the learning sequence is guaranteed. The teacher must know exactly what to do without being observably scripted. Nonscripted preparation, done during planning, can ensure student acceptance and engagement with the new learning experience. As motivator, this is the charge and role of the teacher.

STUDENT ROLE

Students at this level of interactive learning are attenders and questioners. As attenders, students do more than just listen. Attenders cannot only be listeners, they can also be involved in questioning, interacting, discussing, working with each other, and drawing initial conclusions. While students are being exposed to new learning experiences, making links to past experiences, listening, talking with the teacher and with their classmates, as well as exploring media, materials, realia, and resources, they continue to be attenders. Through these activities, they become engaged with the learning and develop interest in the content of the new learning experience. Students, through their role as attenders, go through the process of establishing readiness for this new learning experience. Through establishing readiness as attenders and questioners, their interest and curiosity have been piqued and they interactively begin to dialogue with each other and the teacher, and begin to focus on resources and on the parameters of this new learning experience.

The students can also be described as questioners. Students need to have the opportunity to raise questions, to respond to them, and to gain the information they need through those questions and the resulting responses and discussions. They should consciously be encouraged by the teacher to ask questions and to participate in small-group or whole-group discussions. Students need to be encouraged to ask questions and to wonder about what they are expected to learn. The students need to be able to recap or summarize information, have it clarified for them, and then to project or predict the next steps in the learning experience. These interrogative and summarization activities become apparent as this level of student interaction is completed. Students need to demonstrate to the teacher and to each other that they understand the nature of the new learning experience. They must be able to communicate that understanding to each other and to the teacher. They must demonstrate their engagement with the learning experience. Students are learning about a discourse condition to which they have been exposed and need to be prepared to understand the condition and begin to respond to it. Students, furthermore, need to make a conscious decision or willingness to continue with the learning experience. This can best be done through interaction and dialogue that the teacher must encourage and plan for. It is through interactive discussion and dialogue that this decision can be made. The student goal here is to establish a level of readiness that will enable them to move on to the next level of interactive learning. Through interaction, discussion, and group work, this can be accomplished. When it is accomplished, the students have completed the readiness process and are ready to move ahead in the learning sequence.

EVALUATION

Evaluation in this category of interactive learning is primarily observation. Both the teacher and the students are involved in observation. Observation includes a careful and thoughtful perspective by the teacher on how students are interacting, how they are reacting to the information they have received, and how they have dealt with understanding the new learning experience. The teacher role as evaluator initially is as extrinsic motivator, presenter, and preparer. The teacher takes the lead in observing student work. The teacher's basic task in evaluation is to observe student activities and be cognizant of their engagement and learning needs. The teacher needs to observe how they perform in groups, and how they work individually. The teacher needs to interact with the students and provide help where needed. Student performance is evaluated in terms of the kinds of questions they ask and their responses to information presented by the teacher. The teacher must be a careful observer who takes notes and who knows how the students are reacting to the initial processes in the learning experience. The teacher should stop every so often and have the students express their feelings about what they are learning and raise any questions they have. Evaluation itself has an interactive dimension. The teacher, learning through interaction with students, must ascertain their readiness for moving to the next category of interactive learning (Steinaker 2005).

Students, from the beginning of instruction, should also be engaged in the assessment and evaluation process. They need to know that the teacher is observing their behavior, their interaction, and their personal performance. They need to also be aware that the teacher is responding to their activities through observation and interaction. Students should be asking questions and review their own performance and the process in which they are involved. In this way student assessment and evaluation emerges. Students should begin to take notes and to keep personal and group records about what they are learning. The students should note the information the teacher has provided and to comment on and react to how they have worked together. They also need to come to an understanding of what the learning experience could be and the direction in which it could go. Through these kinds of records and interactive discussions they can ascertain their readiness for continuing the learning experience. Students begin this by demonstrating linkages, establishing a rationale for learning, and understanding materials and resources. They follow this by listening, watching, and recording information. As they interact, students demonstrate more interest and engagement in the learning process. Small-group interaction and discussion are important in creating in students more interest and engagement with the learning process. They present and discuss what they have done. Even at this early stage in the learning sequence, students observe and review their work, demonstrate what they have learned, and share and present.

Observation and interactive processes by both the teacher and the students are the major functions of evaluation at the invitation level of interactive learning. The teacher should note student interest and their willingness to begin to explore more material and resources. The teacher also needs to note the kinds of questions the students are asking and how they interact with each other and the resources available. The teacher must ensure that the students are working within the parameters of the learning experience. The instructional burden of this level of interactive learning is to ensure that

**Motivation
Readiness Levels**

Parameters
Presentation
Preparation

the students have enough information and possess a strong database so that they can continue with the learning experience knowledgeably and with an understanding of its parameters and sequence. Through noted observations, as well as evaluative interaction by the teacher and the students, readiness can be completed. When these things have been done, the students are ready to move to the next level in the taxonomy and toward new ways to evaluate and assess student learning. Observation is a sensory-based evaluation and the teacher and students must note what they see, what they hear, and what they sense.

MOTIVATION

The first step in motivation is establishing readiness. Students should understand that there is a need to learn and to be involved in a new learning experience. It thus is the task of both teacher and students to explore the learning experience and to set high expectations for themselves. During this initial level of motivation, the parameters and the sequence of the lessons or course of study must be made known to students. They should understand that interaction is the *modus operandi* of the learning process. Students need to understand the correlation of the lesson or lessons to real life and to specific expectations and outcomes. Students should know the steps, the processes, and sequence of the lesson or course of study.

The readiness level of motivation has three subcategories: parameters, presentation, and preparation. Each of these subcategories is implicit within the readiness level of motivation. Holm (2002) uses the word *purpose* to define activities at this level of motivation. Students need to establish a purpose within parameters. Parameters define the boundaries of the learning experience, including the dimensions, value, sequence, and meaning of the learning experience. They are defined for student consideration. Presentation involves the teacher and the students interactively. Information is provided for consideration, study, and discussion. Students focus interactively on the value and meaning of the information and resources for themselves and for the group. Preparation is the most interactive subcategory of readiness. During this subcategory of readiness, students are interactively preparing for completing readiness activities and making a decision to move to the next level of motivation. They begin to demonstrate an understanding of the value of the learning experience. Once valuing is indicated from the students, they are ready to move ahead within the interactive learning process.

It is important for the teacher and the students to establish readiness for continuing the interactive learning experience. One of the keys to this readiness is linking past experience and events to the current learning experience and sequence. Other keys, in terms of motivation, are how the teacher presents the material, establishes parameters for learning, and describes potential outcomes and strategies used to motivate students to establish readiness. Motivation includes a positive dialogue in establishing student readiness.

Readiness is the initial step of motivation in the learning experience. Readiness is often the most difficult level of motivation to establish. One important teaching and learning issue is to establish an interactive environment. It is important that students hear about the learning experience and be heard in response to their exposure to information and resources. They are attenders and questioners, and need an opportunity for interrogative interaction and discussion. Students need to establish a dialogue to determine the condition from which they build their learning experience. They need to understand the condition and be ready to challenge that condition. Motivation is linked to the senses, so as many sensory experiences as can be used should be available to the students. If students can see, touch, hear, and even smell the resources, the greater are the chances for establishing readiness. Readiness is identifiable when it happens. Student readiness is expressed through a demonstrated need to continue with the learning process and an evident eagerness to establish relationships at new levels of condition and challenge.

DISCOURSE

Human discourse is intrinsic to the change process (Steinaker 2003b). The first level of discourse is condition. The new learning experience is the new condition for the students. Condition, as it is initiated, is a focused topic. Students and teacher become part of an interactive dialogue. Students and the teacher exchange ideas and perspectives about the new learning experience through discussion, dialogue, and interactive group structures. Students listen to the teacher. They ask and respond to questions and are active in small- and whole-group interaction about the new learning experience. Discourse and change are integral to learning and to classroom interaction. Students need to be aware that change, if it is planned and sequenced, can be a strong attribute within the learning process. Dialogue for change begins with linking what they already have learned or experienced to the new condition that they are exposed to and begin to challenge that condition. Students become aware, during this interactive category, of the parameters of the condition or experience. They become cognizant about possible outcomes of the study and begin to ask questions and challenge the condition. Interaction within the class should be directed toward identifying and understanding the condition and discovering its components and the probable sequence to achieve outcomes. Before students can move to new levels of discourse and learning, they need to clearly understand the current topic and the conditions and parameters for learning. They may even, through questioning and interaction, come up with their own ideas about the topic, including a challenge to the condition.

Questioning, summarizing, clarifying, and predicting can greatly help in understanding the condition, its links to prior experience, and to the nature of its various components. As the learning experience at the invitation level of interaction develops, new ideas begin to emerge from the students as they interact with the teacher, with each other, and with their resources. New ideas and perspectives on the lesson can provide evidence that students are ready for further discourse. There needs to be this evidentiary base for establishing continuing discourse through a readiness to challenge the condition. Challenge is established though asking questions, interacting in groups, and responding to information and resources. Student readiness for next steps emerge from a clear understanding of the content to which students have been exposed. It is through dialogue and discourse that student readiness is demonstrated at this invitation category of interactive discourse. Direction emerges as students begin to challenge the condition and express a need to continue with the study. Students need to demonstrate a willingness to move to new levels of learning. Dialogue and discourse are key elements in establishing this willingness to move to new levels within the learning sequence. It has been said that "the dialectic of discourse is what makes us truly human" (Steinaker 2003b:3). Discourse is the foundation of learning and must be evident at every level of the taxonomy of interactive learning.

> *Students need to demonstrate a willingness to move to new levels of learning.*

CREATIVITY

At this category of interactive learning, creativity emerges as students interact with ideas, components, and dimensions of the condition or topic they have begun to study. The expression of creativity at this level of interactive learning is shown when students demonstrate a felt need to create a product. The teacher needs to provide a climate for creativity through motivation, providing information and resources, and through allowing students the opportunity to interactively learn and create a vision of an outcome or a product. The teacher builds an atmosphere in which the student feels a need to create a product. In this atmosphere, through motivation and planned activities, the students can develop a sense of wonder about this new learning experience. When this sense of wonder is evidenced, the need to create is established and the student is ready for continuing the experience and to move to a new level of creativity. Students recognize that there is something more beyond the stimuli, the initial need, or the information and resources that they have received. Students know there is more to learn and more to create. The need to create is established through the teaching strategies, cognition, and discourse. Creativity is implicit in the teacher and student roles at this category of interactive leaning. Once this need has been established and readiness is in place, the motivation to continue with the experience and to be involved in the creative process has been activated. Creativity is germinated at the invitation level of interaction. The need to create becomes evident as this level of experience.

Creativity is unique to every individual. Creativity is fostered through group work and group interaction. Envisioning group projects or products is a part of the creative process. In the classroom there will be individual and group expressions of creativity. Creativity is fostered in a classroom where there is interaction and articulation about ideas, resources, and realia. "Creativity is a personal interaction with an idea, with material or with a problem" (Steinaker and Bell 1979:91). It is through interaction that students begin the process of creativity, which can be linked to every successful learning experience. When the need to create and the readiness for new experiences is in place, creativity becomes very evident to the teacher and to the students. Through this evidence, the process of creativity becomes a fixed component of interactive learning.

CRITICAL THINKING

"At this beginning level, the critical thinking process involves the recognition of variables. . .within a given context. Learners. . .begin to recognize that there are differences within the given context and respond [to those differences]" (Steinaker and Bell 1979:96). Critical thinking is intrinsic to the structure and organization of interactive learning. It should be a part of the learning process from the very beginning. Critical thinking at this level of interactive learning is the recognition of variables. Students need to recognize something new and different in the lesson or course of study. They should recognize and identify those differences, ideas, and variables. The recognition of differences, variances, and variables is the beginning step in critical thinking and is vital for student learning. Through this recognition, they are able to work closely with all the other components of this level of interactive learning. Critical thinking is a logical process of interaction and making choices within a set of variables. It is always enhanced through interactive dialogue. It is essentially interactive and needs to be a part of the questioning, summarizing, clarifying, and predicting components of interactive learning. Critical thinking and cognition are closely related.

As part of critical thinking, activities need to be carefully planned by the teacher. It is particularly important that the teacher prepare a learning environment where there are recognizable issues and differences or variables. The teacher then uses teaching strategies and motivation to provide a base for the student search for the differences and similarities in variables. If these provide stimuli for the learner, they will enhance critical thinking (Steinaker and Bell 1979). All people are curious. This is especially true of students. Their curiosity and resultant questions about identified similarities and differences can be the impetus for critical thinking. This is why it is important for the students to define the variables and the issues within their resources. At this level of interactive learning, the reason for continuing through the learning experience is to answer the "why" questions raised through thinking critically about similarities, differences, and variables in the learning experience. It is curiosity, a sense of wonder, and the need to find out why that motivates students toward moving on to the next level of interactive learning.

It is curiosity, a sense of wonder, and the need to find out why that motivates students toward moving on to the next level of interactive learning.

PROBLEM SOLVING

Problem solving is basic to interactive learning. A classroom in which students have little opportunity to work together in solving problems has serious limitations. Problem solving can be an opportunity for students to make great strides in personal learning. In this category of interactive learning, both teacher and students are involved in identifying any problems that need to be investigated or solved. An arranged environment along with careful selection of materials and resources can set the stage for identifying issues and problems within the area of study. In the invitation category, the teacher and the students are involved in the identification of these problems (Steinaker and Bell 1979).

Identifying the problem is corollary to understanding the condition being studied. Further, it is also corollary to the roles of the teacher and the student. The teacher invites the students to become aware of issues, variables, and problems. Teacher-planned objectives help students identify the issues and problems so they become willing to pursue those objectives. Teaching strategies appropriate for problem solving are demonstration, use of media and realia, directed observation, and data presentation. Interaction is intrinsic within each of these teaching–learning strategies. Interaction should be between teacher and students. Interaction should also take place among students through groups and interactive discussions.

The teacher needs to set the stage, provide information for the students, and organize the interactive structures they will need. Then the students should be allowed to explore the data and the materials within their learning environment. They need to organize and summarize what they have sensed, thought about, and learned. They can then interact with each other and the teacher as they develop a clear understanding of the problem. Problem solving is one of the strands that needs to be completed to establish readiness for the next category of interactive learning. Problem solving is particularly important at the invitation level of interactive learning.

WRITING

Writing, activity logs, and keeping records of the learning process are important. Together they comprise a specific component of interactive learning. Students need to write, take notes, keep records, and develop learning logs. Students need to use those records to summarize verbally or in writing what they have done. Invitation is the interactive category in which students are focused on defining what are their invitation activities and what they plan to do for their next steps. Depending on the age of the students and their developmental level, this kind of writing and record keeping can range from simple to more complex record keeping and writing.

This is the stage in the interactive learning process when students define the topic, suggest their purpose, and summarize the data they have begun to learn. Their whole purpose in the writing process is to define the parameters of their study, to develop the ideas and the concepts of what they are doing, and to begin an identified and defined process for continuing to study. Definition in writing is a process during which students summarize information, identify purpose, and note sequence. Within their definitional writing they can project ideas toward a descriptive modality of the topic as the next level of interactive learning: Involvement. Writing at this level of interactive learning is designed to be a response to questions, to clarify information, to summarize what has been learned, and to predict next steps. It is important for teachers to build record keeping and writing into the planning. For very young students in kindergarten and primary grades the writing can be sequential drawings of activities with captions or very brief statements or sentences. As students grow older they can keep individual logs and records of group work. Records can become very sophisticated and be specific records of the development of the lesson sequence. Writing, along with oral reports, is an excellent way to ensure that writing is correlated with the learning process. Definition "consists of clear, concise, and coherent characterization of the topic being studied" (Steinaker and

Writing Process Purpose

Define the parameters of their study.
Develop the ideas and concepts of what they are doing.
Begin an indentified and defined process for continuing to study.

Bustillos 2007:vi). This is the goal of writing at invitation. It is incumbent on the teacher to provide a format and order for the writing and at the same time encourage individual and group definitional writing. Writing, in almost all learning sequences, is an essential corollary to the whole learning process. Definition is "the equivalent of memory and translation in the cognitive taxonomy and exposure in the experiential taxonomy" (Steinaker and Bustillos 2007:vi–vii). We can see how writing at this initial category of interaction relates closely to invitation in the taxonomy of interactive learning.

THINKING

We have already discussed cognition at the invitation level of interactive learning. We do, however, want to approach thinking from another perspective. We have defined *thinking* as "the process of associating information to experience" (Steinaker 2002:1). The initial level of thinking involves responding to sensory stimuli. Stimuli are provided by the teacher at this response level of writing. Students respond to the stimuli and link their responses to prior learning experiences. The process of association involves cognition that ranges from memory to translation. These two are evident cognitive expressions at this level of learning. On occasion, thinking can move to other levels of cognitive activity. Sometimes interpretation, application, and analysis occur. These cognitive processes are part of the response to the stimuli and to the information and materials with which the student works.

In preparing information and writing about what they have done, students need to reflect on and think about what they have completed and learned. This is a part of the experience. It is essential that the teacher be aware of the student need for stimuli, for information, and for resources. Thinking and pondering by the student is central to the teaching–learning act. Students must also have the time to not only interact with each other and the material, but also to have to think about their activities and interact with each other about materials, ideas, and processes. Outcomes in terms of thinking, learning, and teaching are dependent on two components: the ability of the teacher to conceptualize the process and then capture it through viable and well-planned instructional processes. This construct in thinking, as we have presented it, is very important to student success and learning at this invitation category of interactive learning. Thinking is an internal process through which the learner progresses. It is sequential and is necessary for learning to take place. Interactive stimuli, through discussion and group work, provide opportunities and focus both for dialogue and for thinking.

> *Thinking and pondering by the student is central to the teaching—learning act.*

LEARNING

Learning is the core element in the achievement of identified goals. Learning is "the process of relating thinking to actions, feelings, and skills" (Steinaker 2002:1). The learning process is concurrent with the thinking process. During the first level of thinking, the students react to stimuli and link what they are expected to learn to past experiences. With learning, that response becomes evident through demonstration and/or interaction. Students show their thinking and how they process thinking in terms of feelings and/or actions. They "expand the feelings or actions within a larger purview of experience" (Steinaker 2002:3). This first step in the learning process is personal. Each student responds in a particular way. When their interest is piqued, they need to interact about how they have responded. Responses and reactions are shared with the teacher and with each other in small-group contexts and formats. Responses, as they occur to each student, foster the need for interacting with others. A sense of curiosity about how other students have responded is built. Learning begins with the individual and is enhanced in small groups; consensus is built in large groups. Learning is optimally accomplished within an interactive context.

The teacher needs to be cognizant of the student need to discover and find out. The teacher can then build a need for sharing within groups. Small groups can respond and then share with the whole class. Responding is a natural part of an initial reaction to stimuli and information. It is a logical and necessary part of the interactive learning process. Students are relating their thinking to real stimuli, demonstrating their interest, and sharing that reaction with others and with the teacher. Responding implies the use of questioning strategies by the teacher and by the students. Interrogative dialogue is part of the responding level of learning. When interest is piqued, questions are raised and students interact in a shared and provocative way. Learning, while it can be private, is also a public or group process. This is particularly evident at the invitation level of the instruction and learning. Interactive learning is an interesting component in any invitation learning setting.

TEACHING

Teaching has been defined as "the process of valuing an action, feeling, or skill" (Steinaker 2002:1). Teaching is a process of validating thinking and learning. It begins with the teacher demonstrating and discussing the value of the content, concepts, and purpose of the learning experience. The teacher notes the cogency of what is to be learned. The objective for the teacher is to work with students to ensure that they too value what is to be learned. Teaching, in sum, is an interactive valuing of a defined learning objective. If the teacher does not value the content, it should not be used for instruction. The teacher must answer the question of why this study is important and how it relates to real life, particularly the real life of the students. The teacher should focus not only on the individual lesson or group of lessons, but on the short- and long-term outcomes. The teacher needs to share how the long-term outcomes can be internalized as part of the student's life and inner self. This may not be easy at the invitation level, but the vision of outcomes and change within the student must be demonstrated at this level of teaching and learning.

Teaching is a philosophical role more than it is an instructional approach. Teachers have their own personal ontology or worldview. Before becoming a teacher, one should also have a grounded epistemology (Ornstein and Hunkins 2004). Likewise, the teacher should be comfortable within an identified personal worldview. A wider discussion of these topics is not undertaken in this work, but it is essential that teachers understand these philosophical and epistemological issues and know why they made the choice to teach. Teaching is both an art and a science, but in the final analysis teaching is good human relating with a purpose. That purpose is to help students learn, apply, and use what has been learned in real-life contexts. It is not an esoteric exercise in succeeding on artificial measures set up by the teacher—or by the district or state.

The first level in the teaching sequence is engaging. "The teacher posits a value or

values in a context of positive or expected outcomes and provides background, data, and stimuli for the students" (Steinaker 2002:4). This definition tells it all. The teacher values the content and provides the classroom environment that engages the students and enables them to sense the value of the learning and to respond to it. This is the essence of teaching and it is what teachers do. Through this initial setting for learning, the teacher and the students work cooperatively and interactively to initiate an interactive learning experience that has meaning, substance, and value for the students. The excitement of initiating and framing this kind of learning milieu is the fit needed for a dynamic and valued interactive learning experience.

LEADERSHIP

In terms of interactive learning, leadership begins with the teacher roles as presenter and preparer. Teaching, as has been noted, is the valuing of the students and what is being learned. This valuing dimension of teaching is basic to teacher leadership. The teacher role in leadership at the invitation category is that of preparer. This is done in two senses. The first is preparation in terms of planning interactive instruction and group work. Planning is essential and necessary during this category of interactive learning. The second leadership role for the teacher is preparing the engagement of students in the learning experience and in the activities involved in the process.

Leadership is a dynamic interaction that is sometimes almost protean in the dialogue and emerging experiences of the learning sequence. Leadership and interactive learning are inextricably bound together. The student role in leadership is as active participant. The roles of preparer and participant come together at this invitation level of interactive learning. The interaction at this initial category of interactive learning is an optimum time for modeling leadership and helping students to begin learning leadership skills. Student leadership grows as interactive group experiences are provided and as students have the opportunity to react to information and stimuli. They dialogue among themselves and interact with the teacher. Through planned activities and the dialogue that occurs, the student role in leadership as a participant becomes evident. Leadership, like instruction, must be shared if the learning experience is to come to full fruition. It is learned and thrives within an interactive setting. Leadership for the students is demonstrated through active participation and can be shared in a positive, activity-oriented, interactive learning environment. Leadership then becomes a positive by-product. In this category, student leadership is emergent. Teacher leadership is evidenced through planning and preparing engaging experiences for the student in a positive learning environment.

> *Leadership, like instruction, must be shared if the learning experience is to come to full fruition.*

FINAL COMMENTS

When the invitation to learn has been given and student readiness established, the next category of the interactive learning can be attained. When the initial strands of cognition, experience, discourse, evaluation, creativity, critical thinking, problem solving, writing, thinking, learning, teaching, and leadership have been established, a readiness for the next level of interactive learning becomes apparent. Readiness is demonstrated when the teacher roles of motivator and preparer along with the student roles of questioner and participant have been completed. Initial levels of discourse and assessment have been completed and the students have fulfilled the definitional role of writing. Invitation is an exciting and illuminating beginning to a learning sequence. Issues of critical thinking, creativity, and problem solving come forward and are being addressed. Elements of thinking, teaching, and learning correlate with the activities designed for invitation. Dialogue and discourse are central to learning at invitation. Careful planning and clear expectations are in place to ensure that this level of the interactive learning taxonomy as well as readiness is established. Through the coming together of all these strands of the learning experience, the students are enabled to transition to the next category of interactive learning. In short, all the elements of the invitation level have been completed and accomplished through thoughtful discussion, dialogue, and discourse. Now the next category of interactive learning is ready to emerge—the category of involvement. Involvement activities at this level of the taxonomy bring students to new kinds of interaction and dialogue. Roles change and new ideas and learning become extant. Involvement becomes active when readiness has been completed.

Invitation promotes openness and dialogue. It is a fitting initial category for interactive learning. Invitation paints a picture of interaction, discussion, and positive relationships. Invitation, carefully planned and executed, can create a climate of efficient aesthetics and engage the student in a rich and motivating experience in learning. Invitation sets the archetypal focus on the art of teaching. It is in this category that successful invitation activities and strategies can ensure optimal student learning. Invitation also provides access for understanding and analysis of the science of learning. Following the development of the lesson and the engagement of the students through specific strands within the lesson can help the teacher to learn about how students learn and what strategies work. Invitation is openness; it is also understanding and analysis of how it happened and why it happened. The art and science of teaching are in place during the invitation activities of learning.

Activities

Remember that all activities are designed to be discussed in groups. They can be done individually, but it is not recommended. Activity eight, and individual and group activity, began in chapter 1 and should continue in this chapter. Everyone should do activity eight. Other activities can be selected or assigned to each group.

1. "Framing the lessons is an essential component of planning" (p. 11). What does "framing" mean? How would you use it in your planning, particularly for the invitation category of interactive learning?

2. Specially designed activities in English (SDAIE) are used with English learners. How would you plan to use SDAIE activities at invitation?

3. Experiential learning can be defined broadly or it can be specifically defined. After reading this chapter, ponder its meaning and develop in your group a statement about experiential learning that identifies your group's perspective.

4. Identify a teaching model (p. 43) and show how that teaching model could be used for this invitation category of interactive learning.

5. How would you plan the interrogative context of learning (p. 45 et seq.) at this first category of interactive learning?

6. Discuss readiness as the first step in motivation. How could it be planned and how would you use it at invitation?

7. Discuss plans for initiating student writing in your group. Identify a grade level and discuss how you would plan for student writing.

8. In your groups you individually selected a strand to follow through in all categories of interactive learning. You began this activity in chapter 1. Write your response.

Involvement

Involvement follows invitation. When students have successfully completed invitation activities, they are ready for involvement. Involvement is a category where it is essential for students to develop new levels of discourse and interaction. Involvement literally means that the students have chosen to continue with the learning experience and are involved with each other and their resources in an interactive setting that has been positively begun through the activities during the invitation category.

Although any teaching model can be used at this level of interactive learning, cooperative learning is one model that is really essential to expedite student involvement. Joyce and his colleagues (2004) noted that "cooperative learning increases learning partly because it causes motivational orientation to move from the external to the internal" (214). Through cooperative group work, students begin to think through the issues and topics within the area of focus. They have the opportunity to discuss them, to share ideas about them, and to interact with each other and the teacher concerning them. Dialogue and discussion are essential for students at this level of interactive learning. Students begin to participate and become more involved within the process. Involvement begins when they cognitively progress through memory and translation toward interpretation.

Involvement is a time when relationships are more firmly established. Students during involvement are able to describe both verbally and in writing their ideas and points of view. Relationships are at the core of the art of teaching. It is at this level of interactive learning that students can begin building relationships. Thinking, learning, and teaching reflect this new level of interaction and creativity. Critical thinking and problem solving become more important to student involvement at this category. Involvement in learning is an exciting and interesting time for students. Interaction invigorates learning. Student attitudes toward interaction and dialogue tend to be positive, and this allows for strong student support for each other and for the learning process. The teacher becomes a catalyst and the student is the explorer of issues and materials.

Interactive learning becomes intrinsically cooperative and more involved with dialogue and discussion at this level of the learning. The art of teaching becomes evident at this level of the taxonomy as students interact with each other and grow increasingly involved in the learning process. The science of teaching can also be understood as we assess each of the strands and define what they show about what happens during the involvement category of interactive learning.

COGNITION

Students during this interactive category use primarily the cognitive levels of memory and translation. These were established at the invitation category and they remain in place at the involvement category. Students continue to make links between what they have known and experienced and what they are thinking about, discussing, and learning in this current learning experience. They need, during this level of cognition, to translate what they have learned to new contexts and understand how they fit together. As translation becomes operant, students use different symbolic forms and develop vocabulary. They are applying old information to new contexts. They are learning interactively and growing academically from their group work. They are clarifying and questioning what they are learning. Students are reflecting on what they know and what they have already experienced. They are explaining or summarizing, interpreting materials, beginning to predict outcomes and effects of what they are learning. This is a time to begin classifying things into appropriate categories and restating them. As students continue through the involvement level of interactive learning, they begin to interpret and predict direction. They conclude this step in interactive learning by beginning to use interpretation as a cognitive function of learning (Steinaker 2007).

When they reach this level of cognition they can explain and summarize issues, interpret material, predict outcomes, and estimate future trends. They convert, defend, estimate, explain, generalize, rewrite, reword, describe, and give examples. This level of cognition becomes more apparent as they predict their next steps and future direction toward investigation of issues, content, and materials. Cognition takes on new meaning during the involvement category of interactive learning. One could say in the vernacular that students are "really getting into it." This is a time when the decision to work with this new learning experience comes to fruition. The student role as explorer is evident in the cognitive style they demonstrate during involvement. The teacher role of catalyst is also central to this level of cognition. The teacher as catalyst and the student as explorer demonstrate the impact of involvement on moving student learning to a new level. The use of cognition enables the students to review and summarize what they have done, validate the decision they have made to continue through the learning experience, and prepare themselves to move to the next level of interaction. When they have accomplished all this, the students are ready to move on to the next levels of both cognition and interactive learning. Through cognition, students have attained a firm grip on their commitment to learn and their involvement in the learning experience that they have accepted.

EXPERIENTIAL

"Participation [involvement] has been described as the level at which one decides, on the basis of data already received, to become physically a part of the [learning] experience" (Steinaker and Bell 1979:24). Some of the activities at participation are

- Discussing data presented
- Structured data-gathering activities
- Reviewing data
- Acting out known situations
- Walk-through, replication, and verification activities
- Group discussion of a presentation or demonstration
- Opportunities to imitate an observed event
- Reading [material] introduced or discussed in class
- Using manipulative or hands on activities
- Counting or quantifying data
- Ordering objects, events, and materials [hierarchically]
- Visualizing, verbalizing, and brainstorming
- Designing questions to recall or to [interpret] data
- Modeling or defining behaviors
- Timing activities and programs
- Generating data through [explaining materials] (Steinaker and Bell 1979: 26–27)

These activities can be summarized as observing, discussing, exploring, assessing, visualizing, directed reading, estimating, manipulating, ordering, collecting, modeling, defining, and listening. The activities and terms listed are but some of the activities and processes in which students could participate at this category of interactive learning. Participation is the experiential category in which students achieve and demonstrate cognitive and experiential involvement. Participation means that students are actively engaged in discussing, interacting, and studying the material and the focus of the learning experience. Dialogue, discussion, and group work should be used extensively at this level of interactive learning. Interactive experience means reaching out, grasping meaning, and interpreting that meaning. Students are involved with each other, with the teacher, and with their resources in generating new ideas and information about the material being studied. Students participate in many activities. They have learned enough so that they are willing to take some risks as they further discover information about the material and begin to work with it. Involvement requires risk taking, and both students and teacher need to be thoroughly cognizant of that dimension of involvement. As the experience develops, students are able to ask more probing questions, to interpret and predict their next steps, and to clarify issues about what they are learning (Steinaker and Bell 1981). Reciprocal interaction with each other, with the teacher, and with the materials moves them steadily toward further exploration of the topic and toward a personal commitment to continue with their involvement in the learning process. Experientially, the students have become totally involved in the experience and are ready for the identification category of interaction.

> *Participation is the experiential category in which students achieve and demonstrate cognitive and experiential involvement.*

TEACHER ROLE

During this category of interactive learning, the roles of the teacher become those of a catalyst and a coordinator. "By definition, a catalyst is an agent of change, something or someone that speeds up the process of change toward planned objectives" (Steinaker and Bell 1979:82). As a catalyst, the teacher must ensure that the interactive components of involvement are present and that the students are participating in the dialogues and discussions as well as in group work. The teacher is more active and direct in terms of the learning sequence and is more closely aligned with student activities. As a catalyst and coordinator, the teacher moves freely around the room and among the students, making suggestions, responding to questions, helping to clarify and summarize problems and issues, and providing direction for additional involvement or direction. As coordinator, the teacher sees that activities are focused, on target, and consistent within the parameters of the learning experience. The teacher is an encourager, a challenger, a confronter, a listener, and a provider of information. The teacher becomes the catalytic and coordinating agent for student involvement. The teacher's roles are essential and vital in making sure the students become completely involved in the process of thinking and learning. The teacher, as catalyst, is valuing the content as well as valuing the contributions of each class member as they jointly interact together.

As coordinator, the teacher ensures that all students are participating and contributing in small groups and in interactive discussions. The teacher must be self-challenged to become the agent of change and the catalyst for group and individual learning in the classroom. It is not always easy, but it needs to be done. The teacher roles of catalyst and coordinator must be carefully planned and sequenced by the teacher (Steinaker and Bell 1979). Thoughtful and careful planning and preparation enhance the roles of the teacher. In addition to being readied through planning, the teacher must also be flexible and able to adjust as different student and group needs emerge during this involvement category of learning. The teacher is an advocate, a helper, a challenger, and a reactor to what the students are doing. The teacher must plan strategies for coordinating. The teacher initiates direction, offers challenges, and works with individual students as well as with groups in keeping the students focused, on task, and completely involved in the learning activities.

Through these roles as catalyst and coordinator, the teacher must ensure that the students know what they have learned and how they have done it. The teacher must also help walk the students through the activities at this category of learning and help form a bridge for the students to the next category in the taxonomy. Students need to feel a pragmatic impetus to continue with the next level of experience and learning—that of investigation. The teacher exemplifies the art of teaching through fostering interaction, sitting down with groups of students and working with them, leading and participating in discussions, and working individually with students at their level of need. The teacher is the careful planner who understands and analyzes what is occurring and then makes any necessary adjustment. In this way, the teacher demonstrates the science of teaching. The teacher is aware of all the strands of interactive learning and coordinates them. The teacher analyzes them and uses the analysis to foster optimum learning. The teacher, as catalyst and coordinator, exemplifies both the art and the science of instruction.

STUDENT ROLE

The student roles at the involvement level of interactive learning are those of explorer and cooperator. Although the student is still attending and listening, the focus of interactive listening has changed and is, at this category, done within a more interactive setting. The student learns the rules of the game, the structure within which to operate, and the issues and sequence of the learning experience (Steinaker and Bell 1981). They also learn to cooperate with each other and with the teacher through developing relationships. The student, during this time, is reviewing what has been learned and exploring the potential for learning within the entire experience. Through an interactive process, the student begins to raise new questions, to explore for clarification, and to classify and order information so that what they are learning makes sense. Through this sequence they can begin to make predictions. Students clarify the tasks needed for the experience, know what is to be done, and have a vision of what the completed tasks will look like when the experience is completed.

Students begin to wrestle with information and to explore the niches and corners of the parameters of the learning experience. They begin to establish relationships with each other through dialogue, discussion, and interactive group work. They interact with the materials being studied and the resources available to them. Through challenge and personal communication with each other and the teacher, students are able to describe what they are doing. They need to be able to explain what they are doing and provide a rationale for why they are doing it. Students respond to the teacher as a catalyst and coordinator and are able, through their role as explorers and cooperators, to summarize their progress, describe the process through this category, and predict the direction their next steps will take them. They must be successful at this level of interactive learning because "success leads to a raising of the level of aspiration and failure to lowering [aspiration]; . . . . The stronger the chance of success, the greater the probability of a rise in the level of aspiration" (Steinaker and Bell 1979:66). Involvement is a time for active and energetic student participation and student learning. It is a time when success should be evident and aspirations apparent. It should be interesting and exciting—a category of cooperative interaction that the students thoroughly enjoy.

When all of this has been accomplished, students and teacher are prepared for the next category of learning, investigation. The building of relationships during this level of interactive learning demonstrates the art of teaching. Student knowledge, understanding, and ability to understand and share their progress and process demonstrate the science of learning. Students have become thoroughly involved in the process of interactive learning.

EVALUATION

Evaluation is again a joint exercise for both the teacher and the students. Evaluation and assessment are daily activities involving both teacher and students. Evaluation has two basic components. One component is process or formative evaluation (Steinaker 2005). The second component of evaluation is product or summative evaluation (Bloom, Hastings, and Madaus 1971). The teacher roles as catalyst and coordinator encapsulate and define the involvement level of evaluation. Through questions, responses to questions, and challenging students to think of other directions, the teacher as catalyst and coordinator keeps instruction and learning moving. The teacher also needs to raise questions about what the students are doing, about their purpose, and why they are actively involved in what they are doing. The teacher needs to link "objective and assessment" (Slavin 2006:446).

Basic Components of Evaluation

Process/Formative Evaluation
Product/Summative Evaluation

The operant role of evaluators and evaluation at this involvement level of interactive learning is that of a questioner. The interrogative dimension of critical thinking becomes evident and evaluation is a matter of demonstrating knowledge and questioning the veracity of that knowledge. The student roles as explorer and cooperator fit into this category well. Students at this level of learning need to explore, to find out, and to gain perspective and focus on the learning experience. They also need to cooperate with each other and with the teacher during this interactive context. Students need to ask each other and the teacher questions. They need to look at how they are learning and the process in which they are involved. Students need to carefully explore the data and make decisions about what the data mean and about next steps in the process. Students are becoming more active in self-evaluation and in raising pertinent questions about the learning experience.

There should be a strong emphasis on student attitudes toward the learning experience, how students feel about the experience, and what kind of achievement is evident. Through interaction and discussion with groups of students and individual students, the teacher should ensure that they are actively involved, have positive feelings about the experience, and are on task in preparing for the next level of the learning experience. This is done through interrogative interaction and through record keeping. The students and the teacher keep careful records of what is happening in the learning experience. Through questions and interaction, students can ascertain from each other their attitudes and demonstrate their levels of interest and involvement in the learning process. There should be interest and excitement on the part of the students and the teacher about what is happening and how it is happening. Written records or logs by students and teacher should be kept.

While the teacher initiates the role of catalyst and coordinator, questioning and verifying become the staples in the teacher's role as catalyst and as a part of the evaluative process. The teacher asks questions, listens to responses, and challenges students to further work. The students raise questions for each other and ask questions about the materials in terms of their validity and functionality. They also interact with the teacher and keep records of what they have learned, what they have done, and what they yet need to learn. Through these kinds of interrogative interactions and learning activities, students become more aware of what they know, what they want to know, and how they can find out what they want to know. The teacher, through interactive questioning, verifies with the students their understanding, their processing of information, and the direction in which they need to go to further enrich the learning experience. The teacher and the students come to value what they have done and are prepared to move forward. Evaluation, in the interrogative context, demonstrates the art of teaching. In the record keeping and directional developments, the science of teaching is emphasized.

Evaluation has become linked to the achievement of standards in this time of teacher and student accountability. Every state has standards or performance expectations (Reeves, 2005). The education paradigm is changing. Johnson, Musial, Hall, Gollnick, and Dupuis (2008) have noted that "two complementary strategies are at the center of today's education paradigm: standards and assessments. In combination these comprise today's instructional model standards based assessment" (p. 359).

**Motivation
Subcategories**

Direction: relationships
establish focus for
exploration and study
Discussion: teacher and
students work together
to ensure a clear
understanding of the
subject
Decision: continue
learning experience
through investigation

As they have noted, assessment and evaluation are being linked to instruction.
Teachers must use standards and the achievement of those standards as central to
their instruction and as a part of the evaluation process of interactive learning.

MOTIVATION

Motivation is a key component at the involvement level of interactive teaching and
learning. Motivation, at this category of involvement, concerns relationships. The
development of relationships energizes interaction, participation, and involvement.
Relationships are threefold. First there is the developing relationship between teacher
and students. Next, there is the establishment of relationships individually and among
small groups and the whole group. Finally, a relationship between students and the
materials and resources becomes apparent through study and involvement with them.
These relationships become the basis for positive and interactive settings for students.
Relationships take planning, effort, structure, and cooperation. Relationships depend
on the roles of the teacher as catalyst and coordinator. Activities, interaction, and group
work are designed to build these relationships.

There are three subcategories at this level of motivation: direction, discussion, and
decision. These subcategories correlate closely with the involvement category of interactive learning. In direction, the first subcategory of relationships, students and teacher
through interaction establish a direction for their exploration and study. Through discussion, the second subcategory, the teacher and the students work cooperatively and
interactively to ensure there is a clear understanding that there is enough information,
knowledge, and evidenced learning in place. This confirms a continuance of the process. During decision, the third subcategory of relationships, the decision to continue
the learning experience through investigation is made.

The whole of the instructional and learning roles in motivation are participatory
and interactive. The motivational focus is to interact, ask questions, explore issues, and
develop clear understanding of the area of study (Joyce et al. 2004). The student roles are
to focus on and explore cooperatively and interactively the information and resources
available. The interactive role is participatory, implying that all involved need to fully
cooperate during this process. A variety of small-group structures can be used to enhance
interaction and discussion.

During this motivation category of interactive learning, students and teacher develop
a joint perception and understanding of the process, the achievement thus far, and
the direction in which learning needs to develop. The level of motivation is relationship. Relationships and partnering in learning are developed. Relationships are built
between students and between students and teacher. Partnering reflects group work and
learning together. Both represent the art of teaching and learning. These kinds of positive relationships are essential in the development of the interactive learning process.
Relationships are needed for substantive learning, for the process to come to fruition,
and for the goals and objectives to be achieved. Relationships are keys to motivation and
to the joint decision to continue the learning process.

Motivation at this level of interactive learning involves direction, discussion, and
decision. Direction means understanding what has happened and the identification of
the continuing process. Discussion is the strong interactive component of motivation so
necessary to establishing relationships. Decision involves the group determination to continue the process as a vital learning experience. The decision to move ahead in the learning
process must be determined jointly by the teacher and the students. Purpose and meaning
may evolve and change as the learning experience develops. The value of the experience
must remain constant. During the decision process, group work and interaction are future
oriented, focusing on the next steps and challenges yet to come, and finalizing a group
decision to move on to the next category of learning. When this level of motivation has
been achieved, and firm relationships among students and between teacher and students
have been established, students have made an intellectual and emotional commitment to

learn, to share, and to complete the agreed-upon joint tasks ahead of them. The interactive context of the relationships is necessary toward establishing this basis for working together, developing rapport, and moving ahead as individuals and as a group toward the completion of the learning experience. When these are in place, the learning process can continue to a new level of challenge and accomplishment. Students are demonstrating the need for building a strong working rapport as they complete activities at involvement and have come to a decision to continue the learning experience together. That emerging rapport will strengthen the relationships already built and will enhance their need to learn together. Students are then able to begin the investigation category of interactive learning. Motivation is built on developing strong relationships and feeling the need to fully commit to the learning experience. Students are beginning to develop a more intrinsic sense of self and connection with the learning experience. They know where they are and where they want to go in terms of the learning experience.

DISCOURSE

Change is a process. It began as understanding a condition, issue, problem, or situation at the invitation level of interactive learning. Here the discourse, discussion, and dialogue become challenge. Challenge is descriptive of this level of change in the process of interactive learning because it embodies the catalyst and coordinator roles of the teacher. The explorer and cooperator roles of students, and the relationship level of motivation, are concomitant with the challenge category of discourse. Challenge is critiquing what is, asking questions about why it is that way, working with emerging issues, and along with this spending the time discussing and interacting. Discourse, discussion, and interaction include the teacher and the students as they dialogue about the condition and raise questions and challenge what exists. Challenge, as a level of discourse, requires interaction in an interrogative context that creates and clarifies understanding of the issues and the process of the learning sequence. Challenge involves exploring and probing the parameters of the focus of the study and requires the student and the teacher to become immersed in the content and the dimensions of the study (Steinaker 2003b).

Challenge is critiquing what is, asking questions about why it is that way, working with emerging issues, and spending the time discussing and interacting.

Change requires a level of challenge in which teachers and students thoroughly explore what is and indicate what could be changed. There is a level of involvement during discourse built around questions, clarifications, summarizing, and predicting what is to come. Challenge is the charisma of change and the catalyst for further direction in the study. The ability to challenge through questions and an interrogative interaction allows the student to be able to describe what is, what has been done, to what is known, and identify next steps toward further study and investigation. Challenge in discourse is interactive and verbal. The style of verbalization is a perspective that students and teacher need to understand. Many time a spoken word, phrase, or comment can mean different things to listeners. Often it is dependent on the context and the cohesiveness of the group. As cohesiveness and relationships within the group coalesce, discourse becomes more open as relationships are established through personal and group involvement. Likewise body movement, expressions, eye contact, and the amount and focus of the discourse need to be considered during discourse. As this is evaluated, the teacher and the students can more clearly understand the known and challenge that which is not known. Both students and teacher must be aware of these elements of the style of discourse to ensure that a consensus of meaning is understood. Both teacher and students need to be aware of the style of discourse to understand its meaning in terms of the interaction at this category of interactive learning so that the transition to the connection level of discourse happens easily and clearly (Steinaker 2003b).

Meeting the challenge of discourse at this category of interactive learning can move the process of discourse and allow it to change smoothly to the next level of interactive—the level of investigation. During interaction at the challenge level of discourse, the art of teaching is demonstrated by the level and quality of interaction. The style elements of discourse, as they become known and understood by the teacher and the students, confirm the science of teaching and learning.

CREATIVITY

Creativity begins with a motive to produce. This was evident at the invitation level of interactive learning. As much emphasis should be placed on the process of creativity as on the product. The how of creating is just as important as the creation or the end product itself. During this involvement category, the creative process develops into a visualizing of the steps to be taken and of the possible product or outcomes of the creative dimensions of the learning experience. At this category of interactive learning, "past experience is used to modify, . . .to clarify,. . . to discover, and to make a decision to create. . . " (Steinaker and Bell 1970:93). To modify, to clarify, to discover, and to decide are essential components of creativity at this category of interactive teaching and learning. Once the students know the parameters of the creative milieu, they can begin to select options, explore possibilities, and deal with probable solutions and possible creative products. It is at this level of involvement that the student begins to discuss and share ideas and creative interests with peers and with the teacher. This is a time to explore, to discover, and to make a decision to translate an idea to a creative product. Past experience and current interaction provide impetus for the student to be creative and to do those things that will creatively move the experience along. Students have envisioned the process and are motivated to continue the process.

Creativity at this category of interactive learning is exploratory, process oriented, and interrogative. It is vital that the student have the materials and the interactive structure of

exploration to develop and to continue the creative process. The roles of the teacher as catalyst and coordinator and the roles of the students as explorers and cooperators are at the core of the creative process and help set the tone and direction for creativity. Personal interaction between the teacher and the students is crucial at this level of creativity. It is fostered through positive group work and through the dynamics of group interaction. During this level, creativity is the essence of the art of teaching. It requires personal involvement, positive interaction, and a pertinent vision of what is to be created.

CRITICAL THINKING

Critical thinking is identifiable and sequential (Steinaker and Bell 1979). Critical thinking during this category of the taxonomy of interactive learning entails data collection and defining variables. It is demonstrated through student focus on data along with identifying the similarities and differences in the data. Information is framed and reframed through an interrogative and interactive process. At this category of interactive learning, students collect data and begin working with those data through the critical thinking process. During invitation activities, they began to recognize that there were variables. Curiosity was the impetus for critical thinking at invitation and that remains the same during this involvement category.

In this category, students also begin to assess and define variables, including specific similarities and differences within the data. They clarify and classify information so they can more easily organize and focus on it. Students "discover why there is a variable and what differentiates it from the rest of the environment" (Steinaker and Bell 1979:97). Here students begin to make inferences about the variable in relation to other contexts and with other resources. Students are enabled, through critical thinking, to clarify, to differentiate, and to substantiate information as well as to interactively discuss and begin to dialogue about the information. They are able to probe more deeply into the data and to understand and gain insight into what it means within the parameters of the learning experience. Students begin to organize, to clarify, and to categorize information for study and discussion purposes. They use this information to help them decide their next steps and the direction for their study. Critical thinking involves the students in an appraisal of the available information, an interactive construct of the information, and an identification of similarities and differences. Critical thinking allows students to categorize and classify information hierarchically and sequentially.

Critical thinking is an organizing activity, necessary to the involvement level of interactive learning. A solution is not always the goal of critical thinking; it is, rather, satisfaction of curiosity and development of a sense of wonder generated through the variables. Critical thinking represents student ability to assess and translate material into functional and usable components and categories. Students note variables and similarities, organize the information, and prepare to move on to the next level of interactive teaching.

A solution is not always the goal of critical thinking; it is, rather, satisfaction of curiosity and development of a sense of wonder generated through the variables.

Critical thinking represents the science of teaching, just as the interaction and interrogative discourse represents the art of teaching.

PROBLEM SOLVING

Students using problem solving at this category of interactive learning are beginning to deal with the issue or problem. The defining activity is exploration of data and information. They are exploring data, examining information, and making sure that data and information are consistent with the problem, issue, or area of study. Students also need

to know if the information or data can be substantiated in terms of the parameters of the study. Students begin to think about the data and define its boundaries. "At this process level the learner must not only clarify what the real problem is but also develop solution criteria and begin to identify constraints faced" (Steinaker and Bell 1979:101). Teacher roles are important at this level of problem solving. As a catalyst and coordinator, the teacher must not only provide data sources, but also provide a format for strong interaction about the data. The teacher needs to ensure that the students can perceive possible solutions. The development of possible solutions and obstacles to be overcome needs to be addressed. The teacher must continue to stimulate, to challenge, to react, and to interrogatively meet with the students in groups or individually. Through this group and individual interaction, the teacher provides direction for the students in their further pursuit of the overall outcomes and objectives of the learning experience. The teacher further assists students in becoming more involved in the learning experience and addressing specific problems and issues.

Students become aware of the problem, understanding the variables and the similarities. They are able to substantiate and summarize the process of which they are a part. In addition, students also interact about their information and work on resolving issues and gaining understanding and clarification of information. Although solutions are not expected at this level of interaction, students can, within an interactive and group process, predict and project direction, possible solutions, and outcomes with more clarity and understanding. Students, through this category of problem solving and interactive learning, demonstrate an understanding of the issues, problems, and concerns about the area of study. They demonstrate their understanding by clarifying the problem and deciding that it is important for them to continue through the learning sequence so they can begin to hypothesize, test hypotheses, and determine solutions. They are, through this process, enabled to proceed to the next level of interactive learning. Problem solving is primarily focused on understanding process, clarifying information, organizing and classifying data, and generally working closely with the resources available. In this sense problem solving represents the science of teaching and learning. However, through interactive and relationship development, the art of teaching is also intrinsic to this problem-solving strand of interactive learning.

WRITING

The writing context of interactive learning at this level is that of describing or telling about what the learning process is and how it has developed. After the definition has been "clearly, concisely, and coherently stated, you will need to describe the topic so the reader understands the focus of your paper" (Steinaker and Bustillos 2007:v). At this category of interactive writing, students are able to describe what they are studying, what they have learned, how they have learned it, and the sequential process through which they have gone to arrive at the culmination of this involvement level of interactive learning. With young students this kind of writing can be done in a group setting, with the sequence being listed and then students copying and illustrating the steps. Older students can keep notes, write narratives, and prepare sequences of learning activities. Written narratives, both individual and small group, need to be shared with the whole class.

During this category of interactive learning, students work thoroughly with the data and the resources. They engage in discourse about the data and discuss it interrogatively. Students further need to write ideas and perspectives on the importance of the topic and why it is important to them to learn the material. In writing, students describe what they have done and what they are learning. They need, in addition, to note what they want to learn. In their writing they describe the parameters and the probable scope and sequence of the learning experience. Describing includes a consideration of questions that still remain to be resolved. Describing includes the clarification of information and data so that they can be read with understanding. Describing involves summarizing so that the salient information and data are highlighted for the reader. It also entails predicting the direction and further steps the students must take to achieve the outcomes and objectives of the lesson or study. Describing these elements gives their document substance, meaning, and purpose. Descriptive writing is the genre most applicable to this level of interactive learning. Through descriptive writing, students are describing the subject matter and informing each other and the teacher.

Writing can, and should, be edited at this category so that the ongoing record is a viable and strong document. Editing can be done by the teacher and by the students. Students can edit individually or cooperatively in groups. When the editing is complete, students can review and finalize their writing. When this has been accomplished, students are ready to move to the investigation category of interactive learning. Writing is a process that requires organization, editing, and clear descriptions. Writing, well done, tells a story effectively and affectively. In this way, writing becomes a part of the art of teaching and learning. At the same time, writing requires careful and thoughtful crafting and organization. Writing, in this sense, is a demonstration of the science of teaching and learning. Writing is both an art and a science.

Levels of Cognition
Primary:
Memory
Translation
Interpretation
Secondary:
Application
Analysis
Synthesis
Evaluation

THINKING

Thinking at this level of interactive learning is demonstrated through apprehension. The students focus on stimuli and resources. They order or arrange the stimuli and resources into a reactive and thoughtful framework. Here students begin to ponder what they have been exposed to in the previous category. They begin to react to the content and the direction of the learning experience. The interrogative structure for this category encourages students to think and to focus their thinking on the content and issues brought before them in this category. Thinking is essential to resolving issues and understanding material. At this involvement level of learning, thinking can be done through brainstorming within the interactive groups set up to foster learning. Brainstorming involves the exchange of ideas, sharing perspectives and what each student has been thinking about. Students react to what they thought about and focus their thinking on what has been presented and they have done; they then project through their thinking brainstorming strategy a direction in which to go. Thinking at this category of the learning taxonomy involves several levels of cognition. Among them are memory, translation, and interpretation. Higher levels of cognition such as application, analysis, synthesis, and evaluation could be used, but are not primary to this level of thinking. When making future predictions and thinking about outcomes, the application level of cognition is used (Steinaker 2002).

Any thinking process at the apprehension level involves memory and translation. Interpretation is the most used level of cognition at this point in the development of the lesson sequence, although application and sometimes even analysis might be used to determine the components of an issue. When student thinking is shared through brainstorming and verbal interaction, ideas will change and direction will develop. Thinking, through interaction, broadens and includes ideas not yet thought about. Thinking individually is good. Thinking together is even better. Group thinking through interactive brainstorming can be used, at this level of interactive learning, to process information and gain apprehended knowledge of the information and the processes involved in the learning experience. To think through the process thoroughly is evidence of focused thinking. Thinking through the issues and content both individually and in groups helps the students make the decision to move on to the next category of thinking.

LEARNING

Learning at this level of interaction is that of personalizing. Personalizing is verbalizing or experimenting with feelings, actions, skills, or attitudes in terms of personal meaning. Students gather additional information, project a direction, and show that they value what is being learned. Students react to what they have done thus far in the process of learning. Learning becomes personal; within the interactive setting, students can share and discuss their personal feelings and attitudes about what is being learned. Learning, as expressed here, adjusts and changes as interaction takes place. Ideas and perspectives grow and change as students share candidly their personalized points of view and what they feel they have learned. Discussion and questioning develops through an interactive modality within the context of this category of learning. Learning becomes apparent once the thinking process becomes focused and ideas are shared and discussed. Learning here needs to be interactive; it involves the students in raising questions, interactively discussing issues or problems, and coming to a consensus decision to continue with the experience. It sometimes tends to be a quixotic yet dynamic interaction at this category of learning caused by the interaction and discussion about the learning topic. We say quixotic because when there is brainstorming there tends to be ideas and opinions from all degrees of the spectrum. Some ideas and perspectives may be far from consensus and the whole must be winnowed. Winnowing these ideas and feelings into a viable focused perspective is a process that needs to be done during this learning category. Consensus and direction can emerge from this energetic exchange of ideas and perspectives. Personalized content points of view are important to share with peers so that a more focused consensus can emerge (Steinaker 2002).

> *Personalizing is verbalizing or trying out feelings, actions, skills, or attitudes in terms of personal meaning.*

At the same time, learning results from thoughtful challenge and discussion of the issues and a focus on decision and direction. Learning takes place positively in an interactive environment where students feel free to exchange ideas, to learn from each other. At this category of interaction, students learn how to use resources and gain personal meaning. They can share with each other, discuss ideas in small groups, and hone their perspectives and points of view. Through developing positive relationships, students are enabled to share with each other and with the teacher. Learning emerges, is enlarged, and becomes integral to the process during this category of the interactive learning process. Here learning is a positive, energetic, and interactive developmental process that students generally enjoy.

TEACHING

As noted at the invitation level, teaching is, at its core, valuing. The teacher values the learning experience, values the students, and values their decision to continue with the learning experience. The teacher also values the potential and direction the students have shown during this category of interactive learning. At this level of interactive learning, the role of teaching is that of particularizing. To particularize means, in essence, to be exacting and extremely careful. Here the teacher works with the students to value what they are learning and to help them focus on the topic and particularize what they are learning for themselves. In this context, particularizing, as a perspective on teaching, fits well into this category of interactive learning. Each of the other roles we have discussed relate directly to this category of involvement. Particularizing does as well. It is closely related to personalizing learning. To particularize, the teacher must ensure that students personalize what they have learned and share their personal perspective.

Through particularizing, students begin to value what they are learning. The teacher needs to affirm this through the teaching roles of catalyst and coordinator. Through these roles, the teacher can ensure that students begin to individually and as a group particularize ideas as well as personalizing them. Particularizing requires building on the valuing of learning and coming to a decision to continue along the path toward further investigating the topic that they have come to value. Here as a catalyst, the teacher holds up the value of what is being learned and coordinates the process of individualizing the value for each student. This is central to the involvement level of the process of learning.

Teaching is attitudinal as well as cognitive. Here the emphasis is on developing a positive attitude toward the learning sequence and deciding to pursue it. Valuing is key to learning, especially at this category of interactive learning. Without learning to value the topic on which they are focusing, the students will not willingly move forward toward investigating it more thoroughly. As the decision to further the learning experience emerges, we learn that valuing is the common denominator of teaching that involves interactive ordering and sequenced student thinking and learning, which will result in actions, feelings, behaviors, concepts, and skills. This is what particularizing is all about.

LEADERSHIP

At the involvement level of interactive learning, the teacher role in leadership is that of a coordinator and the student role is that of a cooperator. The teacher, as leader, still retains a strong and dominant leadership role, but the students at this involvement level of interactive learning have already begun to actively participate in the learning process. Students have begun to value the study and it begins to have substance and meaning to them. They have particularized and personalized the learning and the process in which they are involved. As students begin to more fully share in the vision of the teacher, their ideas, perspectives, and constructs are to be considered carefully by both the teacher and their peers. They are fully involved in the learning experience; the student role in cooperative leadership begins to take shape even though they are still dependent on the teacher as catalyst and coordinator. Their roles as explorer and cooperator enunciate their leadership roles. Students explore their resources and cooperate with each other and with the teacher. Their role in leadership is stronger here than in the initial category of interactive learning. Leadership for the students is cooperative. This means that they can cooperate to develop personal meaning and particularized knowledge. Leadership for the students is emergent and much more obvious at this category of interaction.

> *Leadership is a major component of the art of teaching because it rests on positive interaction and the ability to care for one another and to care for what is being learned.*

Involvement is an active and exciting time for teacher and students. A leader, as noted by Sample (2002), "needs to be able to see the shades of gray" (1) to begin to make "wise decisions and know how to proceed" (1). It is a time for leadership to become a burgeoning partnership between teacher and students. It is at this time in the learning sequence that students can really begin to learn and to demonstrate leadership skills. The teacher needs to plan for helping students learn and use the skills of leadership and to provide opportunities for student leadership to emerge. Leadership is a major component of the art of teaching because it rests on positive interaction and the ability to care for one another and for what is being learned. To be effective at this level of, leadership needs to be cooperative and involve both the teacher and the students.

FINAL COMMENTS

Involvement is an exciting and interesting category of learning for the students and the teacher. Cognition moves from memory and translation to interpretation. Each of the roles come together to make the involvement level exciting and interesting for all. The teacher roles set the tone for this category. They are catalyst and coordinator. These roles exemplify the activities and interaction at this category of interactive learning. The student role of explorer fits into the overall modality of this category of learning. Participation is the experiential level at involvement. Again, the name symbolizes the interactive essentiality of involvement. Participation entails interaction and discussion. Evaluation includes both the teacher and the learner. The evaluation role for both teacher and student is that of a questioner. This role works well with the ethos of the involvement level of interaction. With motivation, the role concerns relationships. Building relationships and starting to work together is part of the experience at the involvement level. Discourse is legitimized through challenge. This is what students do at this category of learning. They need to challenge each other's ideas and their perspectives to built a consensus to move ahead toward new dimensions of learning.

Creativity builds here through actually visualizing possible products. Critical thinking involves the students in reviewing data and identifying variables. Problem solving for students is to further define the issue or problems and to develop possible solutions for them. In the writing process, students are enabled to describe what they have done and how they have done it. Recording experiences is central to the learning process. Thinking, learning, and teaching are strongly emphasized at this category of interactive learning. Thinking involves apprehension, where the student focuses on the stimuli and materials and orders or arranges them in the mind so that the student can decide to move on. Learning, at this category, is personalizing. Learning for the student's transitions to a personal level here and through interaction this personal focus is demonstrated. In terms of teaching, the student comes to value the learning by particularizing it and focusing both on content and value. Leadership at this category of interactive learning is for both the teacher coordinator and for the student cooperator. Students are beginning to be more involved in learning process and have become active participants in planning and cooperating with the teacher. These various roles and perspective summarize the activities and interactions of the involvement level of learning. It is an exciting and very active category in the total process of interactive learning. When all of these are in place, the students transition to the next level of interactive learning. This is the investigation level, where they delve more deeply into the learning process.

During the involvement category of interactive learning, the art and science of teaching and learning are exemplified. Here affective learning takes place. Valuing what is being learned and valuing each other is the interactive art of teaching and learning. An honest, open, and positive sharing of the mind is what teaching and learning is about. Words like *coordinator* and *cooperator* in describing teacher and student leadership illuminate the art of teaching. Providing ongoing opportunities to work in groups and to share with each other to arrive at consensus and focus further exemplifies the art of teaching. The art of teaching becomes very important to teacher and students as they move together toward the investigation level of interactive learning.

To really understand the process, however, each of the seventeen strands needs to be understood and recognized both in isolated analysis and in analysis of how they fit and come together as a total learning experience. The teacher and the students need to know what they are doing and how they have done it. What and how are analytic in nature; as students and teacher review the development of the learning experience, they need to address the science of teaching. Art without particularizing, personalizing, and coming to areas of agreement does not capture the spirit and meaning of teaching and learning. Teachers and students need them both. As all these components of interactive learning at the involvement category come together, the students evolve to the next level of interactive learning, that of investigation.

Activities

The activities for this chapter focus on understanding the theory and providing a basis for analysis of strands and how they pertain to the involvement category of the taxonomy. Every student will work on activity seven. Other activities can be assigned to individuals or small groups. Group interaction is our recommended format for addressing each of the activities.

1. Discuss Joyce and his colleague's (2004) statement that "cooperative learning increases learning partly because it causes motivational orientation to move from the external to the internal" (p. Chap. 3, p. 25).

2. "Critical thinking and problem solving become more important to student involvement at this category" (p. Chap. 3, p. 26). Discuss this statement. What does it mean and how is it shown in this category? Interact about this in your group. Report your conclusions to the whole group.

3. Teacher roles at involvement are catalyst and coordinator (leadership). Student roles are explorer and cooperator (leadership). How do the roles of the teacher and the student correlate and how are they different? How are they expressed in the classroom? Discuss these questions in your group and share your points of view.

4. Discourse at this category of the taxonomy is noted as challenge. What would you see during discourse in the classroom within this category? Interact with your group about this.

5. Pick three of the activities noted on Chapter 3, p. 26. Discuss how they could be demonstrated in the classroom. As you discuss these activities, show how they would be shown in at least four analysis strands.

6. Formative evaluation relates to the process of lesson delivery and learning. Summative evaluation relates to products and outcomes. Discuss these as they relate to the first two categories of the taxonomy. What would you see in the classroom in terms of formative and summative evaluation?

7. Continue with your discussion of the strand you have selected. Ruminate about it with your group. Has it made sense to you? Why or why not? How do you think will be manifested in the next category?

Investigation

Investigation emerges as the third level of interactive learning after the students have become thoroughly involved in the learning activities and in the learning experience. They have focused on the learning, have valued it, and have made a conscious and reasoned decision to continue with the study. As they continue with the learning, they begin to investigate the topic more completely and to use the application and analysis of cognition as they pursue the study. Many models of teaching can be used during this level of interactive learning including all of those clustered in the information processing models, such as inductive thinking, concept attainment, picture word inductive model, scientific inquiry, inquiry training, mnemonics, synectics, and advance organizers (Joyce et al. 2004). All models of teaching that foster interactive discussion should also be used. To achieve a strong level of interaction, a variety of group structures to provide interactive discussion can be used. These can include "cooperative groups, focus groups, pairs, triads, dialectical groups, jigsaw groupings, rotating groups, flexible groups, problem solving groups, exploratory groups, single task groups, panel discussion groups, planning groups, critiquor groups, two kinds of numbered heads groups, and whole class groups" (Steinaker 2007:90). It is essential that the investigation level of interactive learning be organized with discussion and dialogue as central, but also with a strong focus on actively engaging students in academic learning.

Although discourse and discussion are central to the investigation level, there may also be, during this level of interactive learning, some emphasis on direct instruction to ensure their understanding by having students "practice under teacher direction . . . and encouraging them to continue to practice under teacher guidance" (Joyce et al. 2004:315). Student learning time needs to be maximized as they begin to delve into their investigation of the content (Joyce et al. 2004). Interrogative interaction through group structures and with the teacher can be very helpful to students during this category of reciprocal and interactive activity. The teacher roles become more covert and are those of a moderator and resolver who works with students and among groups in a strongly interactive manner. This helps bring about close working relationships and rapport in terms of motivation and working together. Investigation involves a challenge for both teacher and students, In their investigative role, students experiment with their new learning or and investigate. Their goal during this category is to see how things work. Students experiment with what they have learned and strive to determine value and meaning through study and investigation. The student roles are those of an experimenter and investigator who seek to resolve process questions, develop hypotheses, test them, and try optional solutions to problems. The teacher, as moderator and resolver, supports student investigation. Students begin to exercise more leadership as they interact and work

> *Investigation is a dynamic learning time for students and a positive experience for a teacher committed to student learning.*

Information Processing Models

Inductive Thinking
Concept Attainment
Picture Word Inductive
   Model
Scientific Inquiry
Inquiry Training
Mnemonics
Synectics
Advance Organizers

Source: Joyce et al., 2004.

with strong rapport during the investigative process. Investigation is a dynamic learning time for students and a positive experience for a teacher committed to student learning. Interactive investigation is a key component to the interactive learning process.

COGNITION

Although all levels of cognition could be used at this level of interactive learning, three emerge as the primary cognitive functions. These are interpretation, application, and analysis. Interpretation was evident strongly at the involvement level of interactive teaching.

Interpretation continues as students review and interpret material, classify information, build hypotheses, and identify attributes. Beyond interpretation, the students are using application and analysis. They can explain and predict as well as estimate and summarize. Meaning begins to emerge. Students begin to generalize, rewrite, and provide examples. From the cognitive level of interpretation that began at involvement and continues within this category of investigation, students have interpreted material, made predictions, and looked at future activities. During this investigation process, students cognitively move to the application level where they use materials in new, concrete situations and apply rules, methods, laws, and theories. The students demonstrate, solve, show, operate, and apply what they have learned to the new context of investigation. When the cognitive level of analysis becomes evident, students are enabled to break information down into its parts, classify, and organize materials as well as clarify and draw conclusions. They organize, outline, discriminate, and compare and contrast. Students relate all component parts and variables to the whole of the learning experience. These are the cognitive activities associated with the investigation level of interactive learning. The use of at least the three most obvious levels of cognition—including interpretation, application, and analysis—is a major step in learning at the investigation level of interactive learning. Other levels of cognition may also be used as students apply and analyze information. They will use memory and translation, which were evident earlier in the sequence of cognition. The students will also occasionally use synthesis and evaluation. These levels of cognition, while being used in certain learning situations, are not core to this category of interactive learning. The latter two will be more evident as later levels of interactive learning are discussed.

EXPERIENTIAL

At this category of learning experience, the students are experimenters and investigators. The teacher is the moderator and resolver in terms of that experience. When students begin the identification level of experience, they develop an intellectual and emotional identification with the content and focus of the study. They have completed their positive involvement with the learning sequence; now they want to continue to learn more and investigate the information, the issues, and the problems attendant to

Primary Cognitive Functions

Interpretation: reviewing and classifying information, building hypotheses, and identifying attributes.
Application: use materials in new, concrete situations where they apply rules, methods, laws, and theories.
Analysis: break down information, classify, organize materials, clarify, and draw conclusions.

the learning experience. Emotional and intellectual identification with the learning experience becomes evident at this experiential level (Steinaker and Bell 1981).

The teaching mode is research or finding information and details, putting them together for function and use. At this category of experiential learning, the students begin to identify personally and as a group the value, purpose, and meaning of the learning process. The emphasis is on determining meaning and understanding the outcomes of the learning. Investigation, through valuing and seeking meaning, provides "a comfortable framework for learner identification with the experience" (Steinaker and Bell 1979:67).

Furthermore, during this level of experience there needs to be selection and organization of necessary data, using the data, observing, and experimenting. There must also be discussion, conferencing, and interaction through a variety of group structures. Hypotheses need to be developed and tested. Trying conditional solutions in multiple situations should be used. This is a time for students to establish a strong working rapport with each other and work together to achieve projected goals and outcomes. Students, through this level of experience and interaction, are able to demonstrate what they have learned in more than one context. They can discuss what they have learned, respond to questions about their work, and actually perform many of the skills they have learned and developed. For students and for the teacher, this is a time for demonstrating increased efficiency as identification with the experience takes place. It is a time for application and analysis. Investigation is a time for sharing and showing what they have learned. Students, as this level of experience and interactive learning unfolds, have made a strong commitment to the learning, have identified with it, and are taking an increasing level of responsibility for their own learning. They know they have learned well and are ready to internalize the experience. Learning and teaching represent a gestalt approach to human experience. We as human beings interact, ponder, discuss, assess, and analyze what we are sensing, feeling and experience. As students and teacher do these things during the investigation category of interactive learning, they demonstrate both the art and the science of teaching.

> *Experience, at this level of interactivity, demonstrates both the science and the art of teaching and learning.*

TEACHER ROLE

During this category of interactive learning, the roles of the teacher are those of a moderator and resolver. Students have identified with the area of study and with the content they investigate vigorously. During this level of interaction, students work to investigate issues and content and are able to demonstrate what they have learned and what from the perspectives. They investigate the material from a variety of approaches and the teacher moderates their investigation and helps them resolve problems and issues. The teacher moves freely about the room, talking to individuals and to groups of students. The teacher asks questions, responds to inquiries, helps students maintain focus, ensures time on task, and provides direction and information when needed. Although the teacher does all this, the roles of the teacher is

somewhat more passive that it has been for earlier categories of the interactive learning sequence. The roles, however, are more covert because the students have been taking more responsibility for their learning. This is very appropriate for the teacher. Even so, sometimes the teacher may need to use direct instruction or any of the information processing models of teaching during instruction and in whole class meetings. This could also be done in smaller group discussions.

The teacher must be flexible and positive in working with students. The teacher as moderator and resolver recognizes student needs, responds to those needs, and helps direct students toward their goals and objectives. In doing so, the teacher challenges the students to assume new tasks and new areas for taking charge of their own learning process. The teacher also needs to be responsive to expressed student needs and continue to provide reaction, challenge, and emphasis toward deepening student investigation of the material. The teacher must keep things running efficiently and coherently. The process of investigation tends to be a time of strong interactive learning, demanding real thought and analytical understanding from both the student and the teacher. The teacher raises questions and provides information that can help students gain more confidence and direction in seeking to know more about the topic. There is no time for the teacher to sit and wait during this category of interactive teaching and learning. Focusing direction and arbitrating decisions is evidence of the teacher role at this category of interactive learning. "From a dynamic motivator to an active catalyst, the teacher becomes a subtle, but inventive moderator whose job it is to bring reinforcement, personal interaction, and knowledge of results to the learner" (Steinaker and Bell 1979:84). Interaction through challenge, focused direction, and examination of learning are among the hallmarks of this category of interactive learning. It is an adventure in deepening the learning experience. Investigation focuses on the science of learning, but within the interaction and group work, the art of teaching is demonstrated through the interactive process.

STUDENT ROLE

The student roles during investigation are those of an experimenter and an investigator. The question for the student here is how to put their learning into context with their lives and make sense of the information and sources they have gathered. They need to understand how to organize their data, how to review their progress, and how to investigate its meaning and value to them. The descriptor of experimenter and investigator aptly define what the student does during this level of interactive learning. The student begins to look at details, organize information, classify it, as well as develop and test hypotheses. They need to categorize, organize, and sequence information. They also need to plan how to use information and to discover its meaning for them. Students need to demonstrate identified skills they have achieved and use them as a strategy to further the investigation process. Students need to plan what they need yet to do to complete the experience, depending on what they have already learned. Students do this through annotating, sharing, discussing, defining, outlining, creating, valuing, and putting together what they have learned in terms of planning their next steps toward completing the learning sequence. The student needs active engagement in a variety of group settings to have the opportunity to ask questions, to respond to questions, and to investigate through the groups the resources they are using. The students need to verify information, to clarify, and to draw conclusions. The students need to try optional solutions and discover which ones work in particular situations or modalities. In terms of investigation, students need to use skills they have learned to further the investigative process.

The student, at this category of interactive learning, develops an emotional and intellectual bond with the material and with the area of study. The student also builds a strong rapport with peers and with the teacher so that the working relationships can enhance learning and assist in the resolution of issues and concerns about the content. The student is creatively immersed in the study. Through this category of interactive learning, the students have achieved a functional skill level with the materials and resources as well as their study and investigation of those materials and resources, but they have understood how to access and to work with the information they have. Students have developed strong working relationships and strong rapport with each other and with the teacher. These relationships and rapport help make investigation a time for identifying emotionally and intellectually with each other and with the learning experience.

During this category of interactive learning, the student demonstrates time on task, a strong proactive attitude toward the tasks involved, and a willingness to work cooperatively and positively with peers and with the teacher. Students are on focus during their work in this category and have totally identified with the learning experience. This allows them to delve deeply into the content and information they have before them. They also have developed skills and attitudes during their study and need to demonstrate those skills and those attitudes. Students, through their work before this level of interaction and during their investigation, have accomplished much. Through interaction, they have developed strong rapport. Through their investigation, they have discovered new skills and have used them as needed. They have been engaged both in the art of teaching and learning and the science of learning.

EVALUATION

At all levels of assessment, the two components of evaluation are process and product evaluation. This has been true during the first two categories of interactive teaching: invitation and involvement. We reiterate that evaluation and assessment are cooperative efforts by both the teacher and the students, with more and more self and group assessment being done by the students. Assessment is the evaluation modality most apparent at this level of interactive learning. Evaluation is the task both of the student and the teacher. As assessor, the teacher must clearly understand what the students are doing, the direction in which they are moving, and the outcomes they hope to achieve. The teacher must assess and understand student needs. The teacher needs to provide the information, direction, and materials the student might need for this investigative process. Being an assessor is a midpoint consideration of how the students have progressed, what the students are doing within the learning experience, what their attitudes are, how the changing roles of teacher and students impact learning, and what decisions need to be made in terms of direction and internalization. The teacher and the students must assess how well the skills and attitudes have been learned. Both teachers and students need to know whether they can do the tasks, demonstrate the skills, and achieve the objectives that have been developed.

The teacher roles as moderator and resolver fit well with this role of assessor; with the rapport built with students, the assessor role can be a strong asset for the teacher in terms of evaluation. The teacher must verbalize assessments to the students, make notes, and react to student work. Assessment for the teacher is part of the challenge of the roles of moderator and resolver. Students are strong participants in assessing what they are doing, how well they are doing it, and what they hope to accomplish. In their roles as experimenter and investigator, students are expected to develop hypotheses, test those hypotheses, verify information, and have cogent discourse about issues, problems, and successes. They do this with each other and with the teacher. It is very important that students dialogue with each other and with the teacher in terms of assessment and evaluation.

Assessment has two dimensions. Assessment is partly a review of past quality and is, at the same time a preview of next steps and future direction. Assessment, in the hierarchy of evaluation, is at the midpoint. The teacher must assess student performance, achievement, and interaction sensitively and with candor. Both teacher and students need to be interactive in their assessment. Students should be able to verbalize, demonstrate, keep notes and write personal or group assessments about how they are doing

Dimensions of Assessment

Review of past quality by evaluating student:

- performance
- achievement
- interaction

Preview of next steps and future direction by determining:

- positive backward look at accomplishments
- honest review of what yet needs to happen in the course of study
- strongly apparent student participation

and about the effectiveness of what they have done. Students should be able to review their own performance and the process they have followed as they become an integral part in the assessment of the total learning experience (Steinaker 2002).

Assessment is also a cognitive experience during this level of interactive teaching and learning. Teacher and students must carefully and thoroughly process assessments. Assessment requires proactive thinking toward the future and a positive backward look at accomplishments. Assessment can help students build their own scaffolds for future activity as they assess their work and future direction with each other and with the teacher. Assessment here is not focused on scores or grades; it is based on an articulated and honest review of what has happened and what yet needs to happen in the course of study. The teacher roles are to moderate and to resolve issues about evaluating this process and to ensure that the students have indeed gained the insight they need in terms of process, product, and personal assessment to move from rapport to respect in their learning experience and in the continuing sequence of interactive learning. Student participation in assessment and evaluation should be strongly apparent at this investigation level of learning. Assessment interactively accomplished helps students analyze what they have been doing and helps them achieve a level of interactive rapport.

MOTIVATION

Motivation at this level of interactive learning is best represented by the word rapport. It is at this level of instruction that students need to develop more than just a working relationship with their peers and with their teacher. Through rapport and a strong working environment, students are enabled to being to set priorities for their work and the outcomes they expect to achieve (Holm 2003). Students need to establish strong working rapport with each other, with the teacher, and with the process of learning. When these good working relationships have been developed and established, rapport as the level of motivation emerges and becomes operant. Rapport means more than just a strong working relationship. Rapport means that students function as a cohesive and cooperative group. It means that they have identified with each other and with the process and that as group or a class need to do well and to succeed in learning. There is mutual involvement and the building of close working relationships through the process of learning together. Students support each other and the teacher as they more functionally work together. As they work together, they set priorities for work schedules and individual assignments. They have already established readiness earlier and have begun to develop relationships. Those relationships now need to become working relationships with an operating base within an established rapport. When students investigate with focus and energy, they need to do it interactively and within the context of a variety of group settings ranging from pairs to whole-class groups. Students take a greater role in terms of planning, direction, and possible outcomes related to the learning experience. These working functions were exemplified by their role as experimenter and investigator. Students are beginning to move into the role of principal investigator and the teacher should ensure that they have the opportunity to exemplify this role. Where there is rapport there is also involvement, investigation, and insight. Although students work interactively much of the time, there also needs to be a time for personal and individual thought, study, and reflection. The teacher needs to be aware of this and needs to provide for much group interaction, but also allow individual student time for interaction with materials and personal thought and study. The teacher may also need to provide some direct instruction to individual students, to groups, or to the whole class as needed. The purpose of direct instruction with appropriate advance organizers is to deepen the ability of students to complete the investigative process. The teacher must, following the direct instruction, allow for group interaction and study. Through these models and other varied kinds of teaching models, students become more committed to the study, to the process, to the teacher, and to each other.

Rapport means developing and functioning with a strong working relationship interactively developed and utilized. Rapport means that students personally and individually study, review, and investigate problems, issues, and materials. They need to build skills and attitudes and be able to logically put things together. They need to demonstrate what they have learned in a sharing-learning context. They need to build attitudes and develop skills as they work together. Group time at this level of motivation and interactive learning takes most of the work time, but individual time needs to be built into the schedule flexibly and with enough frequency to allow for personal study and reflection. Interaction individually and individual ideas and constructs with the materials and issues can then be brought to the group for further discussion and direction.

> *Rapport means developing and functioning with a strong working relationship interactively developed and utilized.*

Students demonstrate a felt need to really get into the major issues in their study through their own investigation of the resources and the content of the learning sequence. They need to share with each other, with the whole class, and with the teacher what they have learned, reviewed, understood, applied, analyzed, and demonstrated. Student analysis helps provide for the furtherance of the process and achievement of preliminary goals and objectives. Motivation here is shown in an organized working environment where students and teacher demonstrate a cooperative, comfortable, and stable learning setting. As the process continues, a need to put information together and to further define progress and the continuation of the learning experience emerges. It is then that the students move the learning sequence to a new category of interactive learning.

Motivation is a major key to learning and progress through a learning experience. At this point in the learning experience, motivation is exemplified by the development and utilization of strong working relationships among the students and with the teacher. Students begin to trust one another and are able to confidently share with each other about what they have learned and how they have learned it. Trust and confidence are key words in this category of interactive learning and are demonstrated as rapport in motivation.

DISCOURSE

The model for discourse and dialogue for change here is clear, cogent, and content-oriented communication. Discourse during this category is marked by frequent and focused interaction among students and between students and teacher. During this category of interactive learning, the students establish a positive and functional working rapport; they are now able to go into detail about the nature of the content and the sources of the course of study. Discourse is an excellent and basic component of this working rapport. Discourse, through clear and consistent communication, keeps the rapport strong and focused; it is the key to successful interactive learning at this level of the taxonomy of teaching and learning (Steinaker 2003b). Discourse is the format for building relationships and demonstrating the art of teaching. Students need to be focused and on task as they communicate with each other. They need to be clear and concise in their conversations. Students need to learn to keep their mind on the subject and not be involved in peripheral or unnecessary information. They should monitor themselves and assess how well they are keeping focused in their communication.

Students, at this point in the teaching–learning process, know what they need to investigate, to study, to find out, and to learn. They rely on their sources and the interpretation of these sources through discourse and within an interrogative and organizing focus. Discourse is designed to allow students to organize and to begin to put things together in a way they can deal with them effectively and thoroughly. It is at this level of discourse that students demonstrate an understanding of the design and the detail of what they are doing. Students should have a strong preliminary understanding of the process and how they will achieve the final product. Communication implies a straightforward dialogue about the issues and content on which the students are working. Students need discourse to share what they have learned, analyze what they have learned, and apply the results into a personal context of demonstrated use. The teacher and the students should plan a number of group formats to encourage this kind of discourse and to ensure that through discourse and discussion decisions are made, ideas are explored, and the investigation comes to fruition. Communication is an essential component of both group direction and personal learning at this level of interactive learning. Clear and cogent discourse, through effective communication, can ensure that the learning process is not only identified, but becomes a solid interactive investigation. In this investigation process the teacher moderates the discourse and helps students resolve issues within the discourse and learning experience. The student mode is that of being an experimenter and investigator. The art of communicating clearly and cogently is a necessary element of discourse. Learning how to communicate clearly and cogently also demonstrates the science of teaching and learning.

> *Discourse is designed to allow students to organize and to begin to put things together in a way they can deal with them effectively and thoroughly.*

CREATIVITY

Creativity is highlighted at this level of interactive learning, as students conceptualize the product and begin working with it. Experimenting is the definition of this level of creativity. Students experiment with the "idea, product, artifact or behavior" (Steinaker and Bell 1979:93). Experimenting, at this level of creativity, is closely related to the basic structure of interaction during this category of interactive learning. The teacher roles as moderator and resolver correlate with creativity. It should also be noted that the student role as investigator also correlates with this creative level. Through creativity, students try out the concepts and probe the details of the concepts and experiment with them. There needs to be a time for ruminating about the issues and the materials they have before them. Students gain a clear construct of the whole along with its component parts. They ruminate about what they are doing and that "rumination is both active and passive. It involves thinking and doing. Learners need . . . opportunities for rumination during this stage of the creative process" (Steinaker and Bell 1979:93). At this level of creativity, students discover the scope of the creative milieu and begin to "select options, to explore possibilities, and to deal with probable solutions" (93). Students are both emotionally and intellectually committed to resolving issues and to discovering the process toward probable solutions and the final product of their work. The creative efforts of the students thrive in an interactive communicative climate of creativity, dialogue, and investigation. Personal involvement in the learning sequence activates interaction and the creative process. This level of creativity is a time when the students demonstrate a level of understanding and self-confidence in where they are in the learning process. Students know what they want to create and understand the process through which they will need to follow to create their product. Students, through rumination and experimentation, proceed with self-motivation and begin to demonstrate a stronger and more dominant role in the learning experience. When this occurs, the students are ready to move to the next level in the learning experience and the interactive learning process continues. Creativity at this time is a joyous expression of an envisioned product and a clear understanding of how they are going to create it. Students really enjoy creativity because it is an expression of self and an aesthetic expression of doing something new to them.

CRITICAL THINKING

This is a time for organizing and structuring within the learning process. Students function at the interpretation, application, and analysis levels of cognition and the identification level of experience. Critical thinking, at this level of interactive learning, requires the students to critique and organize the resources. Organization is the descriptor of the activities at this level of critical thinking. Students need to do the organizing activities together, discussing them with each other in groups. As noted, this requires application and analysis levels of cognitive thinking and the ability to think through real issues of investigation. The working rapport among students needs to become strong. Students here are ready for really focusing on the details of organization and putting those details into appropriate classifications, formats, and organizational structures. Hypothesizing and testing hypotheses become "a key teaching strategy at which learners should become adept as they move through the critical thinking process" (Steinaker and Bell 1979:98). At this level of critical thinking, there is a shift in teacher and student roles. During this category of interactive learning, the teacher and student roles "reach a balance" (Steinaker and Bell 1979:95). It is here, as the students become critically focused on their study, that they begin to assume a more dominant overt role in the learning process and the role of the teacher becomes somewhat less dominant. The teacher is the moderator and coordinator who helps promote the critical thinking and interactive process, but it is the students who begin to take charge of their own learning experience. Students at any age can do this from kindergarten through graduate school. It is the confluence of critical thinking, the student role, and the teacher role that makes it possible. This confluence of roles is a key component of the art of teaching. Teacher and students need to be ready for transitions in roles and responsibilities that begin to emerge at this level of interactive learning. The changing teacher activities "begin to place the burden for further exploration on the learner" (Steinaker and Bell 1979:98). Critical thinking is an essential element in the learning process at this level of interactive learning. It is wonderfully interesting to work with students who are thinking critically and energetically investigating and critiquing issues, problems, and materials. Students learn how to think critically by being involved with it through an interrogative interaction with each other, with the teacher, and a discussion of the materials they are studying. Critical thinking at this interactive category is a wonderful structural and organizational function of learning. Students wrestle with the issues they are investigating and organize them for functional use during the next category of interactive learning. Critical thinking through interaction is strong in the science of learning and also demonstrates the art of learning and teaching.

Identification Level of Critical Thinking

Critique Resources
Organize by Focusing on
   Detail
Discussing and
   Classifying Information
Testing Hypotheses

PROBLEM SOLVING

The focus of problem solving at this level of interactive learning is trying optional solutions to the issues and problems in the area of focus and to the identified constructs students are developing and detailing. "Alternatives are examined and . . . tried on a trial-and-error basis with less viable solutions being cast aside" (Steinaker and Bell 1979:102). Problem solving is an individual, group activity, and skill that needs to be demonstrated individually and interactively with others. The teacher moderates student interactive work on problems. This is done through discussing the problems with them, helping students resolve issues and problems, then considering logical or alternative solutions to those problems. The teacher remains a strong resource leader for the student but in a more covert role than an overt role. In this role the teacher must develop strong questioning skills to help fully develop the nature of the problem and to narrow down possible solutions. The teacher does this through encouraging and permitting a discursive format of interaction.

Discussion, conferencing, and group interaction are important within the problem-solving process, particularly at this level of interactive learning. Skill at asking questions, responding, and discussing need to be learned by students and modeled by the teacher. At the same time, problem solving is both an individual and group skill. During problem-solving activities, students in "individual situations . . . should be taught the value of interaction with peers as a means of testing their judgments and their hypotheses" (Steinaker and Bell 1979:102). Thus the interactive context of problem solving becomes exceptionally important. Investigation centers on identifying detail and constructing and deconstructing possible ways of dealing with the concepts and ideas within the core of the study. Students need to try optional solutions and begin to narrow those solutions down to arrive at some consensual focus. This needs to be done individually as well as within group settings that are interactive. Problem solving needs to be done interactively and through group interaction. This context of interaction must be designed so that consensus can be built. When students have come to an initial consensus, they begin to demonstrate readiness for the next level of interactive learning. They have critiqued the issues and problems, have arrived at consensus, and have prepared themselves to continue through the interactive learning process. Problem solving at involvement is an important component of student learning and needs to be integral to the interactive process. It is in these ways that problem solving can become central to the learning experience in terms of art and in terms of the science of learning.

WRITING

Written communication is important at this level of interactive learning as it is at all levels of interactive learning. Students not only need to talk about and discuss what they are investigating; they need to keep careful written records of the process they have followed, the problems they have solved, what skills they have learned, and next steps in the process. Students need to address in writing the how of the process and be able to explain why each step was taken and what processes was involved. Through written records, they are involved in self-analysis. Writing is both an individual and a group process.

Written records become very important during this time of study. The definition of writing at this category of interactive learning is detail. In terms of writing, thus far students have defined the topic and have described it. Now, at the investigation level, they go into detail about what they have been learning and what they are currently learning. It is important to keep track of what students have done and have accomplished. To do this ,the student needs to develop writing skills, particularly in formal writing. They need to learn how to organize their work, to outline materials, and to write clearly and concisely. They need to use simple straightforward sentences

and develop a report that is cogent, concise, and coherent (Steinaker and Bustillos 2007). Although we are mentioning this need for skill development at this time, it should have begun at the invitation category and continued through involvement. By the investigation level of writing in the learning sequence, students should possess enough skills to write competently. If they do not, they need to have instruction in writing skills with particular emphasis on writing reports and keeping accurate records. It is essential that they know these writing skills during this level of interactive learning.

At this level of interactive learning, students are recording in their writing the details of what they are studying and how they are learning. They move beyond descriptive writing and are detailing and sequencing what they have done. They are writing primarily in the formal writing style. Students do this through application and analysis. They detail possible direction and solutions as well as specific information about the scope and sequence of the learning experience thus far and about the area of study. Students need to dialogue with each other about what they have noted and written. Shared writing is expected at this level of interactive writing. Students may write individually or they may write a group report. Group reports and writing are consistent with interactive learning. Those reports need to be shared with the whole class for discussion, analysis, and consensus building. Students need to react to each other's oral and written comments and come to agreement on identified ideas, organizational structures, and direction for continuing work. Written communication is as important as oral communication and it needs to become an intrinsic part of the interactive process at this level of interactive learning. Oral communication alone is not enough. Students, here, learn that records and specific written detail must be kept, shared, and reviewed as the learning process develops.

For very young students, the teacher plays an important role in ensuring that this is accomplished by working with students in a language experience setting. Younger students can develop a group writing report with the aid and support of the teacher. They can read it and share it. This works well for these young learners. Older students can take a more active role in writing and assume responsibility for keeping records and preparing a detailed and specific written record of what they have done and what they have accomplished. When these have been accomplished, there is a readiness for the next level of interactive learning and shared writing. The next level of interactive writing is that of insight. Writing is both a learned skill and an aesthetic expression.

THINKING

Thinking at this level of interaction is acceptance of the learning context. Students have moved from sensory reaction to stimuli and information through apprehension to acceptance. Acceptance indicates identification with the learning sequence. It also shows understanding the conditions of the learning experience and the individual and group roles in accepting it and working with it. The thought process has come to the point that the students accept what they have learned, what they are doing, and what they have yet to do. Students need to have time to think, to cogitate, and to groupthink about the learning process. Reflection following the thinking process is needed. Reflection can be done individually, but it is more effectively done interactively. The teacher needs to provide the time and opportunity for students to ponder about and to reflect on the learning process. Students, at this point in the development of the learning experience, need to ponder and reflect on where they began, what they are currently investigating, and where they are going (Steinaker 2002).

> *Thinking helps put the learning process into logical contexts.*

In the interactive mode, they can share their thinking and how they are reacting to the investigative situations. Acceptance means think through what is, to wrestle with it, think about the changes that can be made, and what direction the process needs to take. Time for thoughtful consideration and thinking needs to be built into the process. Thinking can be done through asking questions and responding to them. Students need to feel at ease in presenting their thoughtful points of view and their questions to each other. They need to think about where they are in terms of coming to consensus about the issues and the materials within the learning experience. Thinking is a quiet interactive component of learning. There is a time at any level of interactive learning for reflective conversation and reflective thinking. This kind of groupthink is very important here. Students need to share their thinking, discuss what they have pondered to clarify ideas, to gain focus, and to bring the total group to a cogent decision to move ahead in the learning experience. Thinking individually and in an interactive groupthink is important to the progress of the learning experience. There should be a time for this kind of quiet interactive learning. Focused thinking and shared thinking are extremely important at this level of interactive learning. Thinking at this level of interactive learning has great power.

LEARNING

Learning at this category of interactive learning remains concomitant with the investigation level of interactive learning. Learning is noted at this level as interacting. Interacting, in the learning taxonomy, means having dialogue, sharing, discussing, interpreting, and communicating with the feelings, actions, or skills either personally or in the context of a group. It is at the investigation level of interactive learning that students identify a value or values as a result of their interaction together. Learning becomes experiential and students work with others to process information and ideas.

In a group context, students can share their interpretation of and feelings about what they have learned, what they have done, and what they believe about the ideas and materials with which they are working. Learning becomes integrated for the students at this level. They have learned to work well with each other and they can feel comfortable in sharing their ideas and their findings about the content and the context of the learning sequence. They have established rapport through their interaction. They are enabled through their interaction to achieve preliminary objectives and processes and can demonstrate these to each other and to the teacher. Learning becomes the "union of the learner with what is to be learned in an organizational, emotional, and intellectual context for the purpose of achieving the objective" (Steinaker and Bell 1979:27). Discussion takes place either under the teacher's direction or under student leadership in whole groups and in small groups. Through interactive discussion, students are engaged not only in interpreting, applying, and analyzing what they have learned, but also in exchanging points of view, verifying what they believe with evidence, demonstrating learned skills and attitudes. Also, through interactive groups, students can come to initial consensus about identified components of the learning experience. They are enabled to conceive and use provisional assumptions about what they have learned and what yet needs to be done. They can also successfully demonstrate knowledge and application of identified preliminary skills. In addition, they have identified with the learning sequence and it has become their own.

Students are not reviewing provided resources, they are moving on to collect and review new resources. They are now actively involved in a deepening investigation of the materials they are using and processing the development of the learning. It should be noted that "personal interaction is essential to learning" (Steinaker and Bell 1979:67). Interaction of the individual student with group members results in a pooling of individual ideas and resources, and thus a broader and greater understanding of the total experiences. Interaction also increases the efficiency of the learning process as rapport is developed among students and they identify with the experience.

Functionalizing the Learning Experience

Students should be able to:
    Perform an action
    Demonstrate the skill
    Use the behavior
    Share the concept

TEACHING

At this level of interactive learning, teaching is defined as functionalizing the learning experience. The teacher works with the students, within an interactive context, to complete a walk-through of what has already happened or to engage students in trying out the feeling, action, skill, concept, or behavior. The teacher helps the students to value what they have learned. Within this level of teaching, the students are able to perform an action, demonstrate the skill, use the behavior, share the concept. They are able to demonstrate and use preliminary objectives and outcomes. The students will be involved in "applying, associating, classifying, categorizing, and evaluating data" (Steinaker and Bell 1979:67). They will develop applications learned from the ideas and materials they have reviewed and about which they have interacted. They will conference with each other and with other human resources to discuss individual questions and needs in order to understand as well as to discuss how problems can be dealt with. The teacher and the students work together to develop an emotional and intellectual commitment to the learning experience. Through these commitments, students come to value what they are doing and learning. This is very important and must be done by both the teacher and the students.

The teacher role is to ensure that students value what they are learning. The teacher works with the students so that the teaching–learning environment grows into an organized, contextualized, stable, and functional working environment (Hall and Kidman 2004). Students, through this interactive process, value the learning experience and make it their own, including its purpose, sequence, and meaning. They develop personal and group ownership of the learning sequence. The teacher roles as moderator and resolver are in place to ensure that students develop deeper identification with the vision implied in the learning experience and are interactively involved with it. Through this process, the students have valued what they are learning and show that they have identified with its purpose and meaning. Students are experimenters and investigators. When they have done all of these things, have ruminated about them, worked cooperatively with each other, and developed a functional application of the learning involved, they are ready to move to the insight level of the interactive learning process so that they can fully internalize what they have learned.

LEADERSHIP

At this investigation level of interactive learning, a strong working rapport develops between the teacher and the students. The roles of leadership begin to shift during this category of interactive learning. The leadership of the teacher at this category is that of a resolver who moderates issues, problems, and works with the students in their areas of concern and investigation. The student role as a leader is that of an investigator who takes a prominent, indeed a dominant, role in the investigative process. Students are taking a stronger role in the learning experience. They have identified with experience and it has become their experience. The roles of the students and the teacher are changing here. Students have understood the value and meaning of the learning experience for them. They have achieved initial objectives and have gained skills. Students assume stronger leadership roles in terms of managing their own learning programs. The teacher remains the leader in terms of overall organizational responsibility, maintaining a positive ethos within the classroom, and ensuring the integrity of the learning experience. The teacher is, after all, almost always the only adult in the classroom on a consistent basis. The teacher needs to entrust the students with more leadership in managing their own learning experience and in the development and process toward achieving the goals and objectives of the learning experience. Emerging leadership as well as real leadership on the part of the students is becoming a central focus within the instructional process, as well as within the learning and interactive processes. The obvious, yet subtle, transfer of leadership has begun just as the teacher had planned that it would happen. As student leadership grows stronger, the next category of the taxonomy of interactive learning, insight, begins to become more apparent.

Through their leadership role, the students now own the learning experience. They move toward a more dominant role both in planning and leadership. This is what the teacher planned for and it is a time for the teacher to be very proud of what the students have done.

FINAL COMMENTS

Through the analysis of elements of the investigation category of interactive learning, we have found that it is a time of identification with the experience and of the use of all levels of cognition, but with an focus on interpretation, application, and analysis. The teacher roles of moderator and resolver have been defined and explained. The roles of the student as experimenters and investigators are developed and shown as students identify with the process, are able to perform functional applications of the learning, and demonstrate the achievement of certain objectives and outcomes. Clear, cogent, and constructive communication is established; students can visualize creative ways to complete the experience. In terms of critical thinking, students are organizing and structuring material and making it functional for them. When students perform problem-solving activities, they are experimenting and trying optional solutions. In writing, the students have learned to organize and outline; they are writing detailed, more formal expressions of their ideas and feelings about what they have learned. Thinking is demonstrated through apprehension and organizing material in the mind. Students are then able to communicate their ideas in the interactive setting, which is so important to this category of interactive learning. Learning can be summarized as pooling individual and group ideas and becoming more efficient and effective through developing a strong rapport and working relationship. Students are motivated to learn through the kinds of activities they use at this category of learning. In terms of teaching, they have identified with the experience, they are valuing what they have learned, and they are able to discuss thoughtfully and cogently this sense of valued learning and progress through the investigative category of interactive learning that has been accomplished here. Evaluation is demonstrated in this category because both teachers and students are assessors; it is also demonstrated by pointing out levels of identification, the process of learning, and how well certain preliminary objectives and goals have been met. Assessing is important at this category of interactive learning. Leadership roles begin to change as the student roles of leader become more evident.

Interactive learning is a time of identification within the experience and of the use of all levels of cognition but focusing on interpretation, application, and analysis.

This category of the taxonomy is based on investigation. All strands to teaching, learning, and interaction come together to ensure full identification with what students are doing and to ensure a drive to continue the course of learning to its fruition. Investigation is a powerful and exciting category in which the students become totally identified with what they are doing. It is an thrilling time for both students and the teacher. It is in this category that the art and science of teaching are clearly evident. The art is again obvious within the interactive component of the student work at this level of the taxonomy. The science is apparent as we define and follow the development of the specific strands of the instructional process. Art and science are fully present in this category of the taxonomy.

Activities

Investigation is the midpoint in the process of interactive learning. Use these activities reflectively. Use them for understanding the theoretical basis for this work. Look back at what has already happened in the process of interactive learning. Use these activities to analytically review the strands at this category of interactive learning. Everyone should complete activity seven as you continue to follow your chosen strand through this category of the taxonomy. Group work should be used to complete these activities, although they could be done individually.

1. "Investigation involves a challenge for both teacher and students" (Chap. 4, p. 41). Ponder this statement and define what it means to you and your group. Share what you and your group has determined.
2. "Assessment, in the hierarchy of evaluation, is at the midpoint" (Chap. 4, p. 45). React to this statement and explain what it means for the evaluation process.
3. Trace how motivation has changed from invitation to investigation. How have the roles of students and teacher changed? Prepare a report with your group and present it.
4. Experientially, this category is defined as identification. Explain how identification could be evident for this investigation category of interactive learning.

5. How are reflective thinking and groupthink important for this category of the taxonomy? Discuss this, develop at report, and present what you have developed to the whole group.

6. Students "are valuing what they have learned, and they are able to discuss thoughtfully and cogently this sense of valued learning and progress" (Chap. 4, p. 55). Evaluate this statement in terms of at least four strands in the taxonomy.

7. Within your group you have completed your analysis of a particular strand for the first two categories of the taxonomy. Continue this analysis as you come to the midpoint of the taxonomy. Think about how it has developed, how the strand has changed, and what has happened in the learning process up to this point. Discuss this in your group and share what you have learned with the total group.

Insight

Insight is the category of interactive learning in which the components of the study come together and the total process is internalized. It is at this category of interactive learning that the objectives are fully achieved and the goals are accomplished. When this category of interactive learning is completed, the objectives and goals have been learned, applied, and internalized by the students. While the total interactive learning process is not yet totally completed, the contenthas been learned and is in place. Students are able to demonstrate through a synthesis of materials and evidence provided to each other that they have achieved the expected outcomes and the objectives of the study. The teacher learns, from demonstrated student work and through creative outcomes produced, that all objectives and goals have been achieved. Through the interactive process and focused experiences, students develop respect for each other, consider thoroughly all identified components of the construct, and have measured and shared what they have learned. Students are able to discuss and generalize about both the process and the product of their learning. They have, as learners, extended themselves to a new level of learning and are sustained by the teacher.

Insight is the category of interactive learning where things come together and the outcomes become clear. Insight involves gaining respect for the process, for those involved in the process, and for what has been accomplished. Insight is also a time for beginning to see new challenges for sharing and for dissemination of what students have learned. Insight is not the end of the interactive learning process; it is the springboard for the final dimensions of the total learning experience when it moves toward dissemination and determination of future direction. Insight is a time of triumph and celebration. The achievement of identified outcomes, goals, and objectives can be celebrated. Insight is also a time to interact about dissemination and direction toward using and sharing what has been learned. Questioning, clarifying, summarizing, and predicting are all part of the interactive dynamic of this level of interactive learning. Cognition includes all levels memory through evaluation. Emphasis is, however, on the synthesis level. In some instances the evaluation level can be used. Motivation is at the respect level. New roles for teacher and student emerge as well as new dimensions of creativity, critical thinking, and problem solving. New levels of writing, thinking, learning, and teaching are in place. Evaluation, so important to the students and teacher, takes on a new form. Leadership within the insight category begins to clearly rest more with students. Even so, the leadership role of the teacher remains vital and active.

> *Insight is the category of interactive learning where things come together and the outcomes become clear.*

Interactive learning is a creative and exciting process for students that can be effective in promoting "collaborative work and study skills and a feeling of camaraderie among students" (Joyce et al., 2004:26). Insight is both culmination and challenge for students. The work itself has been completed, but the challenge now becomes how to use it and how to share it. When it all comes together, the insight category of interactive learning is completed. When learning becomes internalized, the insight category of interactive learning is completed. It is then that the next and final level of the learning process becomes apparent.

COGNITION

It is during this category of interactive learning that students put things together cognitively. They have moved from memory through translation and interpretation to application and analysis. During this category of interactive learning, synthesis and evaluation are the major cognitive functions. Synthesis becomes most apparent as the students work together interactively. Evaluation also becomes apparent. Students are actively involved in evaluation at this level of cognition. They need to evaluate the quality of what they have done and how best to use it. As they work at the synthesis and evaluation levels of cognition, they are also using all other elements of cognition from memory through analysis.

Synthesis means that the students have been able to engage in a dialogue about what they have accomplished, come to consensus, and develop final and summative formulations of what they have learned and how they have accomplished their outcomes. At the synthesis level of cognition, students are able to put parts together in a new whole. They are able to prepare a unique communication and develop a set of abstract relationships. They are involved in creative cognition at synthesis. Creating a synthesized statement of achievement is an activity of respect and measured generalization about what has happened, the process of how it happened, and what has been achieved. The cognitive function of synthesis is the bringing together all the details, all the component parts, and all the factors involved in the investigation together in new and creative summative statements concerning their accomplishments and achievements. Some of the terms associated with synthesis are *combines, composes, compiles, creates, designs, rearranges, modifies,* and *develops.* All these verbs taken as a whole substantiate and provide evidence of how synthesis has been developed.

Some evaluation also comes into place at the insight category. Students appraise, judge, make choices, support, select, and value what they work on. This learning strand of cognition, while exemplary at insight, comes to complete fruition at the implementation level of interactive learning. Insight is a time for students to creatively address what they have learned. Cognition, at this point, is self-directing as well as group oriented. Cognition, through synthesis, helps the students probe wider and deeper. Commitment to the achievement of the learning objectives is completely achieved. Insight is a time in the learning sequence to cognitively and creatively finalize what has been achieved and completed. For those involved in the process this is a time to finalize learning, to be ready for conclusions and recommendations, and to prepare to disseminate what they have achieved. In dissemination students utilize, demonstrate, and share what they have done. When they do these, the final step in the total learning experience is demonstrated. Cognition, at this category of interaction, becomes evidence of achievement and completion. Although the interaction has yet to move to another level, this insight level is a coherent and creative expression of a job well done. In its expression of both the art and science of teaching, it is a summative experience that students recognize needs to be shared and disseminated.

EXPERIENTIAL

The experiential level of learning perhaps best summarizes what happens at this category of interactive learning. The experiential level is internalization. When students achieve this level of experience, what they have done impacts their lives and influences their lifestyle (Steinaker 2003a). Here the learning process has impacted the students. What has been learned has been internalized. The concepts they have internalized have expanded the student's experience and have become intrinsic to the student's lifestyle (Steinaker and Bell 1979). Ausubel (1968), who developed the construct of advance organizers, captured the concept of internalization as the advance organizers coupled with the learning experience functioned to move the learner to internalization. Steinaker and Bell (1979) noted that Ausubel (1968) indicated the need for an "advance organizer" that linked up with the learner's "cognitive structure" and provides the learner with the necessary "subsumers" that make subsequent learning "meaningful." In terms of the experiential taxonomy, Steinaker and Bell (1979), referring to Ausubel (1968), suggested

> that there must be Exposure (1.0) through the advance organizers and then Participation (2.0) that uses the learner's cognitive structure or past experience to establish Identification (3.0), when the learning begins to become meaningful. This meaningfulness continues through Internalization (4.0). . . . The relationship of Ausubelian theory to the experiential taxonomy is thus apparent. (18)

This statement from Steinaker and Bell (1979) encapsulates the learning process up to this point. Students have begun the insight category of learning through invitation, involvement, and investigation. Insight is the category of interactive learning toward which they move. Internalization is the level of experience that students achieve during their recognition of success in the activities in which they are involved.

Activities, at this category of interactive learning, reinforce already learned material. Internalization, in this sense, is about learning. It involves transferring learning to different contexts and applications. Internalized experience involves interacting with each other about how the learning experience has impacted each one of the students. In doing this, students learn that internalization means that the learning has changed the their attitude, behavior, and cognitive ability to demonstrate what has been learned and how it can be used. Insight is the result of a sequence of learning activities that culminates with internalized learning and is demonstrated by an attitude, a perspective, or a product that is understood, developed, and made ready for dissemination. Student recognition of success is intrinsic in the learning activities at this level of experience. It is a time to take pride in what they have done and begin to plan for disseminating their success.

TEACHER ROLE

The roles of the teacher at the insight level of interactive learning are those of a sustainer and adviser. The teacher recognizes that the students have achieved the outcomes and objectives of the study and needs to sustain and reinforce what the

Sustainer and Advisory Roles of Teacher

Value-oriented to help students internalize what they have learned
Positively impact student attitude and self-esteem
Extend the learning experience to new dimensions
Help students make creative and critical decisions

students have achieved. The teacher still responds to questions, helps in summarizing the material, clarifies ideas, focuses discussion, and helps predict where and how dissemination could take place. The teacher also advises the students who have taken a more dominant role in managing their learning experience. Yet, the main function of the teacher is to sustain what the students have done and to work with them in an advisory capacity. The teacher does this in positive and even celebratory fashion and to encourage the students toward dissemination. Students have extended themselves into new learning levels and have demonstrated for the teacher and for themselves the achievement and accomplishments they have completed. The teacher must sustain and encourage the students.

The teacher encourages continuing student probing and interaction as well as helping students compare and contrast and finalize ideas and concepts. The teacher should be able to sense that each one of the students has learned. Together, the teacher and the students can then celebrate what they have learned. All this can be done through the sustaining and advisory role of the teacher. These sustainer and advisory roles are value oriented and are designed to help students internalize what they have learned. A positive and sustaining teacher role can greatly impact student attitude and self-esteem as well as generate a need to continue to extend the learning experience to new dimensions. The sustaining and advisory roles are to ensure support for the student for community, continuity, and cooperative interaction.

The teacher and the students do a retrospective of the whole learning experience as well as develop ideas and a vision of what yet needs to be done in terms of sharing and disseminating what they have achieved. The teacher, though the roles are less overt than earlier in the learning experience, remains essential to the learning experience. The teacher, as the only adult in the classroom, can be a strong force for change and development through these roles. As encourager, sustainer, and adviser, the teacher helps students make creative and critical decisions. These roles of the teacher are a powerful influence on students to help make them into continuing and lifelong learners. It is important that these roles be manifest at this level of interactive learning. The teacher roles as sustainer and adviser are exceptionally important at this culminating category of interactive learning. Celebration, coupled with thoughtfully reflecting on how students accomplished their goals and objectives, comprise both the art and science of teaching and learning.

STUDENT ROLE

Students, at this level of interactive learning, have achieved their purpose, their goals, and their objectives and expected outcomes within the study. These outcomes may not be exactly the ones anticipated, but they are within the parameters of the study and the learning experience. The students and the teacher have fashioned a successful learning experience by progressively having the students take more and more responsibility for their own learning and for their own individual and group processes in an interactive setting. They have developed respect for each other and for the teacher through their study. This should be evident in all that they do at this level of insight. The specific roles of the students within this level of interactive learning are those of an extender and creator. These roles need to be understood and demonstrated. Students further need to ensure "clarification. . .between generalizations and concepts . . . abstract ideas, thoughts, and associations" (Steinaker and Bell 1979:44). Clarification is part of the summative process of creating, extending, and internalizing the learning to themselves.

Student working at this level of creative insight should continue in an interactive context. Students need to come to both an individual and a group consensus as to what products they will develop and create. They will also need to determine how the outcomes of their study will finally be shaped and created. Students will further demonstrate an understanding of the transformative impact of the learning experience on them personally and as a group. Any learning experience that comes to fruition needs to be internalizing and transformative. Students are changed because of what they have done and what they have achieved. Internalized transformation within the context of the learning experience is what education is all about.

Students should be very positive about what they have done and need to celebrate their accomplishments in the learning sequence. Students at this insight level of inter-action have learned what they needed to know and have come to value what they have done. This is demonstrated and reflected in their attitudes, in their demonstrated skills, and in the products they have developed. The internalized and transformative learning has impacted who they are and what they believe.

This is an exciting time for students as they extend themselves toward internalization and toward dissemination through interactive group discussion and through arriving at a group con-sensus on product and outcomes. Students dem-onstrate not only strong rapport with each other, but respect for what has happened individually and to the group over the process in which they have been involved. Their roles as extender and creator exemplify their success in accomplishing their goals and objectives. As they extend their learning to new contexts, as they complete projects and products, as their attitudes and perspectives change, they are demonstrating their roles. It is through the culminating interaction during insight that the art of teaching is demonstrated. It is through understanding and internalizing the process that the science of teaching is demonstrated.

> *Students demonstrate not only strong rapport with each other, but respect for what has happened individually and to the group over the process in which they have been involved.*

EVALUATION

Evaluation at this level of interactive learning is summarized with the words *measurer* and *assessor*. Even though these words are indicative of the final evaluation dimension of interactive learning, they are not. Students are measurers and assessors of their own achievement and accomplishments. The teacher is the measurer of the quality of stu-dent success. The teacher is the sustainer who works with the students on the value of their work and on the quality, viability, and visibility of the final product or outcomes. The teacher role as assessor and measurer is a real demonstration of the measures taken during the learning process and during this level of interactive learning. In terms of specific measures to be used, there could be anonymous response questionnaires, rating scales, interviews, review and analysis of products, pre- and posttest measures, collective discussion of what has been accomplished, and a sharing of personal feelings

Specific Measures of Evaluation

Anonymous response questionnaires
Rating scales
Interviews
Review and analysis products
Pre- and posttest measures
Collective discussion of accomplishments
Sharing of personal feelings and attitudes
Critique of products developed

and attitudes about the process of learning and success in achievement. Evaluation also encompasses a critique of any products developed.

Evaluation both by the students and the teacher also involves creating a product or a demonstrated achievement that can be assessed, internalized and celebrated. Evaluation can be both formal and informal in terms of the way in which it is done and in terms of the measures used to evaluate what has happened. At this level of interaction, the emphasis is on product evaluation, or as Bloom, Hastings, and Madaus (1971) termed it, summative evaluation. When the students come to the insight level of interactive learning, the teacher can observe and the students can feel and sense how they have changed. Insight is a time to know and to demonstrate. It is a time to share and relate to others what has happened to them. Process evaluation is important here, but takes a secondary position to product evaluation. Product evaluation is the creative component of evaluation, but process hones in on how the job was done, how the learning was crafted, and how efficiently and effectively the goals and objectives were achieved. Both are very important to the process of evaluation.

The students and the teacher should participate in the evaluation process and should be equally involved. Evaluation should clarify, summarize, and sustain what has happened and what has been learned. Evaluators should both review the process and share the product. Through this kind of assessment, both students and teacher should begin to project how what they have accomplished can be shared. Students and the teacher need to begin to plan their next steps and think through specific activities and a sequence that will lead toward utilization, dissemination, and further learning experiences. The focus of evaluation is on understanding the quality of the products and how they have been achieved. The science of education is dominant during the evaluation process.

MOTIVATION

Motivation, at this level of interaction, is demonstrated through a developing respect. Holm (2003) also used the word *principles* to describe respect. That word is appropriate to use in the same context with respect. It is respect for each other among the students and respect for the teacher by the students. It is also respect for what has been achieved together. Mutual respect is the key to motivation. Respect relates to what has been done and how it has developed through a series of interactive sequences of learning. Respect

also means that students respect each other from the shared process in which they have been involved. Motivation begins in any learning sequence with readiness, then develops into relationships, grows into rapport, and here becomes respect.

At the insight category of interactive learning, motivation is demonstrated by the respect the students feel toward each other, toward the teacher, and through what they have accomplished. By this time in the learning sequence the students have become self-motivated. They want to complete the goals and objectives together. They want to create and celebrate. Furthermore, motivation at this level is also a self-review of what has been learned and its meaning to individual students. Motivation here has become a celebration of achievement and pride in what has been done and what has been achieved. Students have earned respect because of what they have accomplished together and show respect for each other as well as for the teacher. Respect is being strongly supportive of each other and the teacher.

Respect can be subsumed under three words: *continuity, caring,* and *creating.* We could also add *celebration* because students have internalized what they have learned and need to celebrate success. Continuity is both reflective and projective. Continuity is a backward look at the process and a projecting of ideas for dissemination and further learning. Continuity is a visible component both of motivation and of learning. Continuity requires insight and the ability to restructure what has happened and to link it to future dissemination and learning. When this is done in a caring and respectful setting, it becomes a powerful resource for creating new dimensions of self-worth and a motivation to go beyond the learning experience thus far toward dissemination, application, and involvement with new adventures in learning. Motivation provides, at this level of interactive learning, a powerful direction for students and insight for the teacher in sustaining the next steps in dissemination and learning. Respect is the highest level of motivation prior to the student acceptance of responsibility for the direction of the learning experience. It is important that this respect be celebrated.

DISCOURSE

At this level of interactive learning, the descriptor for discourse is *consideration.* The word *discourse* has many dimensions of meaning. Among them are deliberating about what has happened, reflecting and reviewing a successful process, creating and synthesizing something new, viewing and admiring a product and outcomes, feeling a sense of achievement, and pondering future directions. All of these are included in the meaning of consideration and the dimension of discourse at this level of interactive learning. Discourse includes individual and small group exercises to develop new uses for products as well as probing activities. Consideration is integral to the creative process. Consideration comes to fruition at this category of interactive learning. Discourse and creativity go hand in hand when all steps in the creative process are discussed, considered, and completed. Consideration includes activities in which the learner must, in group settings, "determine and [assess] similarities and differences (Steinaker and Bell 1979:32). There is an efficacy for discourse here. It is a positive time because it relates to success and why and how that success was accomplished. Students find that their interactive development and careful construction of learned material has made it so. Discourse and discussion remain the central and essential forces for learning at insight. Discourse that has substance is shown through respectful consideration of each other and the teacher among the students as well as a healthy sense of accomplishment and achievement. All of these are encapsulated in the construct of consideration in the sequence of discourse. Interactive discourse helps sustain the students, demonstrates the role of the teacher, and creates the possible next steps toward dissemination and new learning. Consideration through discourse among students at this level of interactive teaching is important in the learning process.

CREATIVITY

The descriptor for creativity at this level of interactive learning is *creating a product.* Here the students actually complete the process. The students "complete the creative process and achieve a product" (Steinaker and Bell 1979: 94). It should be noted that creativity can be "seen as a series of progressive steps that one. . .may plan" (Steinaker and Bell 1979:91). Planning through the steps in the creative process come to fruition at this category of interactive learning. Through internalization, discussion, consideration, and synthesis, students demonstrate that fruition by creating the summative products and outcomes of their study. They have worked toward this and now they complete it. Students have gone through the process of learning and creating. They are now prepared to allow for dissemination and further extending their learning. The creative results of student work are sustained by the teacher. Students are able to generalize about the product and to extend their own learning toward completion. "The product is finished, the idea formulated, the action done, the picture painted, or the composition completed. Something new to the experience of the learner has been accomplished" (Steinaker and Bell 1979:94–95). The students in an interactive and thorough process have internalized "a unique and creative accomplishment" (95). During this creative process, the students, in a variety of group formats, synthesize material and complete the creative projects they have envisioned. This creative process is something students are challenged by and really enjoy doing. There is self-motivation, as noted above, to complete the product and to admire and share it with their peers in the classroom. Interaction, discussion, and working together toward finishing the project are intrinsic to the creative process. Creativity is accomplished by individuals and by groups of students. The positive sustaining and advising roles of the teacher continue to be of great importance as are the student roles of extender and creator. During this time of creativity, the respect they show toward each other and toward what they have accomplished is demonstrated. Creativity culminates, but there is still one more dimension to creativity. This dimension of creativity becomes evident in the implementation stage of interactive learning.

> *This creative process is something students are challenged by and really enjoy doing.*

CRITICAL THINKING

Critical thinking at this level of interactive learning is focused on generalizing about the variables and about the issues being studied. Critical thinking, creativity, and problem solving coalesce at this level of interactive learning. Students as extenders and creators have designed and finished a product. They have developed a skill, or implemented an idea. Through critical thinking, they begin to make generalizations about the created product and see how it applies in other contexts. Students become interested in ways "to set that behavior, skill, or attitude to a variety of situations" (Steinaker and Bell 1979:99). Critical thinking, through generalizing and transfer learning, needs to be done primarily in an interactive setting. Interacting at this level is a culminating activity. Students need to talk about utility, transfer, and the product or outcome's viability in new contexts. They need to discuss these and interact with each other in small groups, one to one, or as a whole group. Critical thinking requires interaction and a need to ponder and critically examine issues. Students feel the need to complete the creative products on which they have worked. Synthesis and critical thinking are almost synonymous. They happen together during this category of interactive learning. The teacher, as sustainer and adviser, complements the interactive critiquing and discussion. As sustainer and adviser, the teacher ensures that it happens. Critical thinking depends both on reflecting on what has occurred and critiquing what is necessary for completing the goals and objectives. Through their critical thinking process, students are enabled to specifically determine the quality of the process they have gone through and examine the development of the projects they are completing. Students, during this level of critical thinking, may also need some time to reflect and ruminate individually. Because they have already sensed success, their critiquing and critical thinking are accomplished in a positive setting where they know what they have accomplished and how they have done it. Students can both generalize and come to consensus and conclusions about what they have done. They need to generalize because transfer learning is an important aspect on what they have been doing and what they have accomplished. Students need to check out what can happen in new situations and critically assess and analyze how their new product, idea, skill, or attitude will work. Analysis and synthesis are integral parts of critical thinking at this level of interactive learning. When they have done this and have come to consensus and conclusions, they become ready for the final stage of interactive learning.

PROBLEM SOLVING

At this insight category of interactive learning, problem solving entails coming to a consensus, selecting a solution or resolution, and clarifying and drawing conclusion about the issues related to the problem. The choice of solution is based on wider and deeper probing into the actual evidence gathered during the previous problem-solving activities and on a testing of its viability. "The learner is able . . . to verbalize or to demonstrate the evidence that led to the choice" (Steinaker and Bell 1979:102). The process of coming to a consensus and selecting a solution or resolution comes through probing and studying the evidentiary bases from the data collected, from the experiences and activities in which the students have participated, and from the outcomes achieved. Consensus and conclusions are tested and applied to a variety of situations both corollary to the problem and different from it. Problem solving, critical thinking, and creative and interactive group work are closely aligned at this level of interactive learning. Students are self-motivated to finalize the learning sequence and need to work together to see it finished. Students also need to resolve the problem to internalize what they have learned and make the solution to the problems part of their internalized learning. Problem solving is intrinsic to learning at this level of group interaction.

Students need to engage in problem solving interactively and in a variety of group settings. Students also, however, need time to ruminate about their conclusions individually so they can personally transfer new learning to new contexts and to creating the products they have selected for completion. When they have created their products, the problem-solving process becomes a time for interactive discussion to clarify information, raise questions, make predictions, summarize what they have done in groups, and begin developing ideas for dissemination. Through these group activities, consensus and conclusions become viable, transferable, and generalizable. They have completed this category of interactive learning when they have resolved issues, developed solutions to problems, and the synthesized products of the total group. Further, students begin to plan for dissemination activities. Solutions have been attained and generalizations made. When this is accomplished, students are ready for the implementation category of interactive learning. Problem solving is an important component of the learning sequence at this level of interactive learning. Both teachers and students need to be active in problem solving.

> *Students need to engage in problem solving interactively and in a variety of group settings.*

WRITING

Discuss is the descriptor for writing at this level of interactive learning. To be able to interpret material, to analyze constructs and concepts, and to discuss differences and similarities are the hallmarks of writing at this level of interactive learning. The clarity and

Writing Descriptor: Discuss

Clarity and cogency are
    exhibited
Summarizing discussions
Illustrating
Clear and sequential
    organizing
Internalization of
    major components
    and concepts

cogency of writing is exhibited most completely at this level of learning. The writer needs to be able to summarize and interpret and to clearly focus on issues and interpretations. Students have come, through the learning process, to this point of insight. They can now demonstrate understanding of that learning process through their writing. Students do this by summarizing discussions, illustrating, clearly organizing sequentially what they have done, and expressing it in writing. The ability to demonstrate in writing an internalization of the major components and concepts of the learning experience can become evident as they edit and finalize their writing. Students are enabled to encapsulate in writing the methodology and process of creating a product or synthesizing an idea or a skill.

The student writer is able to coherently interpret material and to make sense out of conflicting ideas and perspectives so that the reader can easily comprehend how the process developed and why and how the learning happened. They can also identify the purpose of the learning experience. The reader can capture the interest, the excitement, and the sense of completion that the writers have included in the discussion emphasis of writing. This discussion dimension of the interactive writing process includes a summary and interpretation, as well as conclusions and recommendations. Writing at this level of interactive learning, can, and often should, be done in groups as well as by individual. It is in the group process of preparing summaries and interpreting material that good writing can truly takes place. Individual assignments can be completed and then melded with other individual perspectives into a group report that includes interpretations, and even some conclusions and recommendations.

Writing is, of course, one of the central areas of focus for learning. It is integral to the interactive structure of learning. It is essential for the insight category because, through writing, students can order the experience, explain it, and capture its essence and meaning for future reference (Steinaker and Bustillos 2007). It is at this category of the reciprocal and interactive process that the final written and created product can begin to take shape and begin to be resolved both in writing and in terms of internalized learning. When all these components at the insight category of interactive learning are complete and in place, the final category of interactive learning—implementation—begins to emerge. Written records and student creative writing can be an impetus for ideas about dissemination and sharing what they have learned.

THINKING

Thinking at the insight category is defined as modification. This word is synonymous with the whole perspective of learning at the insight category. Modification indicates that the thinking associated with past experiences has been modified and changed during the experiences at the insight category. It also shows that learning can be transferred and used in different contexts. Modification challenges the thinker to become involved in the dialectic of change. The student needs to identify a thesis and an antithesis. Through these dialectic thought processes, students are then enabled to arrive at a synthesis so that learning is complete and that transfer and new ideas and insights emerge. Descartes said that we are defined by our thinking—and so we are. The students must think through how the learning they have achieved and accomplished can be transferred to new settings and how they can be used. Thinking relates to the creative process of bringing something into being that one has never done before.

Thought and interaction are the constants for creating and completing. Thinking is an active and challenging focus for students as they begin to put together what they have achieved and how they have done it. Thinking is both reflective and projective. It is reflective thinking in the sense that students need to put together the total process sequentially and be able to note the how of the learning process. Through reflection, the elements and strands of interactive learning can be sequenced and understood in their entirety. It is projective in the sense that students need to thoughtfully ascertain a rationale for finalizing their products and how to disseminate what they have done and to project the sequence that dissemination could take. This reflective and projective thoughtful activity can then be used in an interactive session within groups so that a consensus can come from the group.

It is through a variety of activities and through reflective and projective thinking that ideas are transferred and modified, that skills are honed and used, and that modification and growth in thinking can help in the process of producing a synthesized product of which all can be proud. Thinking, through the construct of insight and interaction, is a challenging and creative component to interactive learning. Thinking brings cogency, continuity, and change. Thinking relates disparate components of the learning experience and brings them together. Thinking is central to the process of learning both at the insight level and at all levels of interactive learning. Thinking, in a learning setting, always precedes action. Teachers and students should both learn this truism and think and act accordingly.

> *Thinking brings cogency, continuity, and change. Thinking relates disparate components of the learning experience and brings them together.*

LEARNING

Learning, at this category of interactive learning, is defined as contextualizing (Steinaker 2002). This means that the pieces are put together in a context of clear understanding. The jigsaw puzzle has been completed. Meaning becomes evident through the activities, through the creative process, and through the motivation to produce. We must remember that learning is constructivist in nature. Each student constructs meaning personally. As those constructs are shared with others, meaning grows and is evidenced in broader contexts and in broader areas of meaning. Learning at this category of interaction has come to be valued by the students. Students not only value what they have learned. They transfer the learning to new contexts. They put their learning into a creative process that results in products and attitudes of which they can be proud. Learning comes to fruition at insight. Learning is evidenced by actions, replicating a skill, describing a feeling, valuing a process, and creating and enjoying a product. Learning here is the completion of a sequence and being able to see how that process has impacted students. Learning has ensured the internalization of what they have learned. Learning becomes an individual and group triumph. Learning has been accomplished through an interactive process that has resulted in a meaning-centered transfer of the learning to new disciplines and directions.

Students know what they have accomplished and how they can use it in more than one way. Learning has come together positively at insight. Through what they have learned students, can aptly and cogently demonstrate not only the "how" of the sequence but the "what" and "why" of the concepts and skills they have achieved. Students can make connections through putting it all together and integrating the process to meaning and internalization. Learning is the evidence of skills accomplished, the knowledge of

success, and the insight into the real substance of what they have done. It is here that the art and science of the teaching–learning sequence come together. Learning here has come full circle and the objectives, skills, goals, and outcomes have been achieved. All that remains in the dissemination of what they have learned.

TEACHING

Teaching, as already defined, is a process of valuing. It means valuing the students, valuing the content of the lessons, and valuing the process of learning. At insight, teaching can be defined as verifying. Here the teacher is the sustainer who supports the students in progressing through the insight category toward internalization. Teaching is helping students analyze, synthesize, and evaluate the content, feelings, actions, skills, concepts, or behaviors as they become a part of the student's living and learning contexts. Teaching, with verifying as its focus, becomes an exercise in cooperative interaction and group learning. Teaching becomes more supportive and advisory toward students as they jointly work to bring together all the strands within the learning process. The teacher interacts with the students both formally and informally to ensure that they are self-motivated and totally focused on bringing the learning together and to enable students to transfer what they have learned to substantively new areas of interests and needs. These student experiences of insightful learning must be carefully planned. Both teacher and students need to work together to make the planning emphasize a summative perspective that challenges the students and move the process to fruition.

The teaching roles here are as sustainer and advisor. These roles exemplify valuing and verifying. Success must be valued and evidence must be verified. The teacher must consciously and through careful planning move forward with the students to see that verification is satisfied and success is valued. Teaching is both new and fresh and creative as well as reflective, conservative, continuous, and traditional. Teaching at the insight level of interactive learning spurs a fresh look at direction and destination as well as reviewing and describing step-by-step growth in learning and seeing it as a process that has been continuous and follows the Socratic tradition in learning. That Socratic tradition involves, of course, interaction and cooperative learning. In the Socratic tradition, the teacher often responds to questions with questions. This is the time for the teacher to do this as sustainer and advisor. Socratic teaching exemplifies the art of teaching. Teachers can use it during this category of interactive learning.

LEADERSHIP

Student leadership emerges as even more viable and visible at the insight level of the taxonomy. It is at the insight category that students become deeply involved with and concerned about the nature and continuity of the process. They, during this time of interactive studying and learning, recognize and internalize the value and meaning of the learning experience. Students are assuming much of the leadership in the learning sequence. They have developed a sense of confidence and have internalized understanding of both the learning experience and the products resulting from that process. They become creators, and the teacher serves as their sustainer and their adviser. Sample (2002) calls this "artful listening" (110).

The teacher sustains what they are doing by encouraging, supporting, asking questions, and advising them. The teacher's leadership role at this category is more covert, but it is necessary and compelling in terms of the total learning experience. The teacher's role is to ensure student success and sustain that success. This is a point of success for both the teacher and the students. This is what the teacher has planned for and the leadership that the students have accepted and fulfilled.

At this category of interactive learning, the assumption of leadership by the students in terms of completing the process is strongly evidenced through their creative successes and extending their learning to the achievement of the objectives, products, goals, and objectives of the learning experience. It should be noted that leadership is the passionate exercise toward the implementation of a personal and shared vision. The students have caught the vision and have come to the process of implementation. Their journey has been taken step-by-step through a variety of activities and through the use of many teaching strategies. It has been a journey toward maturing ability to understand, to analyze, to synthesize, and to evaluate. They have done these things. It should also be remembered that leadership is eighty percent art and twenty percent science. The art of leadership is gained through interactive learning and group activities. These are central to the learning process.

> *Leadership is the passionate exercise toward the implementation of a personal and shared vision.*

FINAL COMMENTS

Insight is a wonderful category for learning. It is exciting and interesting. Insight activities bring the learning experience to completion. It is at insight that the learning process comes to a positive conclusion. Although there is one more level of interactive learning that needs to be in place, this is the one where students know they have succeeded and have accomplished their tasks, goals, and objectives. It is fascinating to see how the various strands and roles discussed in this sequence are correlated to fully illustrate this category of interactive learning. Cognition is shown through interpretation, application, analysis, synthesis, and even some evaluation. Experience is defined as internalization. The teacher roles are sustainer and advisor. Student roles are extender and creator. Evaluation is defined through the terms *measurer* and *assessor*. Motivation is shown to be at the respect level. Creativity is demonstrated through achieving and completing a product. Critical thinking is the ability to generalize and to transfer learning to different areas of need. Problem solving shows coming to a consensus about a solution to the problem. Discourse is serious consideration of what has been done, learned, and achieved as well as projecting the learning into new areas. Writing comes to discussion and interpretation at insight. Thinking is exemplified by modification of thought to different contextual settings and this brings it to compatibility with insight. Learning is contextualizing and teaching is noted at verifying. Both of these statements are integrally associated with insight. Leadership from the students is becoming more apparent, but with the strong sustaining role of the teacher as sustainer and adviser. Students are creators and have achieved the goals and objectives of the learning experience. When reviewing, all the terms—*application, analysis, synthesis, extender, advisor, internalization, respect, achievement, completion, consideration, discussion, interpretation, modification, contextualizing, creating,* and *verifying*—come together to fully illustrate the dimensions of insight as a necessary interactive function of the learning process.

Insight brings it all together and displays the marvelous series of activities, interactions, and participatory sequences in which the students have been involved. Every strand of interactive learning has come together during insight. The students have not yet come to the final category of interactive learning, but they have demonstrated to themselves and to the teacher that they have learned and internalized the scope, sequence, goals, objectives, and outcomes of the totality of the learning experience. Insight also prepares the students for the next and final category interaction, that of involvement. Insight is illuminated by the eloquence of success and defined through both the art and science of teaching.

Activities

Insight is a category when things come together for the teacher and the students. Here goals are achieved and objectives met. The activities in this category focus on the theory as it is developed and evident through the completion of activities. Again, these activities should be completed in groups, although they could be done individually. Activity eight is individual, but developed interactively in a small group and then shared.

1. Internalization is the keynote of the insight level. Discuss this in your group and determine how internalization is used in all strands during this category. Relate internalization to several strands of lesson delivery at insight and show what it means in each. Share your findings with other groups.

2. "Thought and interaction are the constants for creativity and completing" (Chap. 5, p. 66). Respond to this statement. How does it relate to cognition, thinking, and learning at insight? Discuss this with your group and prepare a report.

3. Discuss the roles of leadership at insight. Compare and contrast the roles of the teacher and the roles of the students. How have they changed since the invitation category? How do they become evident at insight? How do they point toward dissemination?

4. "It is at insight that the learning process comes to a positive conclusion" (Chap. 5, p. 69). What does this mean and how is it sown at insight?

5. How do critical thinking, creativity, and problem solving come to fruition at insight? How are they alike and how are they different? Prepare to share your findings with peers.

6. "The student writer is able to coherently interpret material" (Chap. 5, p. 66) at this category of the taxonomy. Explain how students use writing to interpret material and "make sense out of" the learning process. Discuss how writing relates to other strands of interactive learning.

7. How do students and the teacher make "the decision to move to the implementation category." How is this done through the various strands of lesson analysis at insight?

8. You have traced the progress of your strand of interactive learning from invitation through involvement, investigation, and now insight. You have kept a log on how your strand has been used at each of these categories. You need to continue your log, discuss what you have learned, and what you have discerned about your strand. First discuss it with your small group and then report it to your peers.

Implementation

Implementation is the final category of the interactive learning process. Implementation is the dissemination and utilization of the changes that have taken place in this process of thinking, learning, and teaching. Change has taken place, and dissemination, well planned by students and teacher, can happen. Cognition at implementation moves beyond analysis and synthesis to a major emphasis on evaluation. The roles of the teacher and the student have nearly reversed since the beginning of the learning process at invitation. At this category of interactive learning, the students have assumed responsibility for what they have accomplished and demonstrate the roles of influencer and disseminator. The teacher, who was initially motivator, now becomes the critiquor and consultant who assesses how the students influence others and to consult with them about dissemination.

Another dimension of the teacher roles as a critiquor and consultant is to ensure that students move toward new learning, based on what they have already accomplished. In terms of evaluation, this is the time when determinations are made both in writing and in evaluation. Students begin to implement and use what they have learned and have come to feel the need to share their learning and accomplishments with others. They are self-motivated to disseminate and to share. During implementation, it is a time of sharing success with others and interactively disseminating what they have learned and what they have done. This is an exciting, challenging, and interesting time for students and for the teacher. It is a celebration of completion and success in a context of sharing and dissemination. Implementation is putting into use what has been accomplished and seeing it work. Implementation is sharing success with others and influencing them to learn or to do the same or similar things.

Implementation is interactive learning in its finest moments. Implementation is an internalized achievement that can be shared with confidence and with the knowledge that much has been done and that it has been done successfully. Implementation is also a time for reflection, evaluating the process and what worked within the process and what problems were ascertained along the way. Students need to comprehend the scope and sequence of what they have done and review the successes and the mistakes so that future learning can be more efficiently accomplished. Implementation is experience revisited and contextualized to future learning and experiences.

Implementation is intrinsic to a maturing learning process. In the final analysis, students in the implementation category of interactive learning continue to raise questions, clarify issues, make predictions, and summarize next steps. It is through prediction that students can be moved from this learning sequence to new areas of learning. Teaching and learning are lifetime experiences and

Implementation is an internalized achievement that can be shared with confidence and with the knowledge that much has been done and that it has been done successfully.

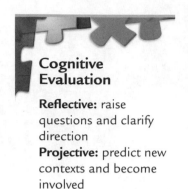

Cognitive Evaluation

Reflective: raise questions and clarify direction

Projective: predict new contexts and become involved

spiral in nature. The strength of interactive learning is that it encapsulates the process and makes is personal and real for the student. Leadership has changed from teacher dominance at invitation to students assuming responsibility for their learning experience at this category of learning. Implementation also becomes the springboard to new areas of learning and toward replication of the process in a new content unit of learning. It is a model both of reflection and expectation at this implementation level of interactive learning. Implementation is laughter and cheers and celebration. Implementation is also planning, projecting, and new beginnings.

COGNITION

Cognition at the implementation level is essentially evaluation. At the same time, students continue to use memory, translation, interpretation, application, analysis, and synthesis. Cognitive thinking at this category of interactive learning is both reflective and projective. It is reflective in the sense that students need to use the opportunity to reflect on process they have gone through and how it was done. Students have achieved the product, and understand the processes involved. They need to evaluate how they accomplished their objectives. Students need to ruminate about the process personally as well as interactively. They need to reflect personally and interactively so that they can clearly understand how and why they achieved their objectives and their outcomes. This process of reflection is very important. Students need to clearly and insightfully understand both the process of their learning experience and why it has been essential to them. Reflection is essential to interactive and personal internalization of the process. Evaluation, as a projective cognitive process, involves a review at possible future learning experiences based on what has been done.

Students need to envision where they go from here. They need to raise questions, to clarify direction, and to predict new contexts of learning. These are activities important for both closure and for continuity in learning. Cognitive evaluation, both reflective and projective, is essential to this level of interactive learning. Cognition at the evaluation level also involves dissemination. Dissemination is a key to learning at involvement. Involvement means interaction with others in terms of planning for dissemination. These are important for success in positive dissemination. Students need to think about how they can effectively share, contextualize, and disseminate what they have done both in terms of process and in terms of product. The teacher needs to critique that cognitive effort and ensure that it is in place. Evaluation is a cognitive function in this process as well as in the reflective and projective tasks involving new learning experiences. Clarification, questions, predictions, and summaries come from evaluative cognitive thinking personally and interactively demonstrated. Evaluation is the highest category of cognition and it is the cognitive category most evident at the implementation level of interactive learning.

EXPERIENTIAL

Exper ientially, the students are at the dissemination level. Dissemination is a time when students know what they have done, reflect on how they have done it, and express a willingness to share and disseminate what they have done as well as what they have achieved (Steinaker 2003a). They also know why they have followed the sequence of learning to this category. They know that they can share what they have done with others. Sometimes dissemination is done within the group as a sharing and discussion of personal experiences and personal reflection on what has been done. This is a valuable dissemination experience and should be planned by students and teacher. Reflection is a valid expression of dissemination and is pertinent to the learning experience. Reflection should be a part of any learning experience. In reflection, students can fully internalize the process of which they have been a part. This is their time to share and discuss, to clarify, to raise and respond to evaluation and process questions, to predict new dimensions of learning, and to summarize what they have accomplished.

Dissemination, however, has another dimension. That dimension is sharing. Students share what they have accomplished with others. They share with peers, parents, and other people. They can disseminate or share through writing, through presentations, through demonstration, and through discussion and interaction with others. This, too, is an important and sometimes essential component of dissemination. Students are responsible, with the teacher, in critiquing their plans for the dissemination. Students plan dissemination, present it, and reflect about it. Students need this interactive experiential activity to validate their experience and to celebrate their success. The processes they have experienced and the outcomes they have achieved need to be shared and demonstrated to others. Dissemination represents experiential learning in its final efflorescence before moving on to another learning sequence. Experiential learning is completed at this level of interaction. Experience is a creative and enriching art. It is also an analytical journey into how and why.

TEACHER ROLE

The roles of the teacher in this final level of interactive learning become those of a critiquor and consultant. These are important roles for the teacher and there is a strong rationale for those roles. Students have assumed here responsibility for reflection, evaluation, and dissemination. They are now managing the learning process. The teacher must be available to critique their role and to ensure they carry it out responsibly and effectively. The teacher helps the students value what they have learned, what they have completed, and what they have accomplished. The teacher helps students celebrate their successes (Steinaker and Bell 1979). This is the overt role of the teacher. The teacher interacts with the students and serves as a resource and consultant for the dissemination process. The teacher responds to student questions, assists in final clarification of process, works with them reflectively, critiques their plans for dissemination, encourages celebration of success, and helps them summarize the whole of their learning experience. The covert role of the teacher at this level of interactive learning is to help students contextualize their learning and to direct their ideas toward new learning experiences.

Concomitant with this dimension of the critiquing role of the teacher is the directional dimension of critiquing. The teacher needs, in the role of critiquor, to encourage transfer of student learning toward a new series of learning experiences. Students need to decide to move on to new curriculum and content, which need to be explored, challenged, identified, learned, and internalized. As this dimension of the role of the teacher is implemented, the teacher begins to motivate the students toward new learning experiences; thus the circular process of thinking, learning, and teaching can begin anew. The teacher is both critiquor of the disseminating activities and the one who nurtures and guides the students to the new learning experiences that have been well planned by the teacher. The teacher celebrates the achievements and the learning with the students and helps the students focus on the need for a new learning experience.

The teacher also helps the students envision a direction and a context for the new learning experience. Motivation toward the new learning experience is intrinsic within the teacher's roles at this category of interactive learning. The teacher roles as critiquor and consultant are vital in this culminating dimension of interactive learning. Their implementation must provide for a new direction for student learning that relates to and follows what they have already done. The teacher provides the motivation for the beginning of a new and exciting student study (Steinaker and Bell 1979). Consulting with students in

> *The teacher roles as critiquor and consultant are vital in this culminating dimension of interactive learning.*

terms of new learning experiences can happen only because of the respect that has been by the students and the teachers. There exists during this category of interactive learning a strong sense of trust developed through the interaction and group work in which students and the teacher have been involved.

Now that success has been achieved, the teacher needs to work with the students to move on to new areas of study, building on what has been accomplished here. This is a major role of the teacher as consultant along with critiquing student dissemination. The teacher roles at involvement are twofold. The teacher celebrates success, but also must ensure that students make the appropriate decision to accept new learning experiences. The roles of critiquor and consultant exemplify the art and craft of teaching and are essential as a major transition from one learning experience to another is accomplished (Steinaker and Bell 1979).

STUDENT ROLE

The student roles during this category of interactive learning are those of influencers and disseminators. The very terms imply what the students do at implementation. They use their experience and the internalization of what they have learned to share with and influence others. During implementation, students are involved in change, evaluation, dissemination, determining, and using what they have done in reflective personal and interactive sharing. They do it first within their own group. In addition, they are developing strategies for dissemination to other groups. Furthermore, students are working with the teacher in determining direction for new learning experiences. Students during this time have assumed responsibility for their activities at this final level of interactive learning. This is a busy time for students.

The student role as influencer has four dimensions. First, being an influencer requires them to look back reflectively on the whole experience to what has happened to them and how they have internalized the learning and applied it to their own lives. This reflective review of the process that they have been involved with requires interaction and discussion among themselves and with the teacher. Second, students need to determine how they are going to use what they have learned and how they are going to implement it. This becomes both process and product evaluation. Third, being an influencer requires students to plan for and implement strategies for sharing and disseminating what they have done. They must consider the message, the methodology, the audiences, and what they hope to accomplish through dissemination. Fourth, being an influencer requires them to look ahead at their own learning experience and to see what next steps lay ahead in transferring what they have learned to new contexts and to new areas of study.

Students need to make a decision to transition to a new unit of study. They do this in conjunction with the teacher as critiquor and consultant. All of this is done using interactive strategies. Students need to talk through what they have learned, how they are going to share it, and where to go in their next learning experiences. They need to determine how they will apply what they have learned to real-life experiences.

Dimensions of Student as Influencer

1. Look back reflectively on the whole experience.
2. Determine how to utilize what they've learned and how to implement it.
3. Share and disseminate what they have done.
4. Look ahead at learning experience to see what next steps lie ahead.

The teacher roles as critiquor and consultant and the student roles as influencer and disseminator come together at this culminating category of the interactive learning experience. The student is very active at implementation and demonstrates that activity in two ways. Students share and disseminate; they make the choice to move to new units of study to further use what they have learned.

EVALUATION

This is a time for disseminating and determining. Determining is the role of the evaluators during this category of implementation. A determiner summarizes what has been done. A determiner knows how it was done, and decides the steps toward developing new units of study. Concepts and attitudes in this sequence of learning have been internalized and the whole landscape of learning has changed. Students have assumed responsibility for what they have accomplished and demonstrate that responsibility in terms of how they evaluate what has happened, how it came together, and how they will develop strategies for dissemination and transfer. All these activities are a part of student responsibility and evaluation at this category of interactive learning. The whole of the learning experience, dissemination, and the nature of new learning experiences must be evaluated. That evaluation involves making decisions and determinations about what is yet to come, especially in new learning.

Students are involved in a process in self-evaluation. They review the process reflectively (Steinaker 2005). They discuss and evaluate strategies for sharing and disseminating, and they project ideas toward transfer and new learning experiences. Decisions and determinations need to be made in all of these dimensions of implementation. Student self-evaluation and self-monitoring are important components within the learning process and the implementation and use what they have learned at this level of interactive learning. Students need, through self-evaluation and through critiquing, to make decisions about dissemination, about how to effectively use what they have learned, and about how to culminate their understanding of the processes involved in the learning experience. They also need to determine, with the teacher's impetus, the next steps in learning. They finally need to determine how utilize and implement what they have learned and to share and disseminate that learning.

Evaluation, at implementation, needs to be both process evaluation and product evaluation. The how and why of what they have learned is process evaluation. In terms of evaluation, the sharing of student learning and their creations are the evidence of product evaluation. The students and the teacher need to establish criteria or standards for dissemination and for choosing new learning experiences. In addition, evaluation means trying out what has been learned, using it, and sharing it appropriately with others. Evaluation means determining which dissemination strategies would work effectively with what groups and then preparing those strategies. Evaluation, interactively determined, is a culminating step in the interactive learning experience.

MOTIVATION

Students have, at this implementation level of interactive learning, accepted overt responsibility for their learning experience. Holm (2003) uses the words *passion* and *perseverance* to describe this level of motivation. They are descriptive in that the students needed to persevere with a passion to achieve the completion of their course of study and to be ready for dissemination. They have demonstrated that responsibility through their success in working together through the learning experience. They have completed the steps in the motivation, beginning with readiness, moving toward relationships, establishing rapport, and earning respect. They have completed all

> *Responsibility is the definition of motivation at implementation.*

these steps in motivation and now they are ready to assume full responsibility for what they have accomplished. Self-motivation is a reflective and projective responsibility. Responsibility is the definition of motivation at implementation. Students take the responsibility for looking back reflectively and review both the process and the products or outcomes of the learning experience.

At implementation, students also look forward to new ideas for implementation, dissemination, and transfer. Students assume responsibility for implementing what they have learned, influencing others through sharing and dissemination. They project new experiences in learning. Students have internalized content and ideas and are thus enabled to disseminate the richness of the experience as well as the problems and the process to others. Students recognize the processes they have experienced and are able to identify the sequence of the learning experiences. This is a positive in motivation and this reflective responsibility can be a real asset for leadership. Responsibility is something all students should demonstrate when they have achieved this level of interactive teaching and learning. Students become the disseminators and assume their roles of helping others to learn about the experiences that they have just completed.

> *Each learning experience has links to new studies and new learning experiences.*

Responsibility means that the extension of learning goes beyond the classroom to other people, to other audiences, and to other groups. Responsibility is affirmation, aspiration, and action. Through motivation the students have come full circle from being extrinsically motivated to intrinsic personal and group motivation and responsibility. Finally, the teacher and the students work together to accept new challenges to learn and new concepts and ideas to discover. Each learning experience has links to new studies and new learning experience. Discovering this new challenge and new direction is the ultimate responsibility of motivation. Responsibility for interactive learning is not only important at implementation, it is an essential student activity.

DISCOURSE

Discourse at the implementation category involves change. Change happens when responsibility for learning is assumed and when students have internalized skills and attitudes and disseminate what they have learned. Change is the end product of learning. When it is internalized, it becomes a part of ethos of the individual and the group. Change in interactive learning is accomplished through discourse, dialogue, and discussion. Change occurs interactively and with a clear understanding of what has happened through the process of learning. Furthermore, change means that what has been learned is to be implemented and disseminated, understanding that others can learn and follow the same experiential sequence to achieve similar goals and outcomes. Change, if it is to come about, must have been internalized and shared. Discourse and interaction are essential to that process and change is the culmination of the process (Steinaker 2003b).

Discourse and discussion become the springboard for new directions and new beginnings. Discourse and dialogue are not only a time for disseminating and sharing. Discourse and dialogue are also a time for critiquing, for planning, and for moving toward new learning and new challenges. Discourse, as defined, has three dimensions at this level of interactive learning. The first dimension is that of reflective critiquing. Reflective critiquing means reviewing what, how, and why learning took place as it did. This must be done before dissemination can take place. The second dimension is disseminating and sharing. If a learning experience is not shared or disseminated, it is not totally completed and the change has not been verified. The third dimension is using change for transfer and for deciding on new challenges in learning. Change leads to new opportunities to grow and to renew discourse in new avenues of learning.

Discourse at Implementation Stage

Reflective critiquing
Disseminating and sharing
Using change for transfer and for deciding on new challenges

CRITICAL THINKING

"At this point in the critical thinking process, the learners are able and willing to relate to others the impact" of the changes on them (Steinaker and Bell 1979:99). Learners demonstrate a need to share the changes that have been internalized in the experiential process of the teaching–learning act. They need to tell others how they have been changed. It is beyond generalizing and involves the use of how they have changed for dissemination and sharing. The focus of the sharing and the dissemination is for the audience to recognize and even to use the change. Internalized learning, the meaning of the attitudes, and the functions of the skill are the focus of the sharing and the dissemination. Dissemination should be a choice freely made by students, not an imposed requirement. Critically engaging the whole of the learning experience leads to making that choice. The student, through critical thinking and articulation, is able to verbalize, demonstrate, and disseminate the process as well as share the developed products. This becomes the culmination of the learning experience and sharing becomes important to the learners. Sharing and dissemination are the overt and positive dimensions of critical thinking. Although this dissemination may only be deemed voluntary, it needs to be done and it brings closure to the learning process. This is the "show how it works" and the "this is how we did it" dimension of interactive learning. Critical thinking culminates with the disseminative process of explaining how and showing what. It becomes complete in an interactive social- and success-oriented construct.

Critical thinking in its final form is the functioning of the student in doing, demonstrating, and detailing the whole dimension of the learning process. Sharing critical thinking leads the students and those with whom the project is shared toward the challenge of implementation and of new tasks. It is important that all these things be done. "The role of responsibility is to see that the continuum of experience continues and that the learner is challenged to look afresh" at new learning experiences (Steinaker and Bell 1979:100).

CREATIVITY

We must remember that "creativity . . . is not esoteric and eccentric but, rather, is a vital and universal human function" (Steinaker and Bell 1979:95). Whitehead (1929) wrote that "it is the universal of universals characterizing ultimate matter of fact" (31). Thus we can sum up the process of creativity. We can also see creativity as a process through each category of interactive learning. All students are creative and all students can demonstrate it. Creativity is an experience that is "a healthy expression of growing human activity, for it is in the creative process that the individual grows and becomes more effective in social interaction" (Steinaker and Bell 1979:95). The pride resulting from successful creativity is shown and shared at this final interactive level of learning. Students are self-motivated and conscious of their success in learning experience. They are also confident about the positive changes they have internalized and know how these changes have impacted them. This consciousness and

confidence should culminate in a voluntary decision to disseminate and share what they have learned. Sharing the created products, the new skills, showing the learned attitudes, or sharing the concepts brings pride and a feeling of success to the students who have achieved the completed creative goal. Students "thrive on creative experiences" (Steinaker and Bell 1979:95). Creative dissemination is a forum in which to share and show. The teacher and students together need to plan this dimension of involvement with care and specificity. Students assume responsibility for planning, but they work closely with the teacher, who becomes their consultant. This assumption of responsibility is the culminating creative experience; it is something that also needs to be planned for by both the teacher and the students. Creativity accomplished provides a threshold for further directions of learning and creativity. Students understand this and together with the teacher they can interactively participate in developing creative new directions and new experiences in learning.

PROBLEM SOLVING

The problems have been solved; now the implementation of the solutions are the problem-solving activities during this final category of interactive learning. The descriptor words for this category of interactive learning are *implementation* and *influencing*. It is at this final level of interactive learning that the students begin to use, implement, and share what they have learned and the solutions they have developed. "Others are made aware of the solution and of the learner's reaction to it, first as they. . .are affected by the problem resolution, and. . .as the student[s]" use or influence others to "use the solution" (Steinaker and& Bell 1979:103–104). Problem solving involves planning the dissemination strategies. This process can be fraught with difficulties; students need to address these through interaction, discussion, and dialogue. This interaction about the development of the dissemination process is an important but necessary aspect of problem solving. The solution is used, shared, and demonstrated in an interactive setting for others to see, observe, and use themselves. Dissemination activities can be planned with a question and answer time between an audience and the students. This kind of sharing is always a challenge for the students, as they to anticipate the kinds of questions they might be asked and to prepare possible responses. They have to know their material exceptionally well and to be able to think on their feet. Activities at this category of interactive learning are the students' dialogue with others on how to use and implement the solutions they have internalized. Within this implementation context there is the necessary dimension of transfer and movement to new content, which can lead to another direction for learning and study.

WRITING

Determination is the descriptor for writing process at this category of interaction (Steinaker and Bustillos 2007). First the writers summarize what they have accomplished. Writers then draw conclusions and makes recommendations. When this is done, the writing process is completed. Students can use the summary along with the conclusions and recommendations for helping to plan new learning experiences. Further, their writing can be used to help identify dissemination activities. Student writing and reports can even be used for dissemination. Through the summary, conclusions, and recommendations students have developed, a format for new ideas for transition to additional learning experiences.

The teacher and the students should be thoroughly involved in the summative process of writing, which brings together all these things. This involvement is achieved interactively and within a variety of group settings. The whole of the writing process has come together during this final category of interactive learning. From defining and through describing, detailing, discussing, and determining, the student writers have brought to the readers the processes and the products of the total learning experience. They have summarized them, drawn conclusions, and made recommendations. They have successfully completed the writing process and can share it with pride.

> *The whole of the writing process has come together during this final category of interactive learning.*

THINKING

Thinking is a process of associating information with experience. Students have completed all the steps of interactive learning successfully to implementation. They have gone through the sensory step, the apprehension level, they have accepted association, and they have modified it. At this implementation level of interactive learning, thinking is focused on the extension element of thought. Thinking becomes more actively involved in extending learning. Thinking in dissemination is extending ideas and concepts. Students then sequence them by showing, sharing, telling, and responding. Thoughtful extensions need to be included in these dissemination activities. Group interaction, groupthink, and brainstorming are activities essential to this level of cognition and thinking. Students must interact, to solve problems, critically discuss, and come to consensus for dissemination and for new direction. Interacting and sharing thoughts and ideas about the learning sequence are necessary. This requires focused thinking with a purpose. That purpose is to develop viable vehicles for sharing and then make sure they are developed, critiqued, practiced, rehearsed, and finally performed (Steinaker 2003b).

Thinking makes the learning process lucid and resolves issues and problems in the ways that come from connecting ideas, considering different approaches, and making final changes as a result of new thoughts being verbalized by all members of the group. Thoughtfully working together is a challenge. It is also an opportunity to learn more, add to what is already known, and embellish accurate and interesting dissemination activities. Thinking is akin to doing. If students can think about a concept clearly, the students can implement it and thus enrich the dissemination process.

LEARNING

Learning is a process. In this analysis of the teaching–learning act, learning has been defined as responding, personalizing, interacting, contextualizing, and expressing. Each of these levels of learning has pertinence as a process within the taxonomy of interactive learning. At implementation, the descriptor for learning is *expressing*. This term clearly communicates what learning is all about at implementation. It is about expressing ideas, skills, and creations. Learning is an expression of self and the process of change that the students have taken in the learning sequence. Expression means sharing and dissemination. This is the learning challenge at this expression level of implementation. Sharing and dissemination become the voluntary final act of the learning process. It is within the sharing of learning that the experience culminates and comes to complete fruition. Learning through expression needs to be done individually, in small groups, and in the whole group. Learning activities here includes, among other things, the following:

> *At implementation, the descriptor of learning is* expressing.

- Seminars structured so that students must defend their views.
- Presentations to illustrate the advantages or excellence of what they have learned.
- Activities that involve determining audience need for the experience.
- Debates between points of view.
- Sales or sharing of developed products and services.

- Skits, plays, or performances illustrating what has been learned.
- Formal reports either orally, in writing, or through PowerPoint (Steinaker and Bell 1979:34–35).

These are a few of the activities that could be used for dissemination. They all could be drawn from students' learning experience. Each can be an expression of that learning and shared with a variety of audiences. Expression can also be done through communicating, debating, influencing, demonstrating, presenting, and motivating. Expression is an important culmination to learning.

TEACHING

The word for teaching at the implementation category is *sharing*. The teacher consults with students about dissemination plans, works with them in developing their plans, and critiques their progress toward completing the plans. The teacher serves as critiquor and consultant.

As critiquor, the teacher works interactively with the students, helping them value what they have learned and their plans for sharing and dissemination. The teacher critiques the process as the students develop ideas and schema for sharing. In addition, through critiquing the teacher brings the students to the point where they value the coming learning sequence and decide to move on to another adventure in learning. The teacher, as a consultant, values student success and helps students make appropriate choices for the platforms of dissemination and sharing. Also as a consultant, the teacher elicits student thoughts and ideas about how to disseminate and help them to make choices about future areas of study. These two roles of the teacher correlate with the student roles as extenders and disseminators. Teaching, at this level of interactive learning, is value oriented and focuses on success and on movement to new learning directions.

LEADERSHIP

The final category in the interactive learning taxonomy is implementation. It is during the activities at this level that students assume responsibility for what they have accomplished. They assume responsibility for disseminating the value and meaning of what they have learned and how they have changed during the process. Students share leadership with the teacher in determining the next area of study and the next direction for their learning. The teacher and the students respect and trust each other at this category of interactive learning; that trust is evidenced as they take what they have learned and apply it to a new course of study. They affirm themselves and their learning through the dissemination process of implementation. **Sample (2002) indicates that through the whole process of leadership "don't form an opinion until you've heard all the relevant facts and arguments" (pp. 7–8). When people come to understand this they can affirm themselves and their roles as leader. He further notes that "leadership is an art, not a science. . . .All of the arts, when practiced at the highest levels of excellence, depend on a steady stream of ideas and creative imagination" (pp. 18–19). It is through this learned process of leadership that students can affirm themselves.**

Students develop aspirations to determine to whom—and how, where, and why—to disseminate. Finally, the students need to take action to disseminate what they have learned and produced. They do this themselves with support from the teacher, who acts as consultant during this category of interactive learning. Leadership is valuing the vision (Johnson et al. 2008). Leadership, unequivocally, plays an important role in the development and continuance of learning into a new experience. Leadership flows from the teacher to the students and finally back to the teacher as the new learning experiences begin. It should also be noted that leadership emphasizes excellence. Six areas of focus must be in place when the learning sequence ends with implementation. Those areas of focus are technical (sound strategies and techniques), interpersonal (good human relating), interactive (participative), collaborative (rapport, respect, and responsibility), cooperative (completion of vision and outcomes), and disseminative (sharing and influencing). These roles encapsulate leadership at all levels of the taxonomy.

FINAL COMMENTS

Through sharing and disseminating, the learning experience comes to its final expression. Through these five categories of interactive learning, we have discussed invitation, involvement, investigation, insight, and implementation. Each level of learning is best exemplified in an exciting and interesting interactive setting. Implementation is no exception. It is a time of celebratory sharing and providing an audience with a view of what they have experienced. It is a demonstration of intrinsic motivation at its finest. Students voluntarily choose to share and report on what they have done. They make determinations in writing, drawing conclusions and developing recommendations. In terms of motivation, they are self-motivated; that motivation emerges during dissemination. The teacher roles of critiquor and consultant along with the student roles of extender and disseminator coincide here at implementation. Part of the processing of the dissemination activities, some of which are listed in this chapter, requires critiquing and consultation. It also requires creative showing and sharing, the utilization of skills and concepts through critical thinking and through problem-solving issues of implementing and influencing. Motivation is intrinsic and students are self-motivated. Evaluation activities are focused on affirming student work, developing aspirations for future learning, implementing disseminating activities and new dimensions of learning. Thinking is summarized as extension, learning as expressing, and teaching as sharing. All these terms capture and illuminate the activities and direction of implementation. Leadership, on the part of the students, has been learned and demonstrated effectively at this final category of interactive learning.

Leadership is learned. It is also experienced and demonstrated. All these activities should be conducted interactively to bring the total learning experience to a strong interactive closure. Each category of interactive learning is exciting and interesting. This summative category of interactive learning brings closure to the taxonomy and a finality of successful achievement. Those who follow this explication of the interactive learning process can experience the same successful finality.

We close out these final comments with a few points of view about leadership. Leadership is very important to the interactive learning process. A major aspect of teacher leadership is to challenge the student to lead. Students need to be allowed to sometimes muddle through leadership experiences, particularly at the invitation and involvement categories of the taxonomy. The teacher needs to continue to listen to the students, interact with them, encourage them, and sustain student efforts to become leaders. Through trial and error learning, the characteristic skills and the interactive

End of Implementation

Technical: sound strategies and techniques
Interpersonal: good human relative
Interactive: participation
Collaborative: rapport, respect, and responsibility
Cooperative: completion of vision and outcomes
Disseminative: sharing and influencing

nature of leadership, as well as with continuing opportunities to lead, students will become competent leaders. Leadership takes time and practice to learn, but it is learned through having leadership opportunities, discussing when and how those opportunities are to be carried out, and what roles of leadership are important within the learning experience. Leadership is the valuing of vision (Johnson et al. 2008). Finally, we need to remember that students can achieve personal excellence and equality through leadership. Leadership can be learned through the taxonomy of interactive learning. Leadership is the essence of the art of teaching. Leadership, wisely demonstrated, shows both the art and science of positive human relationships. Student leadership is the optimal expression of a successful learning experience.

SUMMARY

In the preceding chapters we have presented the process and the theory of interactive learning. We have analyzed the process from invitation to involvement and from involvement to investigation. From investigation we presented insight and from insight we analyzed the last category of interactive learning: involvement. We have included within the analysis of each of these categories specific attention to the roles of a number of continuing strands that are intrinsic to each category. We have followed these learning strands through all five categories of interacting learning. Among them are cognition, teacher roles, student roles, evaluator roles, experiential levels, discourse, motivation, creativity, critical thinking, problem solving, writing, thinking, teaching, and leadership. Each of these strands has a place in every category of the taxonomy of interactive learning. Through these strands we have shown the art and science of the instructional process.

We believe in interactive learning because human beings are gregarious creatures and the context of interaction is a core value of learning and teaching. Interaction encapsulates the art of teaching and good human relating becomes the most effective format for learning. In this work we have noted that interaction takes place in a variety of group settings that the teacher and the students can determine based on defined needs within the course of study. Group structures are essential to ensuring student learning. Students need to learn how to work together before group work can become effectively functional for them. Standards and criteria for group work must be discussed, developed, and learned. Both teacher and students must develop together the interactive skills that make group work pertinent, interesting, and invaluable to learning. Concomitant with group work are skills in questioning, responding, and reporting. These, too, must be learned and demonstrated by the students.

Education is about change. In this work, change and internalized learning have been the dominant themes. We believe that the processes of learning can be identified, sequenced, and analyzed. Change requires leadership and interactive involvement in the teaching–learning act by both teachers and students. Learning is a process that can be defined and studied. Learning has sequence, direction, and substance. The learning process can be identified, defined, and explicated. Students and teachers need to do this regularly as the process unfolds in class. Teachers and students who understand the process can effectively implement a sound learning environment where student achievement is optimized.

Through the process of interactive learning, teachers and students can bring about change. Change can be evolutionary or revolutionary. In either case, change impacts the learner. Indeed, change also impacts the teacher. Humans are always in the process of changing. The one constant in our lives is change. If we understand the process of change and how it can be organized, managed, and sequenced, we can better understand ourselves and better understand the process of learning about and managing change. Strong and effective learning can happen if the teacher and the students follow the steps of each of the fourteen strands through the five levels of interaction. They are invitation, involvement, investigation, insight, and implementation. Synthesized in these five levels of interactive learning is the art and the science of teaching and learning. They emerge, separate, and blend as the learning experience is completed. Finally, they coalesce as the learning experience is disseminated and new experiences emerge.

This processing of the cognitive and experiential levels of learning along with sequencing the teacher role, the student role, and the role of evaluation place a formative and summative context to learning. The sequencing of motivation, discourse, critical thinking, creativity, problem solving, and leadership along with the writing process enlarges the opportunity for understanding the teaching–learning act by teacher and students.

The teaching–learning act is the most dynamic experience in which anyone can be involved. Through this presentation of the teaching–learning act, we hope that teachers and others can use this work to improve their own professional performance in the classroom. It is further hoped that as they more clearly understand and gain insight into what really constitutes the fullness of the teaching–learning act, they can work in concert with learners to bring the rich fabric of teaching and learning to life as they work together to bring about change.

Activities

The activities at this category of interactive learning are fewer than in some earlier chapters. They are also broader in scope than in some earlier chapters. They, as in all earlier chapters, should be done in small groups in an interactive setting. Individual work can be assigned and done, but it is not recommended. This is the last chapter dealing primarily with theory. Later chapters will be focused on organizing activities and groups and then on instruction. Here we want you to ponder each of these. Ponder, from its Greek etymology, means to struggle with the concept and to come to a consensus or a perspective that could change with more information or data. Finally, you will culminate your study of one strand of lesson analysis here as encompassed in the sixth activity. As you continue with activities in future chapters, keep your responses to the theory and apply them to the new information or data.

1. "Implementation is interactive learning in its finest moments" (Chap. 6, p. 71). Discuss this statement. How is it evidenced at this category? Justify the statement in terms of any three strands of interactive learning.

2. Comment on implementation as a platform not only for dissemination, but for deciding to begin a new learning cycle. How does this happen? What does the teacher do and what roles do students play during the decision-making process?

3. Dissemination is the experiential strand of interactive learning. Ponder this strand and discuss how it is exhibited at implementation. Focus on how creativity, cognition, and critical thinking relate to dissemination. Summarize what you have learned.

4. How is leadership evidenced by the teacher and the students at the implementation category? How have roles changed and developed through interactive learning? Discuss this in your group and report to your peers.

5. The term *responsibility* has a number of meanings at implementation. Identify several of those meanings and prepare to share those meanings with your peers.

6. This is your last focus on the strand selected for analysis and sequence through the taxonomy. Summarize your narrative and your findings. Discuss them with the group and be prepared to report to your peers and your instructor what you have found. Within your narrative, note what you found about how the stand is accomplished at each category of interactive learning.

Organization

N ow that you have internalized the theory and have thoroughly understood it, you are ready for the organization section of this work. In chapters 7 and 8 we bring forward two important factors of organization that you, as teacher, must consider as you get ready to teach. We believe in interactive learning, discourse, and dialogue in the classroom. In the next two chapters we bring to you organization as it relates to learning activities and group structures. Our purpose is to present an overview of learning activities and group structures that are viable in the classroom.

In chapter 7 we focus on learning activities. They are presented in taxonomic order with activities suggested for each category of the taxonomy. Some activities can be used at more than one category. These have been noted as they fit into other categories. For each activity we have provided a brief descriptor. We did not, on purpose, provide all the details, but rather give you the impetus to take the activities, fit them into your own classroom organization, and develop the context for their use. We urge you to use the various strands we have presented for putting together these activities. When the activities are over, review what you have done. Identify some of the strands and study how they were used with the activity. Find out how the theory works with each of the activities. You become a partner with us as you do action research on your own teaching.

Next, in chapter 8 we focus on group structures. We believe in groups. We believe in interactive groups. We believe in this from kindergarten through graduate school. Groups are essential in any classroom organization. The different kinds of groups are seldom presented in an organized fashion. We feel that you need to know about many different kinds of group structures that you could use in your classroom. We have identified and discussed seventeen different group structures. Most will be effective at your grade level, a few may not work. Above all, however, use these group structures. They are the heart and soul of interactive teaching. They are the keen elements of optimum learning. To us, they are necessary to interactive learning.

These two focuses on organization are basic to successful teaching. The activities in which you engage your students are vital to their learning. In terms of these activities, build them around group structures. Use a variety of small groups to encourage students to develop their voice and be a part of the change process. You know the theory and you have understood the organization. Review these two chapters carefully and see how you can use the activities and the group structures in your classroom. In the next section, we will focus on instruction.

Teaching–Learning Activities

Interactive learning implies that there are activities designed for dialogue, discussion, and discourse at every category of the taxonomy of interactive learning. In this chapter we present a wide variety of activities arranged by categories of interaction. Several of the activities at each category can be used in other categories, and some can be effectively used at all levels of interactive learning. We have specified only a few. There are many additional activities that teachers can develop and use in which students can participate. Each specific activity will be presented and discussed in the category of first or major use. These activity discussions, although brief, can provide enough information for the teacher to plan them and for the students to be a part of them.

Instruction and how it is delivered and received is an essential element to the success of any learning experience. The taxonomy of interactive learning is keyed at every category to a variety of interactions and activities that are corollary to that level of the taxonomy. The broad rubric for interaction in groups and organized activities in the interactive context are consistent at every category of this interactive taxonomic sequence. The rubric is defined, for the purpose of this work, as interactive instruction and interactive learning. Learning is most effective when there are dialogical and interactive dimensions within the instructional process as they develop from invitation and progress through implementation.

This interactive dimension of instruction, most frequently done through group structures, is most effectively accomplished through a series of activities, interactive in nature, and consistent with each category of the taxonomy of interactive learning. It is through activities within group settings that learning becomes valued and leadership roles can be demonstrated. In the process of interactive learning and in all the categories of the taxonomy, there needs to be the use of specific and interactive teaching–learning activities. We present them in this chapter. In this discussion of the teaching–learning activities, the categories of the taxonomy of interactive learning are noted. Then, within each of those categories of interactive learning, some of the instructional activities that can be used at that category are included. With each specifically identified teaching–learning activity, a brief descriptor is included. We do not go into great detail, nor are these designed as lesson plans. They are a list of selected activities for each category of the taxonomy with a short definitional descriptor, a series of ideas and defined activities pertinent to the category. We suggest that teachers refer to them and use them along with other activities of their own choosing that can be used at the identified category of the taxonomy. These listed activities can be effectively used,

> *Instruction and how it is delivered and received is an essential element to the success of any learning experience.*

but the ones included are only a few of the range of ideas and activities that could be used. There are, of course, many more teaching–learning activities teachers can implement and use. Each teacher, when planning, should determine the activities pertinent to the learning objectives and corollary with the category of the taxonomy functional for instruction and learning. As teachers develop and use their own teaching–learning activities, those activities should fit into one or more category of the taxonomy of interactive learning. Most of these activities correlate well with SDAIE that are used for English language learners. See Appendix C for descriptors of sixteen SDAIE activities.

Some activities can be used at more than one level of the taxonomy. Indeed, some of the activities can be used at all categories of the taxonomy. Among those multicategory activities are interactive and cooperative learning group activities. Interactive and cooperative learning group activities can be used effectively at all levels of interactive learning from invitation to involvement. These teaching learning activities can be used both instructionally and organizationally. A number of these cooperative and interactive group structures are discussed in greater detail in later chapters of this work.

> *Interactive and cooperative learning group activities can be used effectively at all levels of interactive learning from invitation to involvement.*

In the following listing of teaching–learning activities, only a few of the variety of activities that can be used at each level of the taxonomy are listed. Teachers and students may use any activities they wish as long as those activities are consistent with the category in which they are used. Each activity is followed by a brief descriptor designed to provide a definition and/or some additional information. The teaching–learning activities listed in the discussion in this chapter are keyed to a particular category of the taxonomy. They are sometimes generic in their descriptors and this should be taken into consideration when using these teaching–learning activities for planning purposes. There are some thoughtful and easy activities that can be used in several categories of the taxonomy. Let us cite just two. The first activity is a simple one. The teacher needs to be sure to acknowledge every student by name, before, during, or after class. Although simple, this is very important to the students and helpful to the teacher. Second, to ensure that students have an opportunity to work closely with all members of the class in a variety of settings, change the seating arrangements as needed. These two activities coupled with other designated activities help establish readiness, create relationships, and build rapport.

INVITATION ACTIVITIES

Marvin Holm (2003), one of our colleagues, in using the taxonomy at the high school level, posited these needs at invitation or readiness in workshops presented to his colleagues. They are valid at any grade level beginning in elementary school and continuing through graduate school with some adjustment for the age and for the needs of the students. They are as follows:

Students need to understand their need to learn and to be motivated.

Students need know that the teacher has high expectations from them.

Students become involved in activities that make them feel like this is their course.

Students must understand that value and meaning are their top priorities.

Students need to know why the study is valuable and how it relates to them.

Students need to know what steps are to be taken and when action is expected (Holm, 2003:2).

It is important that we keep these student needs in mind as we suggest activities. As noted, these were designed for high school teachers, so make any adjustments you may need for your students. You should keep in mind the students needs at each category of the taxonomy.

At the invitation category of the taxonomy, the teacher's roles are those of a preparer and a presenter. The student roles are as an attender and a questioner. The instructional role is informational. The leadership roles for the teacher is that of a preparer; the leadership role for students is as a participant. Invitation activities need to be carefully planned. They must be designed to provide information, to heighten student interest, and to provide interaction. Interaction can be generated through questioning, working in small groups on specific assignments or issues, and through active discussion of the materials and resources used. What follows is a list of some of the activities that could be used at this invitation level of interactive learning.

- Using audiovisual multimedia materials to create a need, a purpose, or a desire to learn. Audiovisual and multimedia materials can be used at all levels of the taxonomy. Here they are used to inform the student, to present needed information, to emphasize the need to learn, and through this invitation level of interactive learning, to involve the students in the learning experience. Interactive responses can be done in small groups, individually, or as a whole class interactively discussing what they have seen.
- Presenting examples or experiments to illustrate a principle, concept, or skill. This teaching–learning activity is designed to help set parameters and to generate student interest in major concepts or skills to be learned. The teacher usually does the presenting and the students can respond individually or in small groups.
- Locating resources in a specified area. This activity is designed to arouse interest. Under the teacher's directions, students need to access materials, artifacts, and realia. Students generally do this together. Group structure is usually pairs, triads, and small groups. After finding the resources, students interact and discuss what they have found through their groups. Teacher can use questioning strategies to ensure individual and group interaction.
- Identifying and introducing resources. Here the teacher usually introduces and identifies resources, and discusses them with students in a whole-group setting or in a variety of group structures. If there are artifacts or realia involved, students need to have hands-on experience with the resources. Group interaction and focused questioning are among the interactive processes.
- Initial viewing of scenes, objects, and roles. Visual materials are very helpful in this kind of activity where students interact and react to what they have seen. Visual materials are keyed to ideas and concepts within the learning experience. Feelings and ideas can be shared in groups or through interaction with the teacher. Students need to view materials and resources and learn the roles of the people shown in the scenes or objects. This is a good activity for interaction.
- Unstructured interviewing. Some sources are human resources and students may want to respond, interview, or ask questions of their human resources. Students know the skills and the topic that the person will present before the interview. They can prepare questions in small groups and then interact interrogatively with their resource. Although this is called unstructured interviewing, basic questions are prepared in advance.
- Dramatic presentations and skits. These can be done from a script or from a prepared document. The purpose is informational, which is the instructional role at this level of the taxonomy. Practice and rehearsal need to be discussed in groups or as a whole class, and then be dealt with and presented by groups within the classroom.
- Asking fundamental and often naive questions. Students must feel free to ask questions and to respond to them. Students can prepare questions individually or in small groups. They can ask each other or they can ask the teacher or the resource people. All questions must be honored and must have a response. Activities in the interrogative mode can be used during any category of interaction.

- Responding to student questions. This is corollary to the previous teaching–learning activity. Responses need to be designed to be informational and to provide students with essential or needed information. Questions can come from individual students and from groups of students.
- Changing relationships between previously used words, pictures, or activities and their appearance, color, shape, and sound. During this invitation category, students need to become aware of similarities and differences; this kind of activity can help this. This is essentially a sensory experience. Where possible, all senses should be involved in this teaching–learning activity. Discussion in groups can be an excellent way to complete this kind of activity.
- Causing an alerting reaction through any novel, difficult, or unusual circumstance. Activities such as these need to be designed to help students react to the unusual, the difficult, and the novel. Interaction and response are the purposes of this teaching–learning activity. This kind of activity can be used at any category of the taxonomy.
- Projecting what if situations. These are open-ended situational information and questions from the teacher and sometimes from students for the purpose of helping students think about variables and possibilities. The teacher here is preparing the students for further study and movement through the learning experience.
- Use student groups to develop questions, to discuss value and meaning of the experience, and to respond to the presentations of the teacher as well as material in the various resources. This is a good use of student groups, where they can interact with each other with the teacher monitoring them and interacting with them.
- Ruminating and reflecting. This kind of activity is one that needs to be done in groups. Students need to do this kind of reflecting and reacting to what they have seen, found, and asked questions about. They can also ruminate and reflect on what they have learned. It is essential that this kind of activity occur so that the students can affirm the invitation they have been given and react to it. This interactive activity is one that should comes near to the close of the invitation category and helps students move more efficiently into the involvement category of interactive learning.
- Defining parameters and suggesting outcomes. This activity occurs during the closing stages of invitation. Using this activity requires specific interaction that, while generally led by the teacher, can be discussed in groups and even in some circumstances can be led by students. The purpose of this interaction is to motivate the students to continue through the learning experience and to become involved in it.

These are but a view of the teaching–learning activities that can be used by teachers and students at the invitation category of interactive learning. There are, of course, many more. These teaching–learning activities and others like them can help prepare students for further involvement in the learning experience. Through these activities and others, the students finish the invitation category; they have developed readiness for the next category of interactive learning. Completing the invitation to learning requires vision, value, and veracity. The activities must provide for envisioning what is yet to come, valuing what has been done, and providing a sense of fact and reality so the students can recognize the validity of the experience to their needs and aspirations. These activities should be engaging for the students and be within the scope of needs expressed by Holm (2003), or ones that would be closely associated with them but designed for your students.

Teaching–learning activities at the invitation level must be carefully selected and thoroughly planned by the teacher. The teacher needs to know specifically how each teaching–learning activity relates to the invitation level of interaction and how the activities can help provide the student with enough information to make the invitation viable. Roles are very important and the teacher needs to be constantly aware of the roles and ensure that they are used. The teacher roles are preparer and presenter. The student roles are as questioner and participant. Students, too, need to be aware of these roles. The instructional role at invitation is informational. The leadership role for the teacher is that of a presenter and the leadership role of the students is as a participant. These roles must be clearly understood by the teacher in the planning process. Students, too, should know their roles and be cognizant about how instruction is to be presented and what next steps are incipient in the learning sequence.

INVOLVEMENT ACTIVITIES

The goals for the involvement category are straightforward and to the point. Holm (2003) notes them as follows:

> Students connect with each other.
>
> Students develop a sense of togetherness.
>
> Students connect with their teacher.
>
> Students work positively with their resources (Holm, 2003:2).

Involvement activities are designed around a participatory instructional approach. There is a strong interactive component in which students use group structures of various kinds. There is an interactive connection among students, as well as positive student interaction with the teacher. Both teacher and students explore and use the materials and resources relevant to their specific learning project. The teacher's roles are those of a catalyst and coordinator. The students' roles are those of an explorer and cooperator. Leadership roles are coordinator for the teacher and cooperator for the students. All of these roles should be known by the teacher and by the students. The teaching–learning activities at this category of the taxonomy reflect those roles. Suggested teaching–learning activities follow.

> *There is a strong interactive component in which students utilize group structures of various kinds.*

- Discussing data presented. The operant word here is *discussing*. Discussion and participation should include all students in small groups and sometimes in whole-class groups. There should be response and challenge in teacher and student interaction about data being presented. Discussion leads to more active involvement and is a good activity to use at this second level of interactive learning.
- Structured data-gathering activities. Students should begin to gather data themselves. The teacher may have the resources available including Web sites, print material, and multimedia material. The teacher as catalyst coordinator should plan for these and work with the students cooperatively. Students should learn how to gather and organize data. These kinds of teaching–learning activities are essential in the information age in which we live. They should be done in pairs, triads, or small groups so that interaction and discussion can take place.
- Unstructured role-playing (sometimes called dramatic play). This is a great activity. Teacher and students do careful planning and then role-play the life or activities of the people they are studying. It is unstructured because the evaluation of this role-playing is designed to focus on the next steps and further study. This is also a great SDAIE activity. In particular, what they know, what they want to know, and what they have learned (KWL) is implicit in this activity.
- Walk-through, replication, and verification activities. Here the focus is on meaning and value. First, what do the data mean to the students in terms of the learning experience? Second, what do the data mean in terms of usability and value for the learning experience? Again, this can be a group activity in which there is much interaction. Making sure the data are valid and not skewed to particular views is also an area of focus.

- Group discussions of demonstrations and/or data. Group interaction is very important at this involvement, participation, and relationship category of interactive learning. Students need to discuss and dialogue about what they have observed, reviewed, and studies. They need to react to any observations and demonstrations they have seen and need to come to conclusions about them. This can best be done through group structures. Several group structures can be used. These are the purposes of this teaching–learning activity.
- Imitating an observed event. Students have seen an event, a multimedia presentation, a video or a CD, or have observed a situation. They recreate that event in their own way through a skit, a script, a reenactment, or interactive discussions about the event. Students grow in this way and become more involved in the learning experience. This is a good SDAIE activity.
- Reading a story previously introduced or discussed in class. This teaching–learning activity has a specific purpose in providing students with detailed information and allowing them individually and in small groups to react to material to which they have already been introduced and that may have been discussed in class During this activity, students can bring new perspectives for discussion and decision.
- Using manipulatives, artifacts, or realia. This is a participatory activity using anything to which students have been introduced, although sometimes the items may not yet have been introduced to the students. Students manipulate them, apply them, and try to determine their use. This kind of teaching–learning activity is intrinsic to the student role of explorer. This activity can be used in all categories of interactive learning. It is a strong SDAIE activity in its cooperative learning setting.
- Hands-on activities. This is similar to the previous activity, but there are differences. Hands-on can deal with the use and application of print material, building or constructing products, or working together on a project or skill. Cooperative and interactive groups are important in terms of these kinds of activities.
- Counting and quantifying data. Organization is very important to students at this category of the taxonomy. The focus here is organizing, counting, and classifying data or materials. Students have to note similarities, differences, quality, and quantity, and then categorize the materials. Group work, pairs, and triads are essential as students put together data to find organization, classification, and meaning.
- Ordering objects, events, and materials from more important to less important. Students need to learn to sequence materials in order of importance. This is an hierarchical skill requiring higher levels of cognition and should be built into the learning experience at this level of the taxonomy. Ordering can also be a part of activities at all levels of the taxonomy. Again, the structure in class should be within pairs, triads, or groups.
- Categorizing, information, materials, and resources. This activity, along with the last two activities, gives an important dimension to learning at this category of interactive learning. Students need to categorize information, put it into identified classifications, organize it for easy access and use. In doing so, they are building a bibliography of materials and a plan for easily accessing them. In the information age in which we live, this kind of activity is necessary. In groups, students can review materials and categorize them as useful or discard them as being unreliable. Higher level cognition is used along with critical thinking skills.
- Visualizing, verbalizing, and brainstorming. The instructional modality at this level of the taxonomy is participatory. This teaching–learning activity emphasizes participation. It also emphasizes brainstorming where every idea is considered. This activity emphasizes visualization of direction, outcomes, and products. Use of this activity emphasizes interactive participatory formats. This activity is directional in its function.
- Asking or designing questions for recalling and organizing data. The emphasis in this activity is to raise questions about the use of organized materials. Students should question each other and the teacher on how to get data and how to use it.

This is an exploratory activity in terms of dialogue and interaction. Students should question each other and the teacher about the nature and validity of data and how these fits into the learning sequence. They can do this individuals or in small groups. Small-group structures are generally preferable. They are, in effect, practicing their organizational prowess and seeing how it works. They are also demonstrating emerging leadership roles as cooperators.

- Modeling or defining behaviors. All participatory and involvement require interaction and group work. This is no exception. This is a time when students need to review and assess what they have done and what yet needs to be done. This modeling and defining activity can help in this process. Students define standards, review progress, and assess the quality of what has been done. Students also look at direction and their next steps. The use of this activity allows them to develop their next steps.
- Timing activities and programs. How much time does an activity take? Students need to ask this question and considerit in terms of the effectiveness and efficiency of the learning experience. Students need this kind of activity as they prepare to move to the next level of interactive learning. This teaching–learning activity has a strong and definable correlation with accountability and evaluation. Timing and measuring activities can be used at any category of the taxonomy beginning with involvement.
- Generating data through recall or data searches. Here students begin themselves to generate and gather information and sources to use as their involvement in the learning experience grows. They use these data for furthering and continuing the learning information. They reach back and recall information, or search databases and other sources for needed data. There should be considerable reading and writing done in this and other similar activities at this involvement level of interactive learning.
- Organizing and sing interactive grouping structures. Without a doubt these activities span all the learning activities in which students are engaged at this level of involvement as well as in other categories of the taxonomy of interactive learning. Students need the interactive small-group structures to further their involvement and to increase their interest and passion for the learning experience in which they are involved. This strategy relates to all the others at this category of the taxonomy.

At this level of the taxonomy the teaching–learning activities focus on student interaction with materials and resources, with the teacher, and with each other. This can be done in many ways, but is primarily accomplished in small-group structures. The instructional role is participatory and so the interaction among students, interaction with resources, and interaction with the teacher is the major expectation for all teaching–learning activities used at this level of interactive teaching. The interaction and discussion within the small groups is demonstrated through developing relationships and further involvement in the learning process. These activities must be carefully planned. With the inclusion of student ideas and suggestions within the planning process, it becomes a broader and more inclusive process. More student leadership roles emerge during these activities. Every teaching–learning activity is focused on interaction and group work. This is what happens during involvement.

INVESTIGATION ACTIVITIES

Some of the goals for investigation activities as developed by Holm (2003) are presented in the following. Thinks through these goals as you plan your activities. They are sound and can be adjusted to meet the needs of your students. Select, plan, and use activities with these goals and objectives in mind.

Students and teacher build a harmonious working environment.

Students support each other and the teacher in the teaching–learning process.

Students demonstrate a sense of belonging.

Students see each other as important colleagues in the working climate and socially.

Students value their learning experience through investigation, analysis, and meaning (Holm 2003:2).

Investigation activities are designed to strengthen the working relationships among students and with the teacher. They are also designed to move students toward real understanding and conceptualization of the major components of the learning experience as well as the goals and objectives of the learning process. At this category of the taxonomy, the students need to demonstrate and begin to use learned skills, attitudes, and identified outcomes pertaining to the course of study. These skills, attitudes, and outcomes are generated through the learning experience. Activities should be designed to meet identified outcomes. Students and teacher can plan together to ensure achievement of the outcomes. The teacher roles are those of a moderator and resolver; it can be seen that these roles are different from the previous roles as presenter, preparer, and catalyst coordinator. At this category of the taxonomy, the teacher is moving from overt leadership to a more cooperative style of leadership. The teacher's role as leader can be understood as a resolver or one who works with the students to help them resolve issues and problems. The teacher interacts with students individually and in groups to help them through questions and issues they find within the learning experience with which they have identified.

> *The teacher interacts with students individually and in groups to help them through questions and issues they find within the learning experience with which they have identified.*

The student roles are those of an experimenter and an investigator/researcher. This means that the students are trying out skills and beginning to use what they are learning. They are also experimenting with ideas and concepts. It should also be noted that the student role as leader becomes more apparent. They are investigators at this category of the taxonomy and they are evidencing growing leadership within the learning sequence. The teacher as moderator and resolver needs to provide those opportunities for leadership that are needed by the students. The instructional role is investigative and the concept of investigation defines the kinds of activities in which the students need to engage at this category of the taxonomy of interactive learning. The instructional role also links with the student leadership role as investigator. Value and meaning need to be integral to activities at the investigation category of the taxonomy. Focusing on value and meaning is important so that the students can identify those values and concepts and deepen their learning experience. Students should also begin to understand the change process and demonstrate how the experience is beginning to impact them as they identify with it at this category. The following are some of the teaching–learning activities at the investigation category of the taxonomy.

- Use of learning and/or reinforcement strategies to study, to apply, to assess, and to analyze content. Students apply various strategies to clarify and gain understanding of the content. They are, in this activity, beginning to comprehend, apply, and transfer ideas, data, and content to skills and perspectives needed within the learning experience. Students begin to use data and information they have already learned. This activity is done interactively in a variety of group settings.
- Impromptu and scheduled conferences to deal with individual or group needs and problems (student/student, teacher/student). This is an interactive teaching–learning activity designed to ensure that all students have a basic knowledge and understanding of content skills and are able to apply and analyze them. Students who need help or who are having problems can profit greatly from this activity. It is in activities like this that the teacher leadership of resolver and the student role as investigator become very important.

- Discussion under teacher and/or student direction to exchange views and verify ideas. Discussion can be done in small groups or as a whole-class group. Exchanging views and gaining verification of ideas and hypotheses is very important at the investigation category of interactive learning. Students, through activities like these, can begin to demonstrate leadership. This kind of activity is important at investigation.

- Field experience for study in a functional setting. This teaching–learning activity can be done through technology, field trips, multimedia, or a variety of hands-on activities. It is essential that students begin to expand their learning and to see ideas, content, values, meaning, and skills used in a number of contexts. Through field experiences as described here, the investigation of content takes on a much more real focus so students can thoroughly identify with the content area of study.

- Data selection, retrieval, and organizing data activities. Students need to work with data and select those data most pertinent to their learning experienced. They need to organize data for learning and retrieve it as needed during this category of the taxonomy. This is generally done in small groups. This is a very important activity and should be planned carefully by teachers and students.

- Charting events in time; history. Putting events and experiences in sequence in a timeline are important for students to do here. This helps students gain perspective and learn historic processes and sequences within the learning experience. Timelines can be done for the learning experience and these, too, can be very helpful to the students. Timelines and sequencing provide benchmarks for students.

- Focus on specific or particular components of the learning experience. To understand the whole, students need to study the parts or components within their learning experience. This can be done in jigsaw groups or other kinds of group structures with interactive reporting and discussion. This teaching–learning activity requires analysis and acceptance levels of cognitive and focused thinking.

- Application through observation, research, and experimentation. Students at this level of interactive learning are experimenters and investigators. This kind of activity gives them a chance to experiment, to investigate, to test hypotheses, and to observe elements and components of the learning experience. This, again, is best done in a variety of small-group settings.

- Manipulative materials combining of psychomotor, cognitive, affective, and experiential involvement. These kinds of teaching–learning activities are vital for students at this level of interactive learning. All the categories of cognition, experience, affective, and psychomotor taxonomies need to be used to ensure that students really identify with the learning experience and are able to fully express that sense of identification through a series of activities involving all of the these taxonomies.

- Sharing what has been learned through discussion, writing, demonstration, or contests. Sharing is an activity very important and appropriate at this investigation level of the taxonomy. Students need to share, discuss, write, and demonstrate their understanding, learning, and the results of their investigation. This can be done within a competitive or a cooperative setting determined by teachers and students. This can also be a teaching–learning activity that can provide opportunities of demonstrated student leadership.

- Reporting information acquired to other students or groups of students. Reporting here is not to be confused with the dissemination activities at the implementation category of interactive learning. This is only a matter of sharing progress and the skills and processes associated with them to teachers or to other peers. Again, this activity can provide leadership skills for students.

- Demonstrate skills achievement. The students need to show what they have learned and demonstrate what they have done, which can result in reinforcement activities that could be done within the classroom. Each student or group of students needs to share with each other and to demonstrate what they have learned. This can ensure identification with the learning experience and provide an opportunity to use some of the skills they have learned.

- Conceiving and using provisional assumptions. As experimenters and investigators, students develop provisional assumptions about the lessons or course of study. Being involved in this kind of teaching–learning activity helps students to design, create, and demonstrate these provisional assumptions. This kind of activity is best done in small-group structures.
- Testing ideas, assumptions, and/or hypotheses. These kinds of activities are logical follow-ups for the previous activities. If students conceive and develop assumptions, ideas, or hypotheses, they need to be tested for validation or application. Group structures should be primarily used for this kind of activity. Here, too, the students can demonstrate leadership and the teacher can fulfill the roles of moderator and resolver.

Through these activities and other similar activities, the students and the teacher are enabled to establish rapport, complete investigations, and build strong and viable working relationships. The defining focus of all of the teaching–learning activities at this category of interactivity is to establish a strong working relationship and rapport so that teachers and students can openly and honestly share with each other in a safe and supportive classroom environment. Each one of the teaching–learning activities in this investigation category of interactive learning should be conducted interactively. Investigation grows through interaction in groups and through shared activities. This is clearly shown in the type of activities that have been noted and others that may be similar. Students need to investigate, experiment, share, demonstrate, and gain clear understanding about what they have done and what they have learned. These are objectives and goals intrinsic to each of the activities at the investigation level of interactive learning.

The teacher roles at the investigation category are those of a moderator and resolver who works with students to foster their investigative study of the materials and concepts within the learning experience. The instructional role, like the student leadership role, is that of an experimenter. Students' leadership role is as an investigator. Students need to try out ideas, to put ideas into focus, and to develop values and meanings about their initial assumptions and to further develop and test those assumptions and hypotheses. The teaching–learning activities provided at this category of the taxonomy and other activities like them demonstrate the student roles as experimenter and investigator and correlate with the investigative instructional role as well as the teacher roles of moderator and resolver. This is a category of interaction in which the students demonstrate strong identification with the learning experience. Identification becomes theirs through carefully designed activities provided in a positive learning setting and through a wide variety of group structures.

INSIGHT ACTIVITIES

It is during this insight category of the taxonomy that students internalize what they have learned, become cognitively caring, and create products after completing the basic objectives of the learning experience. Insight is the culmination of the learning experience with only implementation to follow. Students during this time achieve the learning objectives and concepts of the experience and have internalized them. The broad goals for this category of interactive learning are as follows

Students demonstrate esteem for other students, for the teacher, and importantly, for themselves.

Students develop and evidence self-respect and pride in what they have accomplished.

Students understand that respect is mutual and positive.

Students relate positively and strongly to the teacher and the teacher with them.

Students internalize their learning and show respect for both process and product (Holm 2003:2).

Insight activities move beyond rapport into new levels of cognition and interactive behavior. Students gain insight into what has developed through the learning experience. This becomes evident as students gain and demonstrate respect for each other and for the teacher as they succeed in the achievement of goals and objectives. The teaching–learning activities at this level of taxonomy promote higher levels of cognition, including application, analysis, synthesis, and evaluation. Experientially, students are at the internalization level. During this category of interactive learning, students demonstrate that they have not only learned the concepts, ideas, and major themes of the learning experience, but that they have made them a part of their lived experience. They have accomplished the goals and objectives of the learning experience and are ready, through a series of teaching–learning activities, to demonstrate their accomplishments. In the process of participation in the activities, the students have gained respect for themselves, for each other, for the teacher, and for the process through which they have come.

The teaching–learning activities in which they participate help ensure that the demonstrated respect will be built and completed. The teacher role is that of a sustainer. The student role is that of an extender. The leadership role for the teacher is that of an adviser. The student role in leadership is as a creator. It is important to note how these leadership roles have developed and changed through the categories of the taxonomy. Students are assuming here many of the overt leadership roles, while the teacher's leadership role has become more covert as an adviser. These roles are demonstrated throughout the activities at this category of interactive learning. Some of the activities are listed as follows.

> *The teacher role is that of a sustainer.*
>
> *The student role is that of an extender.*

- Students describe, clarify, analyze, and evaluate situations and systems. When internalizing the skills and concepts within the learning experience, students need the opportunity to talk about them, classify them, clarify them, understand them, analyze them, and evaluate them. Where appropriate, they should transfer what they have found to new situations. This kind of activity is done most effectively in a variety of group settings.
- Determine and evaluate variables, similarities, and differences. During this teaching–learning activity students are making final determinations and evaluating what they have learned in terms of variable analyses, in terms of similarities and and differences. Here students are making final determinations and evaluating what they have learned in terms of identified variables, likenesses, and differences. They also make judgments about how they fit into their learning experience and why it is important to learn about them.
- Discussions/questions at analysis, synthesis, and evaluation levels of cognition. Cognitive skills are needed at the insight level of interactive learning. Insight is gained through cooperating in figuring out things at analysis, synthesis, and evaluation levels of cognition. Through thinking, concepts, skills, and ideas are modified with new areas of focus and understanding. Insight is developed through cognitive caring and cooperating in figuring out things at analysis, synthesis, and evaluation. Interactive groups can be well used with this teaching–learning activity.
- Identifying and evaluating affective and attitudinal changes that have taken place during the learning experience. This is an important teaching–learning activity that needs to take place at the insight category of the taxonomy. Its use requires reflection on what has been done, how it was accomplished. This activity can be best completed in small-group formats for discussion and identification of values, attitudes, and how they have changed.
- Using data and learning in one or more practical transfer situations. This activity is focused on the transfer of ideas and concepts into useful settings and functions within the parameters of the learning experience. Students need to demonstrate

what they have learned in the study sequences. This activity involves group work, creativity, critical thinking, and demonstrated internalization of key concepts and big ideas through transfer learning and demonstration.

- Creative expressions where learners develop personal styles through writing, art, music, mathematics, poetry, science, and manipulative materials (construction). The descriptor of the activity tells it all. Here students are creatively expressing what they have learned in a variety of contexts and content areas. The cognitive emphasis is at the synthesis and evaluation categories. This is a strong insight activity that should be encouraged for use by students. This kind of activity fits well into small-group organizations and structures.

- Seminar settings and discussion for advanced study and to solve problems of interest. Seminar discussions with a focus toward transfer and advanced studies and toward resolving issues raised in the learning experience are appropriate activities for the insight level of interactive learning and should be used. These are serious and in-depth discussions and focus groups. The use of the seminar here is as in class activity. Seminars as a dissemination teaching–learning activity are also used at the implementation category of interactive learning.

- Developing and using simulations and games. The use of this activity requires students to create simulations and games. This is an activity where real creativity takes place and students demonstrate through simulation or gaming what they have learned and how they clearly understand what and how they have learned. Later students may use them for dissemination.

- Activities requiring originality and creativity. Creating something new and original is a challenging activity for students. They, at this category of interactive learning, enjoy this kind of activity and bringing to it a cognitive and affective insight. Creative activities can be done through a variety of media and formats. Writing, poetry, skits and plays, art, artifacts, models, murals, narratives, and demonstrations are but a few. Using these kinds of activities is also an opportunity for real student leadership. Their leadership role is as a creator. The teacher as sustainer and adviser should strongly encourage these kinds of activities. Small-group work can be a catalyst for bringing out optimum creative expressions.

- Individual and small-group exercises to develop new uses, products, and techniques using data and information learned. Again, the emphasis is on using what has been learned and developed in new ways and new contests. This activity can also involve the development of new products. This teaching–learning activity lends itself well to small group work, but can also be done individually or in pairs and triads. This kind of activity is an important expression of student work at the insight category of the taxonomy.

- Review the learning process and determining future directions/trends. Activities are centered around review and reflection and are essential to learning. These can become a basis for finalizing what they have accomplished and planning for implementation and dissemination. They can also become a beginning point for moving toward future learning and new learning experiences. This kind of activity is one that should be a part of every learning experience. It is pertinent at this category of interactive learning.

- Panel discussions to present ideas and perspectives. Panel discussions can be used to present ideas and perspectives. Panel discussions can be very interesting and helpful to students. They can share what they have learned with each other. In this sharing modality, panel members provide information in specific areas of study and respond to questions. Panel discussions can help students clarify information, assist in transfer learning, and even present new ideas. Panel discussions can be further developed and used for dissemination activities.

- Probing activities, in-depth studies, "behind the scenes" investigation, and research. These teaching–learning activities are designed to help students work insightfully and applicatively into the core of ideas and concepts that have been central to the learning experience. This can be both a formative and a summative review of the whole learning experience. In addition, these kinds of activities help students internalize what they have learned. They, also, in these activities understand why they have learned, how they have learned, and what they have learned.

- Recreating activities using new learning, media, point in time, and/or location. These teaching–learning activities help students recreate the learning experience in new contexts and with new insight. They can reflect on and investigate point in time specifics. These activities also help students use new learning on earlier issues and on issues yet to come. Group interaction is important.
- Role-playing activities designed to provide opportunities to display and express new learning as well as skills and behaviors. Role-playing at the insight category is structured and is based on what students have experienced and what they have learned. Role-playing can be formalized through the preparation of a script. Role-playing can also be developed by informed students and as it is played out. These activities are designed both for review and reflection, but can be used for extending learning to new contexts.
- Developing games in which the emphasis is on strategy, not on skill or chance. Students enjoy developing and using games. A project or activity in which students develop puzzles and games with emphasis on strategy, understanding, application, and analysis is very helpful at this insight category of interactive learning. Games and puzzles are generally developed by students in groups or teams. Other students learn and use the games and puzzles when they are finished. Students enjoy both the creative dimensions of these activities as well as playing the games and solving the puzzles.

The use of these and similar activities will result in the development of cognitive, attitudinal, experiential, and relational insight among the students and with the teacher. These teaching–learning activities are designed to promote the use of ideas, feelings, behaviors, and skills that will result in the students and the teacher not only gaining insight into what they have learned, but also gaining mutual respect for one another. Once these substantive feelings of respect and insight are established, students are ready to assume nearly total responsibility for disseminating the learning experience. The teacher roles of sustainer and adviser are critical at this level of interactive learning. It is during this category of insight that the learning objectives are being achieved and used by the students. The teacher sustains the students' learning, advises them on projects and problems, and encourages students to demonstrate more leadership. Students begin, at this category, to manage their own learning program. They can, and should, make decisions about direction in selecting activities, extending their learning, and in critically and creatively showing what they have internalized through the learning experience.

It is during this category of interactive learning that the goals and objectives of the learning experience have been achieved. Only the level of implementation and dissemination remains. The development of ideas for new learning experiences also has yet to come and will be accomplished at the implementation category of the taxonomy. The teaching–learning activities at the insight level of interactive learning are designed to demonstrate the student roles as extenders and creators. Students apply what they have learned, use what they have learned in new ways and new areas, and creatively develop projects, written materials, products, roles, games, and puzzles. They are truly extenders and creators. The instructional role is applicative and the activities fit well into this instructional role. Much small-group work and interaction are the hallmarks of this insight category of interactive learning.

IMPLEMENTATION ACTIVITIES

Students, when the activities at the insight category have been completed, begin with activities at the implementation category of the taxonomy. During activities at this final level of interactive learning, there are disseminative goals and objectives that need to be accomplished. Along with these disseminative goals are transitional goals to help students move to a new learning experience. Corollary with these kinds of activities are these expressions of student attitudes and beliefs:

> Students feel internally obligated to be accountable to themselves and to others.

> Students see what needs to be done and do it without prompts from the teacher.

> Students become proactive in disseminating their learning process and products.

> Students display their interest intentions, and desire to disseminate.

> Students share and disseminate their experience with others and attempt to move their audiences toward change.

> Students focus on the content and direction of future learning experiences (Holm 2004:3).

At this final category of interactive learning, students assume almost total overt leadership for the dissemination of their experiences in the learning sequence they have just completed. There are two basic areas of focus during this final category of interactive learning. They are, first, to disseminate what has been learned to a number of audiences and second, to determine the next major learning experience. When these two areas of focus have been accomplished, the current learning experience has been completed. The student roles are as an influencer and as a disseminator. The teacher roles are as a critiquor and a consultant. The instructional role is disseminative. The activities at this category of the taxonomy illustrate these roles. Selected activities are as follows.

Corollary with these kinds of activities are these expressions of student attitudes and beliefs.

- Simulations in which students demonstrate what they have learned to selected audiences. Earlier students developed simulation and role-playing to share with each other. Now they can develop those simulations and role-playing activities to share with other audiences. They can also develop them at this category of the taxonomy. The purpose is to share what they have learned in a positive and interesting manner. Simulation and role-playing are excellent vehicles for doing these kinds of activities.
- Campaigning for or selling an issue, idea, perspective, or point of view. This is done in a persuasive modality. The purpose of these kinds of activities is to overtly influence that audiences to accept the students' ideas, issues, perspective, or points of view. In some senses this is the homiletic dimension of dissemination. Students can do this in many ways and through a variety of contexts.
- Debates on differing points of view. Debates are good ways to share information and ideas. They can demonstrate different points of view and explain that sometimes there is no single perspective or point of view that is correct or the only way. Two or more points can be debated. Developing and being involved in debates is a good dissemination activity.
- Reporting what they have learned and achieved to selected audiences. Reporting can be done in a variety of ways. It can be done verbally, in writing, or through difference kinds of media presentations. Reporting to different audiences requires students to focus their report on those who are receiving it. Reports need to be generated through group activities and are often presented by groups of students.
- Seminars organized for students to present and defend views. Seminars were developed and used during insight category activities. They were designed to help deal with issues and concerns at that level. Here they are more complete and are designed for dissemination to identified audiences and are presented to inform and persuade. Seminars are content oriented and their purpose is to share content and processes with different groups. Seminars are an excellent way of presenting views, responding to questions, and persuading people accept the perspectives presented. Seminar preparation needs to be done by the presenters in a small-group setting.

- Demonstration of a product designed and created by the students. Students have developed products or put together packages of materials for dissemination. Demonstrating these products and showing how they were developed and used are positive and interesting individual and group activities for dissemination. Again, these are developed and demonstrated in group contexts.
- Presentations to show advantages or excellence of what students have learned, what they can do, and how they did it. Students, when they have come to this juncture in the learning experience, are proud of what they have accomplished. Through these kinds of activities, students show what they have valued and what they have learned. The can also discuss how what they have done has made changes in them. Students enjoy this kind of positive presentation when disseminating. Here they have the opportunity to show, in positive contexts, what they have learned and what they have accomplished. It is important that students do this at this category of interactive learning.
- Cross-age and peer teaching and counseling. This is an authentic activity in which students are enabled to share and disseminate what they have learned as well as other skills to younger students or to peers who need to learn those skills. To share what they have learned and skills they have developed with other students, particular younger ones, is something most students truly enjoy.
- Developing and showing a multimedia presentation, dramatization, poetry reading, script writing, publishing, as well as arts and crafts. These are creative presentation activities that can challenge the students who are doing the dissemination as well as those who are viewing the presentations. Note that there are a number of written activities built into this generic activity statement. Poetry, drama, formal reports, and publishing have a real place in the dissemination of what the students have learned. In most instances, these reports and presentations should be done by groups of students.
- Activities that involve overtly influencing others to accept and use the information, ideas, attitudes, and skills students have learned. One of the student roles is that of an influencer. Students need the opportunity to show how they have changed and they may want to urge the same changes on their audiences. These kinds of activities are often issue oriented. Teaching–learning activities of this kind are designed to overtly utilize the influencing role with other students or other selected audiences, including adult audiences. These kinds of activities are important for student involvement as disseminators.
- Sale of developed products, productions, and services. This is a self-explanatory activity. Teachers and students will need to check on school or district policy concerning selling student products to make sure that it is legal, permissible, or appropriate.
- Advertising and recruiting activities. Students enjoy developing advertising slogans for the products, ideas, and concepts they have learned about and created. They also enjoy knowing how others react to them and how what they have developed is impacting others. Advertising and recruiting activities are designed for creative effort and for influencing others. PowerPoint presentations could fall into this category of activities.
- Writing to influence, including letters, essays, instructions, and narratives to identified audiences. These are some kinds of writing activities in which students can be involved. The written material expresses student ideas and opinions about what they have done. They can be written to a wide spectrum of people including political officeholders. Students enjoy doing this, especially when they receive replies. If your school has videoconferencing equipment, this teaching–learning activity can be used in videoconferences.
- Designing and producing student-developed learning activities, learning packages, minicourses, and lesson plans. Here students develop learning packages for their peers and younger students. This can be a strong teaching–learning activity for students to put together these learning packages and lesson plan. It is challenging,

and they need to prepare them interestingly and informatively. They are, in effect, doing lesson planning and lesson packaging, which they have already experienced for their peers and for other students.

- Projecting ideas and direction for additional learning experiences. This is the last activity of the implementation level of interactive teaching. It is designed to be just that. Students need to plan with the teacher as critiquor and consultant where they move to from this learning experience and what the next plans are for them in terms of new learning experiences. This is an essential and important activity and closes the implementation category activities for interactive learning.

These activities, as can be seen, relate to the implementation category of the learning experience. The use of these kinds of activities demonstrate that students have not only accepted the leadership responsibility for the learning experience, but have assumed leadership in terms of presenting and disseminating the information, the attitudes, the skills, and the products they have learned and developed. These teaching–learning activities are further designed to focus on new directions and new learning experiences. No learning experience is complete without these dimensions of implementation and dissemination. Likewise, no learning experience is complete unless there is consideration by the students and the teacher about the next learning experience. The teacher roles at this final level of interactive learning are those of critiquor and consultant. The teacher, in these roles, critiques student dissemination activities, helps them focus on effective dissemination activities, and works with students in planning for and projecting new learning experiences. The instructional role is disseminative and that role is demonstrated through all the teaching–learning activities. The student roles are influencer and disseminator. In these roles they demonstrate leadership and creativity through each of the teaching–learning activities. Each of these roles of teacher, student, and instruction shows that leadership and responsibility have come full circle and now rest with the students. The teacher, however, remains a key to finalizing the learning experience and helping the students understand the richness and meaning of the experience they have just successfully completed. Thinking, learning, and teaching coalesce at this final level of interactive learning. Both the art of teaching and the science of teaching are evident during implementation and dissemination.

SUMMARY

All of the identified strategies at every category of the taxonomy of interactive learning that have been listed in this sequence of teaching–learning activities represents only a few samples of the kinds of activities that creative teachers through careful planning can use as they move students through the sequence of interactive learning, culminating with the students assuming personal and group responsibility for the learning they have achieved and for dissemination of their success. Each of the activities can be done in small-group structures and, wherever possible, should be done within the group organization and structure. In the next chapter we will present a series of group structures for use in the classroom.

Every student should participate in all or in most of these activities. It is the teacher's task to see that student participation is at an optimum level and that all students are involved at all categories of the taxonomy and in all the teaching–learning activities. Some of the activities, as noted, could be used in more than one level of the taxonomy, although most are specific to the level in which they are discussed. Each of the activities has a brief descriptor. Teachers should use these descriptors only to gain a better understanding of what the activity is and of the ways the activity can be used. The teacher should then develop a plan for using the activity in the classroom. In many cases, students can also participate in the planning, particularly as the learning experience progresses through the taxonomy. The activities listed here are only representative of many other activities. They are interactively designed to foster dialogue, discussion, and group work within the classroom. This, we feel, represents the optimal learning condition for students. Use of any or all of these activities or ones similar to them in your classroom and you will find student learning enhanced and their interest and involvement in the learning sequence at a higher level.

One should note how the roles of the students and teacher change through the categories of the taxonomy. This is also true of how the instructional roles change and develop. As expectations and outcomes are developed and completed within the taxonomic categories and are achieved by students, we can see evidence of the changes in the learning experience. There is a dramatic change from invitation to implementation in each of the fifteen components of interactive learning we have defined. We have analyzed the lesson sequence from seventeen different perspectives and those perspectives are implicit within the teaching–learning activities. It follows, then, that all the activities as well as teaching strategies and group work needs to be carefully planned. Initially, most of the planning is done by the teacher. However, as the learning sequence develops, more of the planning can be done with and by the students. This should be a major consideration when you plan your lessons or learning experiences. You can use any of these activities or ones of your own, but make sure that a group activity sequence is built into your program and that they are consistent with the taxonomy of interactive learning.

It is important that the teacher invests time and trust in the students. It is through both cognitive and affective interactive learning that students achieve at optimal levels. Through a positive interactive environment, trust and confidence are built and interactive learning processes become natural. These natural processes of interactive learning along with the investment of time and trust are evidenced through the roles of both the teacher and the students. This concept of the investment of time and trust by the teacher, as well as confidence in the student's ability to achieve, help create the condition of caring and support that leads to ethical transformative learning.

In the next chapter of this work, these teaching–learning activities will be further explicated through a discussion of a number of interactive group structures and formats. In that chapter on groups and implementation of groups at all levels of the taxonomy, identified teaching strategies are discussed. Finally, we strongly encourage every teacher to use interactive teaching–learning activities keyed to the categories of the interactive learning taxonomy. If you do this, you will find student participation and involvement in the total learning experience greatly and positively enhanced.

Activities

The activities in the first six chapters were focused on understanding the theory behind interactive learning. In this chapter and the next, we focus on organizing your class in terms of activities and groups. Here we focus on using activities in the five categories of interactive learning. These activities are designed to be done in small groups. We believe this is the most appropriate structure for completing them. They can, however, be done individually, and the last activity is designed to be done by individuals in a small group.

1. On pages 88–90, 91–93, 93–96, 96–99, and 99–102, expectations for each category of the taxonomy are presented. Determine how they correlate with each category and how they change and grow as the learning experience changes from invitation through implementation. Summarize your findings and present them to your peers. *Note:* If you have five or more groups in your class, you can assign one category of activities to designated groups. Be sure that all five categories are assigned. Each group shares. In a whole-group discussion, determine how attitudes change through the five categories of the taxonomy.

2. "Value and meaning need to be integral to activities" at investigation. Discuss this in your small group. Are value and meaning as important at other categories of the taxonomy? What is the role of the teacher in ensuring that students value activities and understand their meaning in terms of the learning experience.

3. Select two activities that you feel would foster critical thinking and creativity. How would you use them in a grade level and content area of your choice? Discuss this within your group and be able to respond to questions from peers about why you chose these particular groups.

4. Students need to learn how to work together in groups. What do they need to know and how would you see that they learn this? How would you monitor their group work? How would you evaluate their work with them? Would you include self-evaluation? If so, how?

5. Pick a different activity at each category of the taxonomy. How is leadership represented in each activity and through each category? Look at leadership both from the student role and the teacher role. What expectations would you have for teacher and students during the activity at each category of the taxonomy? Discuss this in your groups.

6. Pick a content area at a grade level of your choice. Identify at least three kinds of activities you could use at every level of the taxonomy. Provide a rationale for why you chose these activities. Note your purpose for the activities. Tell how they would be organized and what expectations you have for them. Discuss how they would be evaluated. Share your findings with peers.

7. Cooperative learning groups are used at each level of the interactive learning taxonomy. What kinds of activities would you have cooperative groups do at each category of the taxonomy? Discuss this in your group. What would students do through cooperative groups at specific categories of the taxonomy?

Interactive Group Structures

Interaction and group work are themes present through all the strategies and activities discussed in this work. Interactive learning and group work represents a modality for teaching and learning critical to the process of interactive learning and augmented student achievement. Interactive group work represents the process of valuing what is being taught and what is being learned. Positive interaction is at the core of the art of teaching. Interactive learning culminates in good human relating. The science of learning is also present during interactive learning. Group work helps the student and the teacher develop grounded meaning and extend that meaning to a variety of other activities, to their peers, to other people. Interaction and group work are, we believe, essential elements for instruction and learning. Teaching is also about building relationships, earning respect, and taking responsibility. Group work and interactive instruction help students through motivation to establish readiness, build relationships, develop rapport, earn respect, and take responsibility. We see this process as both valuing the students and valuing the learning experience. In addition, when the learning modalities of instruction are established, students can capture a vision, a design, a purpose, and achieve identified goals and objectives within an ethical context of growth and change. Thus, during group work the art and science of teaching come together.

In this chapter we will identify interactive and group structures and formats that can work well in the classroom. These group structures and formats are representative samples of interactive groups. Many other group formats and structures can also be used. We will identify and define group structures that can be used at each category of the taxonomy of interactive learning. Following that, we discuss how group structures can be used and correlated with identified teaching–learning strategies at each category of interactive learning. Group work, for us, represents a level of excellence and performance; when well done, it represents a level of excellence and performance that is the strength and the very core of the teaching–learning process. It is through group structures and processes where relationships are developed and worked out. It is through group work that students develop rapport and respect. It is through group work that they develop responsibility for their learning. Group processes are integral to purpose, decision making, and leadership. The stimulus of interactive group work is challenging and provides an efficacy and ambiance within the classroom that can be exceptional. Positive group work itself is a learning process. The teacher and the students must take the time to provide instruction in how to do group work and then to learn it and demonstrate positive interactive group work. Effective group work must be learned and students must learn how to do it. We feel that learning group processes is essential to

> *It is through group structures and processes where relationships are developed and worked out.*

Table 8.1 Thinking, Learning, Teaching

Teacher	Interactive Category	Student
If I can define, it I can teach it	Invitation	If I can organize it, I can try it out
If I can teach it, I can test it	Involvement	If I can try it out, I can test it
If I can test it, I can investigate it	Investigation	If I can test it, I can use it
If I can investigate it, I can determine meaning	Insight	If I can use it, I can determine its meaning
If I can determine its meaning, it can be demonstrated	Implemenantation	If I can determine its meaning, I can teach it

Table 8.2 Teacher and Student Roles

Teacher Roles	Taxonomy Category	Student Roles
Define: Presenter	Invitation	Organize: Attender
Test: Catalyst	Involvement	Try it out: Explorer
Investigate: Moderator	Investigation	Test it: Experimenter
Determine meaning: Sustainer	Insight	Evaluate meaning: Extender
Demonstrate: Critiquor	Implementation	Teach: Influencer

optimum student achievement. Within any course of study, or series of lessons, enough time must be taken to ensure that students know the process of group work, the roles involved in that process, and how to report and share what they have learned and what they have done. High standards for group function and activities must be expected by the teacher and learned and demonstrated by the students. In addition, students need to be involved in self-assessment and evaluation so they can consistently improve their performance in groups.

Group work is both exciting and challenging, and in using the interactive learning taxonomy, group work can be seen as sequential and is shown to be somewhat different at each category of the taxonomy. It should also be noted that some group structures could be used at more than one level of the taxonomy. To illustrate this sequence of learning and of the interactive process, Tables 8.1 through 8.3 can be used to more effectively develop a perspective of the process. Each of the statements is keyed to a level of the interactive learning taxonomy. Each of them encapsulates the group process. Students learn individually in a constructivist sense, but their learning is enhanced in a strong interactive group setting. In Table 8.1, the sequence shown demonstrates the process of thinking, learning, and teaching. It involves valuing and meaning. In Table 8.2, the teacher and student roles are keyed to the categories of the taxonomy. Each teaching role and each student role has a word or brief phrase that provides another way of interpreting the roles. Finally, in Table 8.3, the leadership roles are presented.

Table 8.3 Leadership Roles

Teacher Roles	Taxonomy Category	Student Roles
Preparer	Invitation	Participant
Coordinator	Involvement	Cooperator
Resolver	Investigation	Investigator
Adviser	Insight	Creator
Consultant	Implementation	Disseminator

Another sequence, as well as a perspective on teacher roles and student roles, is given in Table 8.2. These sequences are linked to the descriptors of the categories in Table 8.1. In each of these roles, both for the student and for the teacher, a word or words are used as a brief descriptor to provide yet another context for learning, which again is enhanced through interactive group learning.

With these roles in mind, we next must consider the leadership roles. As can be seen, they change and are demonstrated in unique and different ways as students progress through the learning sequence and through the categories of the interactive learning taxonomy. Again, the group experiences enhance learning and provide the basis for the changing leadership roles.

We posit that the teaching–learning process can be defined by three words: *thinking, learning,* and *teaching.* We use these three terms as part of the seventeen-strand analysis of the teaching–learning act. We want to reiterate them here and put them into the context of group interaction. We have chosen, for these three terms, succinct definitions to capture and encapsulate what teachers and students are about as they progress through the taxonomy of interactive learning. We also posit that progress through the taxonomy at optimum learning levels is contingent on the effectiveness of group function. As noted, we have discussed these definitions of thinking, learning, and teaching earlier, but they need once again to be brought to our attention with a stronger focus on group formats and functions.

These three definitions illustrate, capture, and encapsulate the essence of thinking, learning, and teaching. The help illustrate the sequence of interactive learning by providing an understanding of the philosophical and psychological base for this taxonomy. Very succinctly, they are as follows:

Thinking is the process of associating information with experience.

Learning is the process of relating thinking to actions, attitudes, skills, concepts and ideas.

Teaching is the process of valuing actions, attitudes, skills, concepts, and ideas (Steinaker 2002).

Within this context of thinking, learning, and teaching, the roles of the teacher and the students are subsumed. Each of these definitions is integral to the warp and woof in the categories of the taxonomy of interactive learning. Also inferred in these encapsulated definitions are the processes through which teachers and students move as the learning experience develops and as the categories of the taxonomy emerge from the dynamics of thinking, learning, and teaching. It is important to keep these definitions and processes in mind as the interactive and group components of the interactive learning taxonomy are discussed. Interactive and group processes are essential if the full potential of the taxonomy is realized by both teacher and students. It is through interaction and group settings that students learn and demonstrate leadership skills. It is through interaction and group structures and formats that students learn to trust one another so they can build relationships, establish rapport, earn respect, and take responsibility. Group processes and interactive learning give students hope and a vision of achievement, accomplishment, sharing, and service.

The terms used in describing the teacher roles and the student roles are important cues toward the kind of interaction and group work used at each level of the taxonomy of interactive learning. Those terms are reflected in each teaching–learning strategy and in each learning activity used in the categories of the taxonomy of interactive learning. For the teacher, the roles change and develop from presenter and preparer, to critiquor and consultant, at the implementation category. The teacher's role changes from dominant in terms of planning and presenting at the invitation level to consultative, supportive, assistive, and critiquing roles during the implementation category. The roles of the students change from an attender and participant trying to understand the material presented during the invitation category, to that of an influencer and disseminator who has surety in what was learned and teaches or presents what has been accomplished and achieved through the total learning experience. Students assume responsibility for disseminating those accomplishments.

The instructional role at the invitation category of interactive learning is informational. At the implementation category of interactive learning, the role is disseminative. This change is the result of gathering and using resources, applying and analyzing those resources; it also results from the development of products as well as the achievement of designed goals and objectives. In addition, the change occurs because of consistent interactive group work from invitation to involvement and then from readiness, relationships, rapport, respect, and finally to responsibility in terms of motivation. Leadership, in the process of interactive learning and valuing, is demonstrated by the teacher's role changes from an extrinsic motivator and preparer at the invitation category to that of a sustainer-adviser and critquor-consultant during the last two categories of interactive learning. The teacher roles in terms of leadership become less overt and more covert as the process of the learning experience develops through the categories of interactive learning. The student role in leadership changes as well. It moves from participator to cooperator, then to investigator, creator, and disseminator. Student leadership changes from covert and cooperative to overt and evident. Student leadership functions overtly, beginning with involvement and grows more overt as subsequent categories of the taxonomy become operant in the learning experience. During the implementation category, students assume almost total responsibility for leadership. It is through the leadership roles that the students gain their voice and begin to understand the nature of change and the transformative power of learning. If they have done this within an ethical context, which we feel is necessary, their voices will be heard and positive changes can be made.

The role of the teacher is, however, always essential to the learning experience and to the process through which it develops. The teacher is almost always the only adult in the classroom. The teacher is always a leader even though leadership at the insight and involvement categories of the taxonomy is more covert and less obvious as the students assume a more overt and visible leadership role. The overt leadership passes, through a sequential taxonomic process, to the students. At the implementation category of interactive learning, the dominant role in leadership, and indeed in self-motivation, belongs almost totally to the students. At the implementation category, the students, through a process of dissemination, become the creative influencers and assume fully their role of leadership while the teacher becomes the critiquor and consultant. The teacher is, however, the one who helps the students determine new learning sequences and helps them make decisions that will lead to new learning experiences. There is also a role for teacher and students in terms of assessment and evaluation at all categories of interactive learning. The roles of the teacher and the students in that process of assessment and evaluation already have been presented and will be further discussed in succeeding chapters.

There are many different kinds of group structures that can be used in the classroom. There are, of course, a variety of functional group formats and structures that could be used at different categories of the taxonomy of interactive learning. We have chosen to present only some of the group structures and formats. Those presented and discussed in this chapter are cooperative groups, focus groups, pairs, triads, dialectic groups, single-task groups, panel-discussion groups, planning groups, critiquor groups, and whole-class groups. Student groups can be long term and continuing. They can also be *ad hoc* groups. Groups can be directly related to a particular issue, area of concern, problem, or specific content area. They can be broad ranging and constant throughout a course of study. They can also be *ad hoc* groups or they can be groups with a single task. Working groups can vary in size from pairs through whole-class groups. Each kind of group has its own particular task, structure, organization, and purpose.

Students need to learn how to function within a group and learn the skills attendant to successful group work. This instruction needs to be done very early in the academic year. Learning how to work in groups and learning skills necessary for positive group function is ongoing and needs to be revisited by students and teachers as necessary. This teaching and learning of group functions and skills is ongoing and needs to be revisited by students and teacher as necessary. It is important that all students become familiar with, and are able to function positively within, each kind of group structure and organization. Be sure to take enough time to ensure this happens. Each kind of group can be used with any teaching strategy or model of teaching in the taxonomy of interactive learning. In the following five chapters, each of these group structures will be correlated with teaching strategies and teaching models at identified categories of interactive learning. All can be used in every category of interactive learning, while others are optimally used at specific categories. In the following material are brief presentations and definitions of each group structure. Also included is how those group structures can be used by students and by the teacher.

Cooperative Group

Group of students meets to address tasks and learning needs defined by the teacher or students within a unit or learning experience.

COOPERATIVE GROUPS

This structure for grouping is one of the most commonly used group formats used in the classroom. A cooperative group structure has sometimes been termed a *collaborative group* based on the necessity of collaboration and cooperation to complete tasks. We use the terms interchangeably. Cooperative groups can be used at all levels of the taxonomy and with many teaching strategies and models of teaching. A cooperative group simply means that a group of students, often ongoing throughout a unit or learning experience, meets to address various task and learning needs defined by the teacher or by the students. Within the group there can be assigned roles that may remain constant or that may change. With each role students have an assignment that will, with the cooperative and collaborative efforts of all members, lead to the completion of the assigned task. Group size for cooperative groups usually ranges from four to six. Making the group larger can cause the group to become less efficient. Roles within cooperative or collaborative groups are generally chair, recorder, reporter, researcher, and a graphic member. Other roles may be needed as the assignment or task is changes. These roles can remain relatively constant or can be rotated and change. The graphic member is the one who identifies pictures, realia, artifacts, leads in creating illustrations; he or she also organizes graphic material for the report. The graphic member is the one who puts the report together in an attractive style. Each of the other roles is defined by its name. Member roles can change daily or regularly as the schedule requires or as needs arise. The final product or report, whether oral, printed, or using multimedia, is assessed by the whole group, who evaluate the report and discuss how it fits the needs of the group within the learning experience. If the final product is to be assessed for a grade, the whole group receives the evaluation or grade for its product.

It is important that each member does the assigned role well because the group is assessed on the totality of the product. Students need to thoroughly understand their roles so that they can function well both individually within the group and collectively as a total group. Dialogue, discussion, and focused interaction are essential within cooperative groups. They also need to regularly self-evaluate their function as a group and their progress toward completing the group assignment. This grouping organization can be used at all levels of interactive learning. Cooperative learning groups can also be used at any grade level from kindergarten through graduate school.

FOCUS GROUPS

A focus group is one that has a specific focus for study and for reviewing information. Focus groups work on one assigned task or defined context within a well-understood framework. The purpose of this group is to gather information and resources and, after reviewing the information and resources, to present what they have learned or found out to the whole group.

Membership can range from pairs and triads up to seven or eight students. Roles are not as clearly designated in focus groups as they are in cooperative groups, but there needs to be a chair, a recorder, and an organizer. This kind of group needs to function as a team. Group members, however, can work individually and then bring their information to the group for consideration and fitting it into the total focus group organizational format. The focus group has the responsibility for bringing needed information and resources from the group to the whole class. The emphasis in reporting is on critiquing what it has found and on how the material and the resources fit into the learning experience. The information needs to come to the whole group in a form that demonstrates the depth of the members' study, critiquing the information collected in terms of how it impacts the study and helps the whole group progress to new levels of learning. The report should be presented, discussed, and acted upon by the class. Once the report is given, however, the focus group can disband or be assigned to another area of focus. This kind of focus group can be used at any level of interactive learning from involvement through the insight category. The focus group can be very useful in providing information, resources, detail, and perspectives on a particular problem or issue needed by the whole group.

PAIRS

This two-member group is defined by its name. Two students work together for a specific reason. There are a number of reasons why students need to be paired for learning purposes. This is not a highly structured group. A pairs group can be set up to help each member with information, skills, and content. Pairs can be designated so one student can help another who needs assistance. Pairs can also be organized to bring information to the whole group or to another group. Pairs can be set up as buddy reading or to help an English language learner with vocabulary and comprehension. Pairs can further be a subgroup of a larger group structure and report back to that group when they have completed their assignment. Pairs need to be compatible and be comfortable in working with each other. Members of pairs need to share with each other, to listen to each other, to dialogue and discuss what they are doing, and to interact positively. They can be friends or share a mutual interest. Several pairs can be working on material at the same time. Each set of pairs can be doing different things from helping each other to finding information and data to be reported to the class. Most of the time there will be a report to the class for accountability and achievement. This is the case when the task of the pairs is to focus on content and material directly related to the learning experience. Although this is expected much of the time, this is not always the case. When pairs are organized so one student is helping another in settings such as buddy reading and to improve the skills of one member of the pair, there is no report to the whole group. Students may prepare a summary of what they have done and provide that for the teacher either orally or in writing. Sometimes they may even report what they have done to their peers. When this happens, their work becomes known to the class. This group structure can be used at all categories of interactive learning. Pairs can be used with any age group and in many different circumstances and learning settings.

> *Members of pairs need to share with each other, to listen to each other, to dialogue and discuss what they are doing, and to interact positively.*

TRIADS

This, by its very name, is a three-member group. Triads are more formally structured than pairs. The purpose for the group is generally defined clearly by the teacher and/or by the students. The three students assigned to the group are expected to work together to achieve the defined purpose. Triad groupings are usually not long term and usually have identified and specific objective and goals to meet. Those goals and objectives almost always relate directly to the learning experience and are designed to provide data and information to the larger group of which they may be a part or to the total group. Sometimes, however, triads can be ongoing if their area of interest and focus continues through additional categories of interactive learning. Reporting their findings and what they have achieved and accomplished is expected. They report to other groups or to the class as well as to the teacher. Student roles in the triad can be determined by the members of the triad. Individual assignments can also be made by the teacher or by other students. Students can work individually or with each other, but need to come together to finalize their report and make that report to the class, to the teacher, or to another group. They are, however, jointly accountable and responsible for the triad group outcomes and the information or material they provide for their peers and for the teacher. Triads can be useful at all levels of interactive learning and can be used with most teaching strategies and models of teaching. Triads can be used with any age group or learning level.

Triad Groupings

More formally structured
Clearly defined purpose
Not long term
Identified goals
Specific objectives

DIALECTIC GROUPS

This group structure is one where the group is responsible for studying and analyzing two or more views on an issue, a concept, or a problem. Much of the time the issue, concept, or problem may have multiple perspectives and options to consider, more than one of which would be viable for the learning experience or course of study. The task of the dialectic group is to study the varying viewpoints, analyze the information, and synthesize what it has learned into a group consensus. The dialectic group then reports its findings and consensus to the larger group or to the class. It generally presents the various perspectives and then its synthesis to the class. Included in that synthesis is the group consensus. In presenting their consensus, group members share their process and their thinking and provide a rationale for why they agreed upon the consensus. They may even present two or more resolutions that would be viable for the total group and have the final consensus worked out together with the larger group. This kind of organization for a group requires critical thinking skills, the ability to analyze issues, as well as to resolve and synthesize the differing perspectives into a consensus point of view. Dialectic groups serve a valuable purpose and are particularly helpful when students have identified with the learning process at the investigation level of interactive learning. While dialectic groupings can be used at all levels of the interactive learning taxonomy, they are very functional

The task of the dialectic group is to study the varying viewpoints, analyze the information, and synthesize what they have learned into a group consensus.

at the investigation, insight, and implementation levels of the taxonomy. Dialectical groups work well at all grade and age levels, but are optimally used from intermediate grades through graduate levels. These kinds of groups are challenging to students and valuable for the learning process.

JIGSAW GROUPS

This group organization can be used effectively at all levels of interactive learning. It is also a group function that most students really enjoy. Several jigsaw groups are organized within the classroom, each of which focusing on one specific part or aspect of the general topic before the total group. One jigsaw is assigned to a specific or particular part or sequence of a major task. Each jigsaw group then focuses on its assigned portion of the total task. Every group has a different dimension of the task. These jigsaw groups work on their specific area of focus, complete their study, prepare a report on what they have learned, and then present the report to the total group. Reports are done sequentially in terms of how the task or problem has been divided into parts or sequences. When all the jigsaw groups have reported, the whole of the task, problem, or issue becomes known to all. A thorough whole-group discussion and dialogue follows the reports to ensure that all the students see the whole of the issues, problems, context, or task. Careful planning must be done by the teacher and by the students before the group activities start. Planning is also involved before the reports are completed. Students need to demonstrate understanding of the various parts of the task and how they fit together. They need to show this in their reports. In addition, students need to develop an understanding of the whole task, issue, or problem. They do this by sharing their part of the jigsaw and then putting it together to see the whole picture. Students must also know how the task, the process, or the information fits into the learning experience. They also need to thoroughly understand the sequence and process of how the task is completed and how it will come together when each jigsaw group has finished its task and the jigsaw is complete. Groups can interact with each other during this part of the process. Jigsaw groups can have from three to six members. Jigsaw groups can be used effectively from late primary through college and university levels. Jigsaw groups are effective learning structures.

> One jigsaw is assigned to a specific or particular part or sequence of a major task. Each jigsaw group then focuses on its assigned portion of the total task. Every group has a different dimension of the task.

ROVING GROUPS

The roving group structure is a variation of jigsaw groups. Within the roving group format, several groups similar in organization to jigsaw groups are organized in the classroom. Each group has specific assigned tasks within designated objectives or sequenced activities. Each group works on the assigned tasks for a designated time frame. What the groups discover is discussed, noted, and written down. At a given signal, one or sometimes two members of each group move to another group or the next sequential group. In the new group, the rover(s) reports what has been developed or learned by the original group. The rover and the new group work together with the new information and augment what they have already discovered. At another signal, a rover or rovers are selected to move on to another group with updated information. They do not need to be the same rovers each time there is a signal to rotate to another group. Each time the signal is given, however, one or two rovers needs to move to the next group. This process is continued until all groups have gained the information needed for finalizing their presentation or their report. All groups have, when the process is completed, essentially the same information, which has been given to them by the rovers. Each group participates in the reporting experience. It is interesting to see how each group interprets the information and how similar or different their reports are. It is important that each rover present the new information gained in his or her previous group to the group into which the rover(s) move. Roving groups are of particular value in that groups are focused on organization of content and its reorganization after the rover comes with new information to the new group. Group members must synthesize the new information, meld it into what they already know, and prepare it for the next group in a clear and understandable way. The task of the rover is to present that information succinctly and with clarity to the new group. Higher cognitive and thinking skills are necessary for the positive function of this kind of group. The success of this group structure depends on the substance and meaning of the information taken to each new group with a focus on how it relates to the learning sequence. At the end of the small-group

Value of Roving Groups

Focus on organization and reorganization based on the presentation of
   new information
Synthesize new information and prepare it for the next group in a clear way
Learn to present information succinctly and with clarity

sessions, the whole class should have the same information. A sharing of findings, a report of information, and a discussion should follow this group-sharing time. It is important, too, for the class to see how each group interpreted the information and how well the rovers related the information to different groups. Roving groups can be used at all levels of interactive learning, but can optimally be used at the involvement and investigation categories of the taxonomies. Roving groups have been used successfully with students from late primary grades through graduate students. Students learned from the experience and found that in the sharing and discussion process they gained a much broader perspective because each of the groups usually have a slightly different interpretation of and reaction to the information. This makes for excellent discussions. Roving groups can be used at any grade or age level, but as mentioned earlier are more optimally used from late primary through middle and high school and into college and graduate school.

NUMBERED GROUPS ONE

This group structure is related both to roving groups and jigsaw groups. It can also be done in the context of numbered heads. In the jigsaw or roving group context, the primary group works together on one piece or part of the jigsaw problem or material to be studied. The group works interactively and creates a statement about their part of the jigsaw. The primary group counts off by numbers. There may be four or five groups working on various components within the total focus of the group. Primary groups should count off as ones, twos, threes, fours, and fives, depending on the total number of groups in the class. At a given signal, there is regrouping. All the ones meet together, as do the twos, the threes, the fours, and the fives. In each of the numbered groups, the members work together to get the whole picture, the whole study, or all the information. Each of the numbered groups, after they have discussed the big picture or the major points, develop a statement or a list of salient points it have learned through its discussion and dialogue. When each of the numbered groups has finished, its list of salient points or its statement is shared with the whole group. Numbered groups can be asked questions about what they have discovered and their major points. Each group presents

Numbered Groups

Primary group works on one part of the problem or material to be studied.
Primary group counts off members by numbers.
Regrouping occurs at the given signal.
Numbered group members work together to get the whole picture.
Numbered group develops statement/list of salient points.
Information is shared with entire group.

its summary, statement, including salient points. These can be compared and contrasted so that the whole group gets more than one perspective on the totality of what it has been studying. It is important that the discussion and the compare–contrast aspects be integral to the work. After each numbered group has shared and has responded to questions and participated in discussion and dialogue, the groups can come together and by consensus identify the most important points the class needs to know. Sometimes this elicits a lively interactive discussion. This is positive. This group strategy can be used at any grade level and in a variety of settings. One of the authors has used this group format frequently with graduate students and they responded well to it. The numbered group structure can be used by elementary students beginning at late primary. It can also be used effectively at middle school and high school. It is a group strategy that works well and can be easily developed. It will work at any category of the interactive learning taxonomy.

NUMBERED GROUPS TWO

This is a variant of the numbered group one format. It is sometimes called numbered heads. We call it numbered responsibility groups. In this setting the groups remain constant. They are numbered one through four or five depending on the number within the group. Each group is responsible for a defined area of study or skill to be learned. Each group could be focused on the same area of study or skill, or each group could have a different content area. Each group interacts together with its resources and is responsible for learning as much as it can about the topic. After the time limit for the study time has elapsed, the teacher or the leader in the classroom can ask a member of a group to respond to a question or a statement based on what has been studied. No one in the group knows who will be asked a question or be asked for a reaction to a statement. In this way each group member is responsible for knowing the information and responding effectively to it. When the numbered group member has responded, the teacher/leader then asks another group numbered member a question. This is how the process works until as many group members as possible can respond. Interactive dialogue is the key to ensuring that all members of the numbered groups thoroughly understand the material. Dialogue and equal responsibility are necessary to the success of the group. Everyone in the group is responsible for everyone else in the group because no one knows who will be asked the question. In some instances the questions or statements to which the students respond may be given to them in advance. This sometimes spurs the students on toward interactive dialogue and discussion. This is a strong interactive group structure and one that can be used at any level or age. This group structure can be a real impetus to learning.

FLEXIBLE GROUPS

The use of flexible groups involves students in a continuing focus on learning content specific to the learning experience. Flexible groups work on identified skills, content, or sequences related to a particular area of study as needed by the students to achieve defined expectations and skill levels needed within the learning experience. Flexible group membership changes as the skills or content is learned by one group of students. Another group of students or those from the initial group who need reteaching then focus on the same or similar skills, content, or sequences. This rotation of students in flexible groups can continue until all students have learned the skills and the content needed for that content or skill within of the learning experience. When all students have learned or mastered the designated content of skills, the focus of content or skills, and the processes involved, the groups change. The purpose of flexible groups is to provide for reteaching, a more

Flexible group membership changes as the skills or content is learned by one group of students.

in-depth approach to content or skills, and for special learning needs. A flexible group can also be used to introduce new content or a new concept. The membership in flexible groups is based on student learning needs. Because of the specific focus of the group, membership changes so that all participating students in the group at a given time have the same opportunity to learn designated material. If a student knows the content or the skill, that student does not need to participate in the flexible group.

When there is a need for a small-group focus on content, concepts, or skills, flexible groups can meet those needs. Content and learning needs are a major focus of flexible groups. They are designed to ensure that all students have learned specific content or have been introduced to a new concept. Flexible groups can also be used to ensure that all students have the content and skill base needed to move on through the learning sequence. Flexible groups can be led by the teacher or by students who know the material well. Flexible groups are designed to help those students who need an extra focus on the content of the learning experience, who need to evidence skills necessary to the unit of study, or who need to have a skill or content material retaught.

New concepts or new areas of content focus can be done within the context of flexible grouping. Group size can range from three through ten to twelve, although groups of three to six are preferable. Reteaching, content insight, and skill building are areas where flexible groups can be very effective. Flexible grouping structures can be useful at all categories of interactive learning. It is generally most used and needed during the invitation and involvement categories of the taxonomy. Students of all grade levels and ages can participate in this kind of flexible group structure.

PROBLEM-SOLVING GROUPS

Again, the title of this group format defines it focus and purpose. Students are assigned to the group for the purpose of resolving a particular problem or an issue of concern encountered in the learning process. Groups should range in size of between four and six so that they can function well together. The group can assign particular tasks to each member by consensus or by an agreed-upon process. There are no formal rules, although a chair, a recorder, and a reporter could be designated. The group members' assignments are to arrive at a consensus or resolution to the problem or issue and report their findings to the class. The group is responsible for presenting the consensus or the resolution of the issue or problem assigned. It is also responsible for providing evidence justifying the reasons for how and why its particular perspective, resolution, or consensus was selected. Members of problem-solving groups need to be able to cite sources, to provide an evidentiary base for their resolution or consensus, and to provide a rationale for, and defend, their resolution. This evidentiary dimension of their report is especially important because group members are dealing with data and information, not with opinion or personal points of view. They are presenting a resolution or a perspective based on a careful review of sources and information. Their judgment must be based on sound resources, built through critical thinking skills, and applied through an effective decision-making process to

come to consensus. Group members need to ensure that the class understands the processes they followed and can accept and use the information, the resolution, and the perspectives they have developed. Their report and their findings are, of course, open for discussion and questions from the class and by the teacher. The discussion could be lively, particularly if class members have different views. Consensus then needs to be worked out by the total group. This group structure, although it can be used at invitation and involvement, tends to be more viable and more effectively used at the investigation, insight, and implementation levels of the taxonomy of interactive learning. We recommend that this grouping format be used from late elementary school through graduate school.

EXPLORATORY GROUPS

This group structure is designed so that the members can explore a body of information and report the important elements of that body of information as they pertain to the learning experience in which the class is involved. Group members are charged with the responsibility for determining if the body of information they are exploring is pertinent for their study or can be used by the group as a whole. Exploratory groups are generally small in size, ranging from three to five or six. They frequently may have a great deal of information to review, to analyze, to synthesize, and to report what they have found to the class. Thus, this kind of group may need some time to review, to study, to reflect, and to relate the material to the learning experience, then report back to the class. It is also important that they report what they have learned with clarity and for the purpose of helping the class more fully understand the essential information needed to continue efficiently through the course of study or through the learning experience. The student members present the information to the class based on the completion of their review, their study, and their best judgment. Their major purpose is that of expanding the database so that students can use what has been reported for further study in the learning experience. This group organization is used mostly at the invitation and involvement levels of interactive learning, but can be used at other categories of interaction as well if more information is needed about a particular subject. There may be some need for this kind of group at the investigation level of interactive learning, but only occasionally at the insight and implementation categories of interactive learning. The exploratory group structure can be used from late primary through graduate school.

SINGLE-TASK GROUPS

Single-task group structures may also sometimes be designated as *ad hoc* groups because they serve for a specific purpose and for a specific assignment. In this *ad hoc* context, the group meets to complete a single task assigned by the teacher or assigned by the students. One variable, one problem, or one issue is to be studied and its findings developed, completed, and reported to the class. Single-task groups can be flexible in size, but a small group of four to six functions well. Students need to be very aware of the parameters of their assignment and know that when it is completed their group will disband. Single-task groups, as their name indicates. have only a single purpose. Members of the group also need to be aware of the process they follow and ensure that what they discover and learn could help the class gain important and necessary information, thus assisting in processing through the learning sequence more efficiently. A single-task group may also have a time frame for completing its task so that the

> *One variable, one problem, or one issue is to be studied and its findings developed, completed, and reported to the class.*

class can have the information expeditiously. This grouping structure can be useful at all levels of the taxonomy of interactive learning. For example, at implementation, students may want to know the process involved and the information needed to disseminate what they have learned. A single-task group can serve that purpose well. The single-task group likewise is important at the invitation and involvement levels of the taxonomy when students need specific information about a topic they need to learn about and use in their lesson sequence. Single-task groups can be used at all grade levels.

PANEL-DISCUSSION GROUPS

Panel discussions are sometimes very important to the learning situation. The panel members can, through this kind of structure, focus on a problem or an issue and present information about it from one or more perspectives. Panel discussions are presented to the whole class and the views are discussed through a question and answer session following the panel presentations. In preparation for the panel discussion, a panel group is organized. A panel can consist of two or more students. It can be an extension of pairs or triads and can be as large as four to six members. The panel members study an issue, an area of concern, or a problem facing the class in terms of the learning experience. They prepare thoroughly, take notes, develop a plan for the panel discussion, then present their ideas, opinions, and findings to the whole-class group. Preparation and planning are most important for panel members. They must be thoroughly prepared to present information and respond to questions or comments from their audience. The information they have learned is first presented to the class and then discussed by the class. Class members can ask questions, respond to remarks, or exchange ideas with the panel and each other. Discussion and interaction are major components here and the student panelists are the leaders of the discussion. Students not on the panel need to take notes and have time to develop questions for the panel. Students not on the panel also must understand that they need to interact with the panel. The panel members need to carefully format their presentation and then share their information in an open forum. They need to be prepared to respond to questions and, as expected, lead the discussion. Panel groups usually have three to five or six members. Panel discussions are most pertinent at the investigation and the insight levels of interactive learning. They can be used at other levels of the taxonomy, but do not work as well because students may not necessarily have enough information to thoroughly discuss the issues brought to them. Furthermore, at earlier levels of the taxonomy, they may not yet have totally identified with the learning experience. Panel discussions are seldom used at the invitation or involvement categories of interactive learning. At the responsibility category, panel discussions, however, can be used for dissemination or reporting to other audiences about the completed course of study or the learning experience. They are very effective in this dissemination format and should be used for dissemination purposes. Panel discussions can be used at all grade levels, but are most useful from late primary through graduate school.

> *Panel discussions are presented to the whole class and the views are discussed through a question and answer session following the panel presentations.*

PLANNING GROUPS

Planning groups are almost always essential to any learning experience. Planning groups are organized for the purpose of planning direction, clarifying processes, and suggesting the next steps within the learning experience. Planning groups can range in purpose from "what we need to know" at the invitation category to "how can we best share this information with others" at the implementation category of interactive learning.

Planning Groups Purpose

Planning direction
Clarifying processes
Suggesting following
  steps in learning
  experience

Planning groups are integral and essential at all levels of the taxonomy. Planning groups usually have from four to six members, although these numbers could vary as needed. They need to have a focus and a commitment to the planning process. Their focus should be identified and defined by the teacher and the students. The role of the planning group is to respond to the charge they have been given and do it in the time frame allocated. Group planning, both in small groups or in class groups, is an element of almost every teaching–learning strategy and is an activity used at every category of the taxonomy. Planning groups must always report to the class and to the teacher. Members may present the information as well as their suggestions for the next steps or direction in a variety of ways. The information and the direction should be learned, cogent, and consistent with the learning experience. When the planning groups present their ideas and suggestions, as well as future learning activities for their possible next steps, those ideas are usually discussed with the whole class to determine how to use and follow what the planning group has shared. Although their findings are generally well accepted, there is sometimes a need to rework their plans and present revised plans to the whole class. Plans and direction can be implemented or changed by the whole group as needed. Planning groups are effective at all grade levels and with students at any academic level. For primary grades, the simple question of what do we do next is a way to provide purpose and focus for the group. As the students grow older, more sophisticated roles for planning groups can be used.

CRITIQUOR GROUPS

Critiquor groups have a specific and special purpose. They are designed to critique the learning process and identify progress toward defined goals and objectives. Critiquor groups are the process or formative critiquors of the efficiency and effectiveness of the learning experience. Critiquor groups are used mostly at the investigation, insight, and implementation categories of the taxonomy. They may be used at the involvement level,

Critiquor groups are designed to critique the learning process and identify progress toward defined goals and objectives.

but less frequently. They are the monitors of both the processes and the products of the learning experience. They are, in effect, the quality control managers for the whole class as the sequence of learning develops toward implementation. Critiquor groups may work with a rubric or a checklist. They may develop these themselves or the class with the teacher can develop them for the critiquor group. They may work with a rubric or checklist that is very simple for primary grades. For older students the rubric or checklist could be more specific and broader in range. Critiquor groups in middle school and beyond could work with a semantic differential scale to assess and study the learning process. This group critiques what the class has done and what they are doing. They also focus on how it is being done and what progress has been made toward the achievement of goals and objectives.

When preparing its materials, members of the group meet to plan its work and assignments; then, with the rubric or checklist, they observe the work and function of the class. They do not participate in other group work or with discussions. They simply observe and take notes. After they have completed the observations, they meet together and discuss what they have observed. They then begin the process of preparing their 1reports.

The report of the critiquor group can be presented in one of two ways. First, the report could be given to other functioning groups within the classroom with little or no commentary. Second, the report could be presented to the whole group and used as a stimulus for discussion toward improving process, progress, and product. In essence, critiquor groups initiate and provide a platform for class self-evaluation of the learning experience. Members of the group, with this kind of responsibility, need to have strong critical thinking skills and the ability to summarize information in a clear and concise manner. They also need to be able to respond to their peers and to explain why they came to the conclusions they developed. Again, it should be emphasized that this kind of group is designed for use when the class has reached the levels of investigation and insight where critiques are needed and generally appreciated by all. Critiquing should always begin and be presented in positive terms by noting first the good things that are happening. Yet, the records and reports should also include suggestions for improvement or change in how students work together. The focus is on improving or changing the learning process. Again, student membership needs to be carefully selected, but most students should have the opportunity to serve on a critiquing group. It is good experience in leadership and critical thinking.

WHOLE-CLASS GROUPS

The whole class can meet as a group. Whole-class groups can also be described as the committee of the whole. Whole-class groups are used when all class members need to work together in considering an issue or a problem, to make a decision, or to explore material. In such cases there must be a specific need and an agenda. The class should be notified, whenever possible, in advance of the topic and the agenda so members of the class can prepare for the meeting individually or in small groups. When the entire class needs to discuss the issue or problem and come to a consensus or make a decision, the meeting can be organized and begun. The teacher or identified students can lead the discussion. Whole-class groups can also become very important during assessment or evaluation of the process, the products, and the achievement of objective. They can serve to design the next steps in the learning experience. Often whole-class groups are held following reports of critiquor groups. Whole-class groups are often led by the teacher during the initial categories of interactive learning, but can and should be led by students as they take stronger leadership roles related to the learning experience at succeeding categories of the taxonomy. Whole-class meetings can be formalized through the selection of class leaders or class officers who lead the discussion and work with the group on making necessary decisions about issues on the agenda. The whole-class group can also receive reports from all other groups; based on the information brought before the whole-class group, a decision can be made. It is very important to have, whenever possible, a whole-class meeting on a regular schedule or an as-needed basis. The class should have the opportunity to do this regularly so the total group can learn more about what individuals and groups are doing and make whole-group decisions about major issues or concerns. Whole-group meetings keep the class together on the nature and direction of the total learning experience.

SUMMARY

Interactive groups are, in our view, an essential and critical component of learning. We homo sapiens are a gregarious people who grow in learning and maturity through interaction. Students in school are no exceptions. They enjoy working together and learning together. They do this through the kinds of groups we have presented in this chapter. We have presented but a representative sample of the kinds of group structures and formats that can be used in the classroom. There are, of course, many other grouping formats and structures that could be identified and used by students, but the ones discussed in this chapter are generally the ones most commonly used in the classroom. The concern we have is that students use a variety of group structures in the classroom. We believe strongly and have posited that interactive group structures used positively and effectively by students will greatly augment student learning. The interactive learning generated through group activities is absolutely essential to ensuring a positive and successful learning experience. In the following chapters we develop this perspective even more through a discussion of teaching strategies at each category of the interactive taxonomy. Next, the use of the interactive group formats and structures are specifically correlated with identified teaching strategies and are aligned through the strategies with the taxonomy.

Activities

In chapter 7 and in this one, we have focused on organization within the classroom. The activities in the previous chapter were related to teaching–learning activities and their place and use in the classroom. In this chapter we have focused on group activities and how they are organized and used in the classroom. These activities are designed to be done in a group context, but can be done individually. The outcomes of each group should be shared with peers and the total group.

1. "Positive interaction is at the core of the art of teaching" (Chap. 8, p. 105). How does this statement relate to group work? Interact with your group about this. Relate the statement to group work. Develop your group's point of view and share it with your peers.

2. Review Tables 8.1–8.3. How does the information in these tables relate to group work? How do they relate to groups? Begin your focus with Table 8.1. Discuss the roles noted in Tables 8.2 and 8.3. Report your ideas and perspective to the whole group.

3. "Students need to learn how to function in a group" (Chap. 8, p. 108). Discuss this statement with your group. What steps need to be in place to ensure that students have learned how to function within a group? Share how you would do this.

4. Select a group structure and follow how it works at each category of the taxonomy. Choose a group other than cooperative learning. What kinds of activities or work would the students do at every category?

5. How would you use pairs and triads? Choose two content areas at any grade level and determine how you would use them. Provide a rationale for their use. Share their function and your rationale with your peers.

6. How would you evaluate group work at each level of the taxonomy? Name some evaluation strategies to be used at each category. Talk about this in your own group. Report what you have determined.

7. How would you use numbered groups (numbered groups one)? Select a content area and show how you would use this group format at all levels of the interactive learning taxonomy.

Instruction

We have discussed the theoretical base for our work. We have focused on organization through learning activities and group structures. In this section we focus on instruction. Our purpose in these next five chapters is to present teaching-learning strategies designed for each category of the interactive learning taxonomy. We also present two additional chapter in this section. They are on lesson planning and on the process of change. We built our instructional section on specific teaching strategies for each category. There are, of course, other teaching strategies that you could use. If you use other strategies, be sure to key them to a category of the interactive taxonomy. For each category of the taxonomy we have defined five teaching–learning strategies. We go into detail about each of the strategies and explain them in a way that you can study them and then use them in your own classroom. That is our purpose for each of these chapters.

Any effective lesson will require the use of several teaching strategies. Using the interactive lesson planner, you will see a list of these teaching strategies. Simply check off the teaching–learning strategies you will use for your lesson or series. Keep the material from these chapters before you as you check off those strategies so that you will know what it means if you use a particular strategy. The material in these chapters can be invaluable to you as you plan and deliver your instructional plan. Think about the strands we have presented in the theory section and think about how they could be observed in your lessons.

We have included in Appendix B a list of the teaching strategies and how they are linked to cognition. You can do what we have done in the appendix with any of the strands of the taxonomy. Do this whenever possible. Make the linkages of theory and organization to instruction. This kind of discipline will help make you a more professional teacher. It will also help you learn to value your students and value what you teach. Through the intertwining of theory, organization, and instruction, you can improve your interactive skills in working with students and become a more effective teacher.

After the five chapters delineating the teaching–learning strategies, there are two more chapters relating to instruction. These are on planning and on the process of change. In the chapter on planning, we discuss the elements of planning. We talk about the process, how it needs to be done within the context of interactive learning, and how it can be planned to include group structures and interactive learning activities. Your planning can be done through the ILP included in Appendix A. Directions for filling out the ILP are provided in Appendix B. Thorough planning is an instructional imperative. Thorough planning includes students in the planning process as the course of the lesson sequence or unit of study is completed. When you are at the implementation category, student planning is dominant in the process. As teacher, your role is still vital, but it does change. Review the process of planning and the teacher and student roles in leadership as you work in planning in all categories of the taxonomy of interactive learning.

We close this section of the work with a chapter on the change process. We felt it was important to focus on change as an instructional process. Within the change process, a number of the strands become evident and you should now be able to recognize them and analyze how they worked in your own teaching. We have included comments on critical pedagogy, our views on critical pedagogy, and on what we call "ethical transformative learning." These comments can help you understand critical pedagogy and our views on it. Ethical transformative learning, as a perspective, can be a powerful force in your classroom. It can bring positive and considered change in your teaching.

Now you have learned the theory, studied the organizational factors, and have carefully reviewed the instructional strategies, planning, and change. You are ready to professionalize your teaching. You know the why, the what, and the how of teaching. You know the theoretical underpinnings of your work, how to organize the group work and the learning activities. You can plan your instruction and you know the process of change. You are professionally ready to implement an interactive learning format in your class.

One final chapter remains in our work. It is not specifically a part of this section on instruction, but is a coda for the entire work. The final chapter deals with implementing interactive learning and how you will be implementing this in your classroom. This final chapter is a series of vignettes and stories of how we, and our colleagues, have implemented the taxonomy at all levels of instruction. This is on implementing interactive learning. It is that, but more importantly it is a series of vignettes and stories of how we have implemented the taxonomy at all levels of instruction. It is the most personal of all the chapters and one we wanted to share with you. Finally, we hope you use the taxonomy, understand the strands, plan and implement with professional care, and become what you can be in terms of teaching and learning.

Invitation Teaching–Learning Strategies

Selected group formats and structures were identified and discussed in chapter 8. In this chapter we link these group formats and structures to the identified teaching–learning strategies at each category of the taxonomy of interactive learning. We will provide only a brief description of each strategy. The key in this chapter is to demonstrate that every identified teaching–learning strategy has within it an interactive component and that interactive component is well served through a variety of group structures and formats. For each category we have identified five teaching strategies. The teaching–learning strategies at each category of the taxonomy are included in this and the following chapters. We begin the presentation of teaching–learning strategies with those in the invitation category.

The teaching–learning strategies at this category of the interactive learning taxonomy are incentive exposition, data presentation, demonstration, directed observation, and interactive data review. Interaction and group work at this level of the taxonomy of interactive learning are designed to build interest and focus for the students so that they will accept the learning experience and decide to continue with it. Group structures at this level of the taxonomy and within these teaching–learning strategies can include cooperative groups, pairs, triads, jigsaw groups, flexible groups, single-task groups, exploratory groups, planning groups, and whole-class groups. Interactive group work is very important here to ensure that the interactive process takes place. Students need to know how to function in groups, so a learning process to help build confidence in working effectively in groups needs to be in place. Instruction about the group process and how to work within groups is essential; time needs to be taken to ensure that students learn how to work together in groups. Group work needs to begin with the initial activities and lessons in any course of study. When the student-felt need for groups begins to emerge, students should know their roles and their responsibilities, including group and individual responsibilities. They need to know how to organize, how to function as a group, how to assign and sequence individual and group tasks, and how and to whom to report what they have done and the information they have learned. A variety of group structures can be used with every teaching–learning strategy at this category of interactive learning. In this chapter, each teaching–learning strategy is noted and appropriate group structures are associated with each of the teaching–learning strategies.

INCENTIVE EXPOSITION

This teaching–learning strategy is usually the initial teaching strategy used in the teaching–learning process. At this beginning of a teaching–learning experience and within this teaching strategy at the invitation level of interactive learning, the teacher's roles are those of a motivator and preparer, with preparer being the teacher's leadership role. The student role is that of an attender while the student leadership role is as a participator. Incentive exposition is usually the first teaching strategy used at the invitation level. It denotes the beginnings of an interactive learning process that can continue through implementation. Through this teaching strategy, the beginnings of exposure and knowledge about the experience yet to come is established. It is important that from the very beginning of the learning experience there is an interactive context. This means that there is a need for group organization and function. The teacher asks questions, elicits answers, links what is presented to previous learning, and explain the value of what is being presented. Students respond to questions, ask for clarification and information, and talk about linkages to previous learning. The teacher encourages these questions and may even prompt them.

> *Incentive exposition is usually the initial teaching strategy used in the teaching–learning process.*

Planning and exploratory groups can be used and are very helpful during this strategy. Within this strategy, the teacher can frequently have students meet in small groups to review and discuss the information they have and to develop questions. They also, through interaction, demonstrate that they understand the links to past learning experiences. Focus and single-task groups can be very helpful in making those links. The teacher, as motivator and preparer, has the expectation that from the discussion, from group work, and from responses to questions, the students will become more active in discussing the information presented and develop an interest in it and a curiosity about the lesson sequence. The student role at this invitation category is that of a questioner. The student leadership role is that of a participator. Students as questioners and participators can become active group members and be involved in group settings during this initial interactive process. The purpose of the interaction and group work here is to elicit interest and to expose students to the information and materials they need so that they will seek to know more. This can be effectively accomplished through carefully planned group work. The teacher, as motivator and preparer, must plan questions, materials, and activities designed for student response. These questions and activities should be at all levels of cognition so that students have the opportunity to think about and discuss the information and materials presented. Discussion and responses can emerge through group work.

Interaction and group work can act as a stimulus for students and help them to achieve designed goals and objectives. It should also be noted that with the beginning of group work there should be a discussion about and instruction concerning the importance of group work. There should be instruction and indeed some practice about the roles and tasks of each group member, and the expected outcomes of the group work. By practice we mean a guided walk-through by the teacher and students covering all elements of group work. Students can then be organized into cooperative groups, pairs, triads, and focus groups. Other kinds of groups such as exploratory groups and single-task groups could also be organized. The task of each group needs to be focused on the content and material being presented and studied. The groups also need to have specific assignments that will provide opportunities to explore and discuss the information from the perspectives of both interest and information needed for the study.

Careful and thorough teacher planning is essential for these group formats and structures. Tasks and identified expected outcomes must be clearly understood by students and there must be a planned time for discussing, responding, and sharing. In terms of interaction and leadership, the teacher's roles are those of a presenter and preparer. The teacher must understand these roles and be aware that integral to successful interaction is ensuring that the students have an active role in responding to the information, discussing it, and organizing the materials and any realia that may have been introduced. If done in the interactive mode, along with participation in appropriate kinds of groups, the students are much more likely to feel a need to learn more and thus will evidence an increasing interest in the content and ideas within the material be presented. They are, through this teaching–learning strategy, developing a readiness for accepting the learning experience.

DATA PRESENTATION

The interaction of teacher and student, student to student, and students to materials continue in this teaching–learning strategy. Group organization strategies similar to the ones noted for incentive exposition can be used with this strategy. The teacher, in the roles as motivator and preparer, is the one who plans for and presents the information. The teacher needs to plan for both interaction and group work because each is an important component of this teaching–learning strategy. Students, during their use of this teaching–learning strategy, continue to build a base of information. This needed information base can be used as a foundation for students becoming more actively responsive to the learning process. Students interact with the teacher, with the materials, and with each other. They can and should interact in all these ways as they work together in groups. The teacher who has carefully planned, has built opportunities for group work, and has developed a format for active interaction ensures student interest and willingness to continue with the teaching experience. The use of interaction provides an opportunity for discussion, questions and responses, and peer focus on the materials and information. The teacher needs to work with the students in setting up and planning for group work. At the invitation category of interactive learning, this process continues to make sure students can function positively and together in groups.

As a result of the teacher's careful planning, students participate in a variety of group structures. One group structure that is very pertinent during this teaching–learning strategy is exploratory groups, where the group is assigned to research a particular set of data. Data exploration is also defined as a teaching–learning strategy at this level of interactive learning. Exploratory groups can begin here and can also be used in data exploration as well. The focus of the exploratory groups here is slightly different than in the data exploration strategy. Here their focus is narrower and more limited. Exploratory groups focus on a particular set of information, organize it, and bring it back to the rest of the class in the form of a report.

> *Data exploration is also defined as a teaching–learning strategy at this level of interactive learning.*

Cooperative groups and flexible groups are also pertinent within this strategy. Jigsaw and numbered groups one and two can also be very pertinent as the students respond, in groups, to the information and data presented. Whatever group organization is used needs to have the students focused on the data presented and work within defined limits usually set by the teacher. Interaction and group work are integral components of instruction and learning within this strategy. Pairs, triads, and whole-class groups are also valuable and can be used as strong components within this teaching–learning strategy. With the data presentation strategy, there is a sense of beginning to set goals and objectives for both the short term and for the long terms as well as looking ahead to the next steps in the learning experience. Planning groups and whole-class groups as well as jigsaw groups and the two numbered groups could be very useful in organizing and categorizing data. Organizing and categorizing data is a strongly interactive dimension in this strategy. The interactive focus of groups and the class is also very important to the goal-setting process implicit within this strategy.

Data presentation is an important strategy, and interactive learning demonstrated through group work is one major component of this teaching–learning strategy. Within the context of data presentation and the interactions used, there emerges the need for valuing the data and learning what is being presented and discussed in groups. Students can be expected not only to discuss the importance of the data with each other and the teacher, but also to recognize its value to them and to the learning experience. Thus the valuing process begins. Valuing is begun in this strategy and continues as a *leitmotif* of teaching, learning, and motivation throughout the learning experience. Students also need to learn to organize, record, save, and store data they may need later in the learning experience. Furthermore, students need to learn about and demonstrate record keeping and begin to maintain records through notes, logs, and other narratives. If technology is available, it should be used. This is a part of the teaching–learning strategy and students should learn how to do this as they work together during this data presentation strategy.

DEMONSTRATION

Because demonstration involves showing how to do something, going through a sequence step-by-step, and showing and explaining models and realia, there is no question about the importance of interaction and group work when teacher and students work together in this teaching–learning strategy. The teacher, in the roles of presenter, preparer, and motivator, is responsible for most of the demonstrating. Students attend carefully to the demonstration and are participators through the demonstration. They ask questions about the demonstrations and, in most cases, react to the demonstrations and interact about them. This teaching–learning strategy is designed to ensure that student interest is engaged and enhanced. Interaction and group work are a strong fit within this teaching–learning strategy. Demonstration can be done through whole-class groups or in smaller cooperative groups. Cooperative learning groups, single-task groups, and numbered groups fit well into this teaching–learning strategy. Their task is to respond to a specific demonstration. Single-task groups can review and study a particular demonstration and any realia associated with it. Their focus is on the content, sequence, meaning, and value of the demonstration. Sometimes the demonstration is itself a group activity. Students can participate in the demonstration in groups, review it, and study it. They then report about their reactions and any findings about the demonstration to the whole class.

Cooperative group members can help explain and provide answers to problems or issues brought up during the demonstration. Interaction and group work designed at this category of interactive learning are used to ensure, engage, and enhance student interest in the learning experience. The use of pairs, triads, flexible groups, and planning groups can contribute to this enhanced student engagement in learning. Students, through these three invitation teaching–learning strategies, are building a functional database by dealing with the information and material presented in an interactive and group context. Their role as attenders is demonstrated here and they have begun to participate in the learning experience. Also, through their work in groups and through an inquiry approach to demonstrations, students can develop questions and interact with the teacher, the materials, and with each others. As students interact with the teacher and with each other, they become further engaged in learning and interested in finding out more about the learning experience. The teacher, through careful observation of student interaction, group work, and their responses to demonstrations and presented material, can develop questions and provide students with understanding and direction as they are involved with interactive group work. Demonstration also includes coaching. Demonstration and coaching are critical to teaching and learning (Dechant 1991). Demonstration is a teaching–learning strategy that strongly involves the students with interaction and group work. Group structures are pertinent formats to ensure student involvement in demonstrations.

**Invitation
Teaching–Learning
Strategies**

Ensure student interest
Engage student interest
Enhance student interest

DIRECTED OBSERVATION

Within the context of this teaching–learning strategy there is a focus on particular stimuli or specific components of the data and the study underway. Directed observation is more focused than the three previous strategies within this category of interactive learning. The teacher, as extrinsic motivator, preparer, and presenter, directs the observations and provides opportunities for interaction and group work. The use of the senses is generally integral for this teaching–learning strategy. Directed observation engages the students in the use of many, if not all, of the senses. They can see, hear, smell, taste, and feel the materials being observed. Activities included in this sensory strategy encourage interaction and discussion. Discussions emerge and groups can be formed to react to the particular and specific components and stimuli on which the observation has been focused. Verbal interaction through questions from the teacher and from students as well as reactions to comments is effective as this teaching–learning strategy unfolds.

> *Directed observation engages the students in the utilization of many, if not all, of the senses. They can see, hear, smell, taste, and feel the materials being observed.*

The teacher needs to demonstrate questioning skills at higher levels of cognition and students need to learn how to develop and ask questions. Thinking and cognition are basic in this strategy. There are opportunities to learn associated with this strategy and, indeed, all teaching–learning strategies at the invitation level of interactive learning. Cooperative groups are especially helpful within this strategy as students work with the materials, the realia, and the other stimuli within the study and learning experience. Flexible groups could also be organized to ensure that all the class members understand the information and the context of the study and that they all have an opportunity to manipulate the stimuli and use their senses to learn. Pairs and triads are excellent formats for this teaching–learning strategy. Whole-class groups with interrogative discussion as their focus are important within this strategy because this large group activity provides students an opportunity to respond to questions and issues together as well as to share information and points of view that can come together with a group consensus. Other group strategies could also be used. The teacher's roles are to ensure that the students remain focused and that the discussion is pertinent to the materials being reviewed and observed. The teacher also needs to keep the focus on the learning experience and help students become more cognizant of what it is and what the next steps might be. Planning groups, if used, should be put into place toward the close of the directed observation; their information and findings are then shared within the whole-class group. Interaction and group work are integral to and very important during this teaching–learning strategy. This interaction in a group setting continues to help students develop and enrich their database for the learning experience.

INTERACTIVE DATA REVIEW

The name of this teaching–learning strategy suggests that it is built around the premise of interaction and group work. This is indeed true. Interactive data review is the culminating strategy at the invitation category of interactive learning and there is a strong emphasis on interaction through the interrogative modality, through discussion, and through group interaction. Two kinds of groups are especially important during this strategy. They are cooperative groups and planning groups. Cooperative groups can be very valuable in helping students review material, make sense of it, and report back to the class. Cooperative groups can review and study material, use their senses to understand more about the material they are reviewing, provide a hierarchy of importance, and even lead class discussion about the material. Much of their task is to look at the developing database and to determine if it is substantive enough to move on through

Groups in Interactive Data Review

Cooperative Groups: review and study material, use their senses to understand more about the material, provide a hierarchy of importance, and lead class discussion.

Planning Groups: review what has happened, project the next steps to take, and to identify possible outcomes, goals, and objectives.

the learning experience. Planning groups are also essential in that one of the major purposes of this strategy is to review what has happened and to project the next steps as well as to identify possible outcomes, goals, and objectives for the learning experience. These two kinds of groups can function very positively during this teaching strategy because they can help build a positive climate for interaction and an overview of the process up to this point.

There are other group structures that could be used by the students and the teacher. Jigsaw groups are very good ways to involve all the students and have each jigsaw group resolve one part of what has been learned for review and then share it with others. When the jigsaw is put together, the whole picture is complete. Roving group formats as well as flexible groups where designated students move from one group to another for content and skill review and study can be very helpful to students, particularly for those who may need some reinforcement or reteaching. During group work, the teacher needs to move from group to group, ensuring that they are focused on the study, asking pertinent questions, or challenging students to think in another way. Through these kinds of teacher–group interaction, students are enabled to review the process, assess what they have done, resolve issues and problems, and project direction and next steps. After there has been a lively participatory interaction among the students in groups, with the teacher through questions and through reports of group work, a whole-class discussion is appropriate to finalize what has been done.

Finalization here has three functions. First, the whole-class grouping is designed to ensure that all students have an appropriate common information base. Second, it is designed to ensure that all students have accepted the learning experience and are committed to continuing with it. Third, whole-class groupings are designed at this category of the taxonomy to help students project next steps and to visualize possible goals, outcomes, and objectives. Students have learned to value of what they have learned and have grasped its meaning. This is vital to not only this teaching–learning strategy, but to all the strategies at the invitation category. When all this has been accomplished, the students have completed, through strong interaction and interrogative group work, the readiness category of interactive teaching. They are ready to move into the next category in the taxonomy of interactive learning.

SUMMARY

In the group work associated with this initial category in the taxonomy of interactive learning, it should be remembered that the teacher roles are those of an extrinsic motivator, a presenter, and a preparer. The student roles are those of an attender, a questioner, and a participator. The instructional role is informational. With these roles in mind, interaction and group work is organized *vis-à-vis* these roles. The teacher, in terms of planning, must build a series of interactions and group work associated with each teaching–learning strategy used at this category of interactive learning. There are sets of interaction and group teaching–learning activities that have been discussed and that can serve well at this level of interactive learning. The teacher needs to plan for the use of those sets of group structures and forms as well as for specific learning activities. It is through these teaching–learning strategies and through the intensity of group work that students begin to find their voice.

The quality and kinds of questions and discussion modalities are major issues to deal with in terms of teacher planning. Questions and discussions should be planned around higher levels of cognition so that they will cause the students to respond not only with memory, translation, and interpretation, but with application, analysis, synthesis, and evaluation. Small-group interaction and whole-class discussions should be planned in the same way. The purposes of questioning and discussion are to ensure that students become involved in the learning experience and to help students make choices that bring forth a felt need to continue with the learning experience. Discussion and the nature of the group interaction should pique the interest of the students and elicit a positive response to the learning environment and experience. The use of discussion, group work, and interaction in these teaching–learning strategies and activities help students begin to value what they are studying and become motivated to continue with the learning experience.

The purpose of group work is very similar. Group work is designed to involve the students in thinking about and exploring the information with which they have been presented. Small-group work in pairs, triads, or cooperative groups provides students with the opportunity to explore information, to learn to work with each other, and to become immersed in the learning experience. Group work, while planned by the teacher in the roles of extrinsic motivator and preparer, provides the impetus for student acceptance of the learning experience through a level of involvement and interest that becomes their rationale for seeking more information and wanting to continue with the learning experience. Organization of the groups and the goals and objectives for each group meeting should be planned initially by the teacher; with growing interest on the part of the students, however, they can begin to participate in the planning. The earlier in the learning experience that the students become a part of the planning process, the more effectively the plans are developed and put into place. Through being a part of the planning process, the more rapidly the learning experience progresses and the more focused the students become in making the learning experience their own.

The structure and nature of particular groups are related to the nature of the invitation category of interactive learning. Not all kinds of groups work well for the teaching–learning strategies used at this category of interactive learning. Pairs, triads, cooperative groups, planning groups, focus groups, single-task groups, flexible groups, jigsaw groups, and roving groups work very well at this category of interactive learning. All these group structures and formats not only work very well at this level of interactive learning, but serve specific purposes planned by the teacher and can be used effectively for gathering and exploring information. They can be used to learn specific skills and to reteach identified student needs. Group work fits well into the informational–instructional focus of the teaching–learning strategies at this category of the taxonomy of interactive learning. Interactive and group strategies planned carefully for this category of interactive learning can be very valuable to the learning experience. Students, through the teaching–learning strategies used, the planned learning activities, and the interaction and group work, can develop a strong database and make positive and considered determinations to become more involved in the learning experience. They learn to value the experience and are ready for the next category of interactive learning.

In terms of cognition, although the major focus is on memory, translation, and interpretation, along with some application, there are instances when analysis, synthesis, and evaluation become a part of student work in dealing with the resources they are studying. Higher levels of cognition become more apparent in the discussion and interaction that take place in small groups. Likewise, the emphasis in terms of creativity, critical thinking, and problem solving remain primarily at their initial levels. Sometimes, even this early in the learning experience, students will demonstrate higher levels of creativity and solving initial problems. In both cases, they need to think critically as they begin to delve more deeply into the learning experience. In terms of writing, students define the components of the learning experience and are beginning to be able to describe it. In terms of thinking, students have responded and are ready to personalize the learning experience. Students become engaged in the learning process at this category of the taxonomy. Students and the teacher will know when they have completed this level of interactive learning and have come to value what they are learning. When all this has been accomplished, the students are prepared for the involvement category of interactive learning.

Activities

In this third section we are focusing on instruction. We have developed activities for the chapters on theory and activities for the two chapters on organization. Beginning with the activities for this chapter and for the next four chapters, we will be focusing on instruction. The activities for these five chapters will require the interactive groups to review theory, apply activities, and select group structures to identified teaching–learning strategies. We strongly recommend that the activities be done in groups, although they can be done individually. They are generally broad based and require discussion, review, application, and thoughtful pondering.

1. Select one teaching–learning strategy at invitation and identify appropriate group structures to be used with that teaching strategy. Provide a rationale for your findings. Show how at least four strands of lesson analysis could be identified using with the group structures selected for the teaching–learning strategy.

2. What is the role of motivation in the teaching–learning strategies at invitation? What group activities would you use with these strategies? Discuss this with your group. Prepare a report and share it with your peers.

3. How is the interrogative modality shown during interactive data review? Discuss this in your group. Identify how interaction through the interrogative modality is demonstrated. Share your information with other groups.

4. Discuss with your group and share with your peers your group's views on how students develop a strong database for learning using invitation level teaching–learning strategies.

5. "Students become engaged in the learning process at this category" (Chap. 9, p. 132). What does this mean? How is it shown? Why is a database essential at this category of interactive learning? Respond to the statement and the questions. Validate your responses and share them with the rest of the group.

6. How would you assess student readiness to move from invitation to involvement through the completion of the teaching–learning strategies at this category? Discuss this, develop an information report, and share that report.

Involvement Teaching–Learning Strategies

When students move from the invitation category of interactive learning to the involvement level of interactive motivation, a new set of teaching–learning strategies as well as new roles for teacher, student, and instruction become operant. Those teaching–learning strategies are linking, review data, participatory hands-on activities, unstructured role-playing, and ordering. Each of these strategies is integral to involvement activities and learning. The use of each causes students to become involved in learning and to make a decision that the learning experience is valuable for them. Different interactive purposes and group strategies are used to initiate involvement category activities and to move students through these activities, teaching–learning strategies, interactions, and grouping structures. At this category of the taxonomy, the teacher roles are those of catalyst and coordinator. The role of coordinator is the leadership role the teacher demonstrates. The student role is that of an explorer, while the student role in leadership is that of a cooperator. These roles of the teacher and the student are descriptors of the activities and teaching–learning strategies and are demonstrated at this category of the taxonomy. The instructional role is participatory, which implies interactive learning and the dynamics of group work. The three subcategories at the involvement category are direction, discussion, and decision. These, too, exemplify the activities at this level of learning. Throughout this category of interactive learning, students are gaining direction, discussing, and working with the information presented. They are reviewing their learning and projecting the next levels of learning. They are establishing relationships with each other, with the teacher, and with the resources they use. Furthermore, they are making firm decisions about the direction and the next steps in the learning experience.

The student roles as explorer and cooperator and the teacher roles as catalyst and coordinator help foster and promote the participatory interactive working relationship characteristic at this category of interactive learning. In addition, the instructional role is defined as participatory, which means that all involved in the experience take part in the learning experiences at this level of the taxonomy. Interaction and group work are essential here. The teachers and the students develop a need to work together in the participatory modality and to interactively move the experience step-by-step through this category of interactive learning. Selecting and using appropriate teaching–learning strategies are very important at this level of interactive learning. Likewise, selecting and using activities that correlate with the teaching–learning strategies is also very important.

Cognitively, students are beginning to apply what they have learned and to analyze data and information. They are able to describe what they are doing in terms of writing about their learning experience. They begin to visualize some of the products they will create and clarify and define variables they encounter. In terms of problem solving, they are exploring databases for possible resolution of issues and problems in the material they are exploring. In the thinking sequence, students are at the apprehension level, where they focus on the stimuli and information, and order or arrange the stimuli into a reactive framework. Students, at this level of the taxonomy, demonstrate learning by participation in and personalizing the learning sequence. The student does this in terms of personal meaning and reviewing information so he or she can project a value. The teacher is working with particularizing or focusing the students on the process of achieving the already valued experience and projected outcomes. The teaching–learning strategies of linking, reviewing data, unstructured role-playing, participatory hands-on activities, and ordering, as noted above, are designed to help students focus on the learning experience and becoming more involved with the experience. A number of group formats and group structures, coordinated with interactive strategies, are used with each of these teaching–learning strategies at this involvement level of interactive learning.

LINKING

Linking is the teaching–learning strategy where the new learning experience along with information gained during the invitation category need to be linked both with past experience and with the new projected learning to which the students have been exposed to and in which they are now involved. These kinds of linkages need to be made to help contextualize what is being learned with what has been learned. Some links were made during the invitation teaching–learning strategies, but within this strategy those links are made more evident within the context of the new learning experience. Linking becomes multidimensional in this strategy. Students make those linkages through working together as well as sharing and discussing. Their discussing and sharing focuses on what is happening now and what has happened in earlier learning and personal experiences. Cognitively, this is represented through memory, translation, interpretation, and analysis. Through these levels of cognition, students can identify linkages and contextualize them in terms of relationships with older experiences and new experiences. Through apprehension in the thinking sequence, students become more focused and are able to arrange the stimuli for personal interpretation and for a reactive setting where they can discuss and order them. Learning becomes personalized, while the teacher is focusing and particularizing the learning. This kind of interaction is enhanced through a variety of group activities.

Linking becomes multidimensional in this strategy. Students make those linkages through working together as well as sharing and discussing.

Many kinds of groups can be used within this teaching–learning strategy. Among the group structures and formats that work well here are pairs, triads, single-task groups, focus groups, exploratory groups, cooperative groups, and whole-class groups. Others group formats can be used as well. Among the others could be both kinds of numbered groups and roving groups. It is important that linking past experience to the present learning sequence be articulated, discussed, and identified. These can be accomplished very effectively through well-planned group activities. Whole-class groupings for the purpose of discussing what has been learned and firmly establishing links is important; this can be used to share individual and whole-class experiences and to formalize the linkages. Linking, by its very name, implies a discussion modality in which interactive group work is integral. Group work, as noted, is essential at this involvement level of the taxonomy. It is particularly essential in this teaching learning strategy. The teacher roles in this teaching strategy are catalyst and coordinator. These roles mean that the teacher brings the students in contact with ideas, constructs, past learning, and present direction. Linking is a key strategy for bringing new meanings as well as making past experiences a base for the new learning. There is also an expectation that the students react to those contexts through interactive study and group structures. Students relate information through a number of group formats. They have dialogue, they discuss, and they work with the information. They understand the linkages and the challenges for new learning presented. Recognizing the links and using them in the learning experience is the end result of these kinds of group interaction at this level of the taxonomy. The vehicle for this linking process is interactive group work. Valuing the links between past and present is at the core of the teacher's roles and is an essential component of this and other teaching–learning strategies at the involvement level of interactive learning. The student roles as explorer and cooperator coincide with and complement the teacher roles as catalyst and coordinator. It is through these corollary roles that the interactive process of linking is completed. Linking is the first teaching–learning strategy used during the involvement category of interactive learning. It is during this strategy that relationships are being established and strengthened, where there is the visualization of products that can be developed. Students begin to personalize what they are learning and to apply elements of the learning experience. It is a strategy that can bring great promise for learning to the students.

REVIEWING DATA

Reviewing data is a teaching–learning strategy in which the use of interaction and group work is exceptionally important. Students are reviewing data for two purposes. First, they are organizing and categorizing data to find out whether the data has pertinence to the study. Second, they are establishing hierarchies of importance to establish what elements or components of the data will be the most useful to completing the study. In any learning experience, this strategy needs to be used when students have decided to become active participants in the learning experience. Once linking has been completed, this teaching–learning strategy should be used.

By the time students are using this strategy, they have made the decision to move ahead with the learning experience and need to continue to build their knowledge about the content of the study. Students need to validate what has been done and to determine what can be used and the level of its importance to their learning. Although these activities can be done individually, they are much more effectively and efficiently accomplished through group work, including the use of a wide variety of group structures. Students can work in pairs and triads. They can do jigsaws. They can use cooperative groups, dialectic groups, flexible groups, numbered heads groups, and single-task groups. Students, as they work in their groups, need to understand that they are responsible to the whole-class group for their review of the data. They are also responsible to the class group for summarizing and suggesting the usefulness of what they have reviewed and studied to the class group.

Peers need to know what others in the class have done, how they have done it, and what they have learned. Within the reporting context, there is a defined component of sharing, discussing, and valuing their review. This can be done through a whole-class discussion or through reports of the various groups with an application to the study. Students, in terms of cognition, may also use analysis, synthesis, and evaluation. They need these levels of cognition to review the data. Most of the focus for cognition is,

Purposes for Reviewing Data

1. Categorizing and organizing data to determine pertinence of the study.
2. Establishing hierarchies of importance to establish useful elements and components of the study.

however, at the application level. Students are reviewing information about a condition and are beginning to challenge that condition.

It is during this strategy that students begin to develop interactive relationships with each other. The whole class can work together and assess their review of data. Generally, this is done first as they work together in small groups. Each group then reports to the class. After the small-group reporting is completed, the whole class, working together with the teacher, reviews the data during a whole-class group meeting. Reviewing data is a strategy in which group work is a strong and compatible classroom structure for success. The dynamics of group work and discussion are intrinsic to the success of this process of data review.

The learning experience is becoming personalized through this strategy and will continue through other teaching–learning strategies at this category of interactive learning. Here students begin to recognize variance and are able to put materials in order of importance. They, in their writing, describe what they have reviewed and report to the class. Here they work cooperatively with each other and with the teacher. Through their group work they are exploring the data to resolve issues and to determine which data they can effectively use. The teacher is working with them to continue to focus on particular areas of content in the review of data. In terms of experience, students are participating actively in the learning experience and are exploring the data to determine its meaning and relevance to what they are involved with in the total learning experience. Students are beginning to raise questions about the material they are reviewing and are determining how the data fits into their study. It is an important strategy at the involvement category of interactive learning and one that students find personally valuable as well as valuable to the learning experience in which they are involved.

UNSTRUCTURED ROLE-PLAYING

This teaching–learning strategy can play an important role for learning and in moving a learning experience forward to new categories of the taxonomy. This strategy is not, however, used as often as it should be. Then, too, this strategy may work better with some units of study than with others. Once students have reviewed their data and have discussed its importance, they need to show evidence that they have understood what they have reviewed. To do this, they need to apply the data to different contexts. These new contexts could include some of the objectives they selected for their learning experiences. Or they could try out what they have learned in fresh contexts. When using new contexts, students need to experiment with new roles and relationships. Unstructured role-playing can help accomplish this. Using unstructured role-playing, the students can assume roles or take positions on learned data and can demonstrate them to their classmates through group work and unstructured role-playing. Careful planning on the part of the teacher and the students is critical to unstructured role-playing. Planning groups, panel discussions, problem-solving groups, and dialectic groups can be a part of the group process of preparing the role-playing scenarios. Pairs, triads, and cooperative groups can also be used. Each group can focus on a phase of the information and data needed for the role-play.

Using unstructured role-playing, the students can assume roles or take positions on learned data and can demonstrate them to their classmates through group work and unstructured role-playing.

This teaching–learning strategy is called unstructured because there is no written script, nor any kind of formal structure for the role-playing. Groups working on the unstructured role-playing can plan how to conduct the role-play. It is usually informal, but formal roles can be defined. Group structures can be single-task groups or focus groups. Each group needs to report to the class as a whole and after whole-class discussion and the working out of details, the role-playing exercise can begin. The purpose of unstructured role-playing is to show by the role-play what the students know; what they want or need to know in terms of their roles can better represent the real issue, problem, or social situation they are demonstrating. The role-play itself is a group activity. The first time and on a continuing basis, it is generally the shortest part of the lesson. Planning takes more time and so does evaluation.

Evaluation is extremely important because it is through evaluation that students analyze what they have done, how they have done it, and what they need to make the role-playing more realistic. Also discussed in the evaluation is how the role-playing works into the total learning experience of which students are a part. Usually all, or nearly all, participate. Those who do not participate are expected to be active observers and participate effectively in the discussion and evaluation that follow the role-playing. The focus on the evaluation is related to how well the role-play was performed and what yet needs to be learned. The evaluation can be done in cooperative groups or it can be done in the whole-class context. What still needs to be learned is how the role-playing can be more realistic, what realia or artifacts are needed, and how it fits into the learning sequence—these are some of the focus areas of needed for the evaluation. Unstructured role-play should be used more than one time to ensure that students have thoroughly understood what they have learned and the learning direction they will take from this strategy forward. Each time unstructured role-playing is used it should become more sophisticated, more specific, and more realistic. Each time it is used the same evaluation process must be used at the close of the role-play. It should also be remembered that teaching, at its very core, is valuing. The use of this strategy can help build within the students a sense of the importance and value of what they have learned and are learning and will continue to learn. Unstructured role-playing fits well in social science lessons, language arts, and to a lesser extent in other content areas.

PARTICIPATORY HANDS-ON ACTIVITIES

The first word, participatory, in this teaching–learning strategy becomes the orientation for group work and group activities. Within group work and activities there must be a strong emphasis on interactive discussion and participation. *Participation* literally means involvement and interaction between students and among students individually and in groups. Students need to use realia, artifacts, and a wide spectrum of materials. In addition, they need to contact and work with people and resources outside the world of the school. The use of this strategy is an opportunity for the students to broaden their perspectives on the learning experience. Technology can be used to support this strategy, although it is not totally necessary. This teaching–learning strategy provides the framework for rich experiences with people, resources, materials, realia, and artifacts. Group work is essential and integral to the success of this strategy.

Many kinds of groups can be used with this teaching–learning strategy. Small groups such as pairs and triads can work well with the resources and materials. Focus groups and single-purpose groups can work with single concepts or ideas. Students can also work on specific and defined task assignments. Cooperative groups, jigsaws, and flexible groups can be very effective using this strategy. Roving groups could even be used here. Within this strategy, students reach out to each other and to communities, resources, and people to find information, to process it, and to use it within the context of their learning experience.

> *The use of this strategy is an opportunity for the students to broaden their perspectives on the learning experience.*

Participatory hands-on activities are excellent structures for discourse, for problem solving, for critical thinking, and creativity. The student role of explorer is particularly apparent with this group structure as is the teacher role of catalyst. Experientially, students can demonstrate participation within this strategy. Critical thinking, problem solving, and creativity are shown as students work with hands-on materials. Student leadership as a cooperator in the learning experience can be observed during this teaching–learning strategy.

Three Components of Ordering

1. Students must have thoroughly explored, studied, and interacted with the data and materials they have used.
2. The students must have personalized the data and materials through interactive, participatory, and group learning settings.
3. The students must be willing and able to envision and project a sequence of activities necessary to complete the learning experience.

ORDERING

Use of this strategy involves the students reviewing the learning up to this point, projecting final outcomes, determining a possible or probable sequence of activities to achieve those outcomes. It is through this strategy that real commitment to learning and to the projected outcomes becomes evident. Ordering involves the students in sequencing data and materials, establishing a hierarchy of those materials, defining frames of reference, and projecting and structuring a further process for learning. Cognitively, the students are using interpretation, application, and analysis. In terms of writing, the students are defining and describing. They may even touch on detail. Students are particularizing the information, thinking about it, and projecting new directions within the learning sequence. They have established relationships, and those relationships are working toward the completion of the learning sequence.

Through this process of thinking, organizing, and learning, the students become more cognizant of direction and are ready to make the decision and commitment to complete the tasks before them. Students, through their activities during this strategy, are defining variables and visualizing the outcomes of the study and the products to be achieved. The roles of the teacher as catalyst and coordinator during this strategy are to ensure that the students value the experience and that their decision to commit themselves to the learning experience is based on their relationships. Those relationships are with the materials, the media, artifacts, and realia as well as with with each other and the teacher. They have accepted the challenge and are able to describe it. Relationships represent the art of teaching and learning. The strategy itself and the activities within it represent the science of teaching and learning.

Three components are necessary to this teaching strategy. First, students must have thoroughly explored, studied, and interacted with the data and materials they have used. These need to have been accomplished through the use of teaching strategies and learning activities at the readiness and relationship levels of motivation and during the invitation and involvement levels of interactive learning. Second, the students must have personalized the data and materials through interactive, participatory, and group learning settings. Third, the students must be willing and able to envision and project a sequence of activities necessary to complete the learning experience. They must be comfortable with this projected vision and understand it as necessary to them personally, to the group, and to the continuance of the learning experience.

Ordering is the final teaching–learning strategy in the involvement category of interactive learning. Ordering is both reflective and projective. Its use culminates the strategies at the involvement level of interactive learning. Using this strategy, students look back and review what they have accomplish, then begin to plan and order the process toward completion of the learning sequence, with the teacher acting as the catalyst and coordinator. Students are demonstrating their roles as explorers and cooperators. Ordering is an important, even necessary, strategy for the students as well as for the teacher. It is the students, however, who must make the decision to continue the learning experience. They must reflect on what they have done and project the direction in which they need to continue the learning experience and achieve projected outcomes. They, during this teaching–learning strategy, commit themselves to further activities and to the projected goals and outcomes they and the teacher have envisioned. They have explored data, personalized it, and have accepted the challenge of continuing the learning experience.

The teacher must value the experience and ensure that the students also value the area of study. Students need to reflect on the value and meaning of the learning experience as they organize and order the next steps in their decision to continue the learning experience. Students also need to show evidence that they can indeed achieve the outcomes that they and the teacher have projected and to which they have made a commitment. Finally, the students need to show that they are ready to continue their progress into the investigation category of interactive learning. If a decision to move forward is not made, or if there is no student commitment, the learning experience can fragment, with less and less involvement on the part of the students. If the decision and the commitment are accomplished, the students have demonstrated that they are ready for the next steps and a new level of interactive learning. That category is investigation.

SUMMARY

Involvement and the teaching–learning activities and teaching strategies associated with this level of interactive learning become an exciting and interesting time for both the students and the teacher. Strategies used at this category of interactive learning require strong teacher involvement as well as strong student involvement. The teacher roles of catalyst and coordinator, although still strong, are somewhat less directive than at the invitation category of interactive learning. Students as explorers and cooperators have become more involved in the experience and are gaining a clearer understanding of the parameters of the experience and have visualized its projected outcomes. The students are demonstrating emergent leadership and need to practice these learned leadership roles during all the strategies at this level of interactive learning. At this level of interactive learning, they begin to assume more and more involvement in the direction of the experience and begin to envision purpose, process, products, goals, objectives, and outcomes.

Through participatory activities and much group work and discussion, students evolve in the learning sequence toward a well-designed and definitive decision to commit themselves to the totality of the learning experience. They have developed through identified teaching–learning strategies and a variety of learning activities. Students have also developed clear working relationships with each other and with the teacher. Students have developed a strong affinity for the materials and resources they have used. This affinity has been important to them in making their commitment to continuing the learning experience. Students have developed a projected sequence and have determined to continue toward the fruition of the learning experience. The teacher, in the roles of catalyst and coordinator, has had a major role in this process. Through probing questions, interactive involvement, and careful planning and organization, the teacher not only ensures that the process will continue, but that the students truly value what they have done, what they are doing, and the process through which they will go. When this has come to pass, students and teacher are ready for the next category of interactive learning. That category of interactive learning is investigation.

Finally, there are two major emphases at the involvement level of interactive learning. These two are building relationships and students demonstrating that they are valuing the learning experience and beginning to sense its meaning to them. The teacher is responsible for much of the preplanning as well as for the interactive activities and involvement with the students individually and in small- and large-group structures. The teacher in the roles of catalyst and coordinator dovetails nicely with the student roles of explorer and cooperator. An explorer needs a navigator, a compass, and a map. The teacher is the navigator and the students use the compass to generate a map for their commitment to the learning experience and the expected outcomes of that learning experience. Through careful planning and increasing student involvement and leadership, this has happened. Student success in valuing learning and developing relationships are essential to the continuance of the learning experience.

Students during this category of interactive learning are beginning to take a more active role in learning and are demonstrating emerging leadership skills. They, too, are involved in building relationships and understanding and valuing the learning experience. They participate experientially in identified learning activities and build relationships with each other, with the teacher, and with the resources they use. They have personalized the learning experience and have comprehended the scope and sequence of the experience. They have explored data. Ideas and concepts have been particularized. As evaluators, there have been questions generated by both the teacher and the students. Visualization of the outcomes has been accomplished. The culmination of positive relationships and coming to value the learning demonstrate that the students are indeed ready to move to the investigation level of interactive learning.

The involvement category of interactive learning is marked by the series of five of teaching–learning strategies, a variety of group structures, and many instructional activities. These are the hallmarks of interactive learning. At involvement, both the art of teaching and the science of teaching are demonstrated. Through the building of relationships and group interaction, the art of teaching is demonstrated. Through cognitive levels used, through critical thinking and problem solving, and through the use of each of the teaching–learning strategies, the science of teaching has been demonstrated. No group decision or commitment to the learning experience could happen without the positive relationships and the artful crafting of these relationships. Relationships and valuing are built by understanding what the learning experience is and what it could be. This is evident in the way the students and the teacher use the activities and teaching strategies for analysis and directional learning. These kinds of interactions demonstrate not only good human relating, but also an ability to analyze what is happening, and thus demonstrate the science of learning and instruction. Student acceptance of the challenge of learning and their ability to visualize a path toward the achievement of the total learning experience becomes evident. Involvement represents not only the personalization of the learning experience; the projection of next steps is also very important at this level of the taxonomy of interactive learning. Involvement implies strong organization, careful analysis, and positive interactive relationships. These are the qualities that help most the students through involvement and into the investigation category of interactive learning.

Activities

In this second of the instructional focus chapters, we are at the involvement category of interactive learning. The activities here will require you and your group to look back on the theory as well as to the organization of learning activities and group structures. Probe all the activities. Refer to previous chapters in terms of theory and organization. Discuss these activities in your groups. Build your rationale for these activities and defend that rationale. Ponder the substance and the meaning of your responses. Interact with your group about the activities. Prepare to share your ideas and point of view with your peers.

1. How is reviewing data at the involvement category different from interactive data review at invitation? Discuss the differences from the perspective of at least four analysis strands.

2. Identify five activities listed for the involvement category and show how they would be used with each of the teaching–learning strategies.

3. Cognition is important to these teaching–learning strategies. What categories of cognition would you use at involvement? Which ones would you use more than others? How would you recognize cognition at the involvement category?

4. Describe the changing roles of teacher and students as they are shown in the teaching–learning strategies at invitation and involvement.

5. Relate cooperative learning and three other learning activities to the teaching–learning strategies at the involvement category of interactive learning.

6. "Students are demonstrating emergent leadership" (Chap. 10, p. 140). Study this statement in terms of the changing roles of students and teacher leadership at this category of interactive learning.

Investigation Teaching–Learning Strategies

Once relationships have been developed and the student decision has been made to commit to the learning experience, a new category of interactive learning becomes operant within the learning experience. This new category of interactive learning is investigation. The process of working together has become natural to the classroom setting during involvement activities and teaching strategies. At this category of interactive learning, students begin the investigative process and establish rapport with one another. During the strategies and learning activities they experience at this level of interaction, a strong sense of rapport with each other and the teacher becomes evident. There comes, with the strategies and activities at this level of interaction, a sense that "we can do this together" and a willingness to get on with the tasks attendant to the process. Rigor, always a part of the learning experiences in the previous categories of invitation and involvement, becomes even more essential and evident at this investigation category of interactive learning because students have already made a felt decision to commit to the learning experience and to be a part of this ongoing process.

All seventeen strands of instruction analysis, or the science of learning, are in place during the teaching strategies and activities at this category of interactive learning. Cognition is demonstrated at the application level. This is the identification level of experience. The teacher roles are those of a moderator and resolver. Students demonstrate the roles of experimenter and investigator. As evaluators, the students and teacher begin to assess progress and process in terms of defined outcomes. Rapport is the level of motivation that is most evident at the investigation category. Discourse is shown through connection and thinking by acceptance. Creativity is experimenting and critical thinking by organizing. Detail is the dominant expression of writing at this level of interactive learning. In terms of problem solving, trying options is representative of investigation. Learning is interacting and teaching is functionalizing. Teaching is shown through making activities functional. Finally, the category of interactive learning that is exemplified here is investigation. That is what happens at this level of learning. These strands are shown through all teaching strategies at this level of interactive learning. Investigation is a dynamic category of interaction for students and the teacher.

As at every category of the taxonomy of interactive learning, there are basic goals for students to achieve. At the investigation category of interaction, these goals are designed to lead to a positive and productive work setting where students are at ease working together and see the need for individual and group success in the learning

Teaching Strategies for Investigative Interaction

Field activities/making
  connections
Applying data
Interacting/sharing/
  conferencing
Hypothesizing
Testing

experience. Having a productive work setting and a work situation that demonstrates a positive rapport are among the major goals of this category of interactive learning. These generic goals are implicit in each of the teaching–learning strategies noted for this category. In addition to these generic goals, students develop harmonious working rapport. Students support each other and the teacher in the learning process. Students investigate resources and data. Students develop a sense of belonging. Students work with the teacher as moderator to help resolve any issues or concerns. Students continue to develop and demonstrate leadership skills. Students participate actively in planning. These are the results of activities at this category of interaction. When the strategies used for instruction and learning are completed at this category of interactive learning, investigation is well established.

Within the investigation category of interaction, the roles of the students and the teacher change as does the instructional role. The teacher here serves as a moderator and resolver. The student roles are experimenter and investigator. The interactive instructional role during this category is investigative. These roles provide the frame of reference for building rapport, achieving goals, and for performing the activities, using the instructional strategies and completing the tasks associated with the learning experience. Through the use of a variety of teaching–learning activities and through the use of the five teaching strategies, students not only build rapport with each other, the process, and the teacher, but prepare themselves to move into the next level of the taxonomy of interaction—that of insight.

The five identified teaching strategies associated with the investigative category of interaction are field activities/making connections, applying data, interacting/sharing/conferencing, hypothesizing, and testing. They require higher levels of cognition, including application, analysis, synthesis, as well as some evaluation. Application, however, is the cognitive level most evident at this category of interactive learning. In terms of experiential learning, students achieve the stage of identification through the teaching–learning strategies at the investigation sequences of interaction. Some of the teaching–learning activities associated with these strategies are virtual or real field trips, data selection, retrieval, and organizing activities. Other activities could be charting events in the learning experience, conceiving and using provisional assumptions, application through observation, research, and experimenting. Students should be involved in sharing their learning through writing, discussion, demonstration, and contests. Reporting to each other, demonstrating learned skills, and trying and testing provisional conditional hypotheses in multiple situations are additional activities. Activities listed for the investigation level of interactive learning can be used. There are many other teaching–learning activities that could be associated with the teaching strategies used at this category of the taxonomy.

These activities can be used with any or all of the five identified teaching strategies associated with this level of interactive learning. Other teaching strategies can be used at this level of interactive learning, including those listed for earlier categories of the taxonomy. The teacher and the students use only those learning activities and teaching strategies necessary to the learning process and the projected sequence toward planned outcomes. This context of functional use of activities and teaching–learning strategies remains constant through this category of interactive learning as well as into the next categories. It should be noted that as the students use the teaching–learning strategies at this category of interactive learning, they show increasing intrinsic motivation and demonstrate a felt need to participate in planning their learning experiences. As this felt need is demonstrated, the teacher provides more opportunities for students to have leadership and planning experiences. The teacher roles as moderator and resolver help make this apparent. Students show more overt leadership as investigators while the teacher's role in leadership becomes more covert. Leadership and planning roles have begun to change from those exhibited at invitation and involvement. The first of the teaching–learning strategies discussed is field activities/making connections.

FIELD ACTIVITIES/MAKING CONNECTIONS

This is a teaching–learning strategy with many dimensions. At this category of interactive learning and during this teaching–learning strategy as well as corollary strategies used at investigation, students begin to show an emotional and intellectual identification with the learning experience. They have chosen to continue with the learning experience and are consciously involved in the strategies and activities associated with this level of interactive learning. Their decision to identify with the experience and make it their own has been both emotional and intellectual. Here in this teaching–learning strategy and others used in this category, they identify experientially with the learning process. They are experimenting, organizing, and going into detail about the information they have learned and new data they encounter within this strategy. Within this particular strategy students become involved in real field activities both on and off campus. Through the use of technology, they can become involved in virtual field activities. Students can also be involved in field experiences through the Internet, e-mail, telephone, written and personal communication, and videoconferencing. With visitations and field trips both on campus and campus, students can become involved in a variety of field activities designed to broaden the experience and to accept different points of views and interact with a variety of resources.

By the use of this strategy, students can make connections with people, resources, and ideas. Their ability to apply what they have learned is broadened. They can gain new ideas of how others see the concepts and ideas they are studying. Much interaction and group settings need to occur during this strategy. Students need to interact with each other, with new materials, and with human resources. They can have these interactions within the classroom, within their groups, and within settings outside the classroom. The use of this strategy can open the world to the students and help them make connections and communicate with others. They need this strategy to enhance and enrich their learning experience.

> *By the use of this strategy, students can make connections with people, resources, and ideas.*

Students at this level of the taxonomy of interactive learning develop an investigative sense in which they begin to study materials more carefully; they start to pose questions indicating higher level thinking to each other and about the materials and their field experiences. They also build questions for the human resources they have encountered in the field. They have these interactions within group settings in the classroom and with other human resources. As they are involved in this strategy, the students will usually demonstrate a need to get together in groups to discuss what they are learning and to reflect on their field experiences. They can use a number of group formats to reflect on what they have learned and to apply it to the learning experience. Field experiences provide a link connecting the students with the material and resources they have encountered and allow them to communicate with each other about those experiences. The teacher roles as moderator and resolver continue to be essential as issues and problems are discussed and resolved. During this strategy, there continues to be an expression of focused interaction among the students and with resources. The teacher needs to participate with the students to challenge them, to prod them to explore materials, to identify ideas, and to make connections with various resources and people. The teacher needs to be familiar with the materials and with the kinds of information the students are reviewing and studying. The teacher expects to have the students emerge from this teaching–learning experience having made connections within the whole spectrum of materials they are studying.

At the same time, students must explore and review materials and check resources. Students may do it in large groups, small groups, triads, pairs, or individually. In any case, there needs to be consistent and cooperative interaction among students. While engaged in this teaching–learning strategy, students should be able to identify how their activities and interactions relate to identified objectives and outcomes. They need to see how they are moving toward the purposes and anticipated goals of the activity. Students need to relate to the long-range outcomes of the unit of study. The information they have learned, and the connections they have made, should help them understand that what they have done will lead them toward the planned and anticipated outcomes both short and long term.

The student roles as experimenter and investigator become more apparent and evident during this teaching–learning strategy. Students respond, review, evaluate, and make connections through their interaction with each other, with the teacher, and with their resources. Students need to understand that through this strategy they need to interact, do the necessary research and review, and assess and evaluate what they have done. They focus on the selection of data and the retrieval of data appropriate to the needs of the learning sequence. The purpose for this teaching–learning strategy is to solidify student involvement by identification with the learning experience. Another purpose is to make connections with people and with resources. It is during this and other strategies at this category of interactive learning that the students really begin to demonstrate intrinsic motivation. They become more closely associated with and involved in the process of learning and completing the experience. They become involved, initiate the investigative process, and then begin to gain insights into direction, process, and ultimate outcomes. Motivation, as a process, is beginning to be more and more recognizable as intrinsic among the students and less extrinsic on the part of the teacher. The teacher's roles as moderator and resolver and the student's roles as experimenter and investigator mesh well with this teaching–learning strategy. Students begin, at this category of the taxonomy, to demonstrate more participation in the leadership of the learning experience.

APPLYING DATA

The next teaching–learning strategy at the investigation category of interactive learning is the application of data and applying those data to real situations and issues students are dealing with in terms of the learning experience. Further, students need to be able to apply the data to their own lives and to the community in which they live. The students have had a series of interactions with the material and with a variety of resources. They have made personal and intellectual connections with these resources and materials. Students have also begun to investigate and determine for themselves the process through the total learning sequence that they need to follow. They have become associated and involved with the learning experience. Leadership and self-motivation are beginning to emerge. The activities within this strategy demonstrate their stronger leadership role in learning. Along with this growing leadership role comes the meaning and value of what they have learned as well as its application to themselves and their real life.

With this teaching–learning strategy, the students use, assess, and interpret data through observation and experimentation, through recording data, and through explaining data. Students now begin to organize the data into clusters, categories, and/ or usable sets. They continue to work with their resources, but in a somewhat different context. In their field activities they have gathered and investigated the data and made connections. Now students need to organize these data into usable structures so they can further apply the data to the learning process to which they are committed and to real situations. Not only do they need to organize the data, they need to be able to explain the selection of the data and how they have been organized and categorized. They also need to verbalize and share how the data can be applied to a variety of instructional activities in which they are involved and toward the expected outcomes of the experience. As this happens, students take a more active role in telling why they have selected the data and how they are going to use it. Using this teaching strategy, students learn why they are dealing with the data in certain ways. The students also need to be projecting some of the possible or now more probable outcomes of the learning sequence. Students use, apply, and experiment with the data. They begin to interpret data and, if needed, reorganize the data into different sets, clusters, or categories. The teacher, as moderator

Teacher Roles as Moderator and Resolver

Teachers must ensure that the students have learned the necessary review skills
   and organizational skills needed to work with the materials and resources.
The teacher must allow the students to assume an active leadership role in
   considering how to apply and use the materials.
It requires keen insight into student work and an understanding of when to
   allow the students to assume increased management of the learning sequence.

and resolver, interacts with students, offering suggestions, making observations, and encouraging students to apply data in different and/or unique ways. The teacher must have a strong understanding and knowledge about the resources the students are using and be able to work with students so that they can use the resources efficiently and effectively and within the context of their identified objectives and goals.

There are two components associated with the teacher roles as moderator and resolver. First, teachers must ensure that the students have learned the necessary review skills and organizational skills needed to work with the materials and resources. The teacher should also help students resolve issues about how to organize, categorize, and manage those materials into workable structures consistent with the learning experience. Second, the teacher must allow the students to assume an active leadership role in considering how to apply and use the materials. The teacher needs to have the students participate fully in the consideration of direction for the learning experience and have some freedom in deciding how to apply the materials and ideas they have learned to new settings. The roles of the teacher as moderator and resolver are ones requiring both keen insight into student work and an understanding of when to allow the students to assume more and management of the learning sequence.

In terms of this teaching–learning strategy, students are becoming increasingly self-motivated. They are at the acceptance level of the thinking sequence, the interactive level of learning, and what they have learned has been functionalized through the roles of the teacher. Students are beginning to assume more and self-direction and leadership in their efforts toward achievement of what has now become their objectives and their goals in terms of the learning experience. The teacher, as moderator and resolver, helps students negotiate the new learning circumstances and the new processes and problems that begin to emerge. Students have, through their involvement with this strategy, begun to use and apply data in a variety of learning settings and through identified activities associated with the strategy. They are involved and they are investigating resources. They have shown evidence that they are ready for another learning strategy.

INTERACTING/SHARING/CONFERENCING

Once students have begun applying data, the need for activities engaging students in interacting, sharing, and conferencing begins to emerge. It becomes necessary in the learning sequence to plan for a specific time and strategy where students have the opportunity and are encouraged to discuss, interact, share, and conference with each other. That is what this strategy is all about. During this strategy students exchange ideas, points of view, and opinions about the materials they have explored and applied. Through their exchange of ideas and perspectives, they continue to identify more emotionally and intellectually with the learning experience in which they are now deeply involved and toward the prospective outcomes they expect to achieve. The exchange of ideas results in more involvement, increasing investigation, and the beginnings of insight. The interaction consists of three components. Those components are interaction

The exchange of ideas results in more involvement, increasing investigation, and the beginnings of insight.

between teacher and students, between students and their peers individually and in groups, as well as interaction with materials and resources. Interaction with resources can also include human resources in person or through distance learning and video- or telephone conferencing.

The interaction, sharing, and conferencing necessitates questioning, information giving and receiving, clarification of information, and expressing ideas, points of view, and opinions. The purpose of the strategy is to review the data and information gained from previous learning and to collate them with new information and resources into useful organizational structures that will lead toward the development of hypotheses. This is accomplished through a variety of group formats focused on discussion, organization, and sharing ideas. In any learning process there comes a time when students need, in a group setting, to interact to bring out group ideas, discuss structures, data, and resources, and come to a consensus. This is the time and this is the learning strategy.

The use of this strategy also illuminates sequencing and organization; it enables students to begin developing hypotheses. Interaction, sharing, and conferencing used by students in the process of interactive learning serves two purposes. First, it allows the students to report to each other, share what they know, indicate where they are in the learning sequence, and tell how they feel about what they are doing. Second, the use of this strategy can cause the students to process the information and to move themselves toward the development of hypotheses. Through the use of this strategy, students are interacting together, investigating materials, and gaining new insights into their resources. The use of this strategy can also help students understand and conceptualize other levels of learning and categories in the interactive process. Students can get new ideas and additional information from each other and can discuss their own ideas, perspectives, and feelings. Students, through their interactive sharing and conferencing, can arrive at some areas of consensus and can begin the process of thinking about hypotheses and testing those hypotheses.

Interaction, sharing, and conferencing as a strategy involving dialogue and discussion can take a number forms and used in a number of contexts. It can be done in a large group, in small groups, in committees, in *ad hoc* groups, in triads, and in pairs. The teacher moderates the discussions and the interactions. The teacher does this by asking appropriate questions, helping students keep outcomes in mind, helping them interact positively and in context, and helping students establish a means and format for sharing and sequencing. The teacher, as leader, helps resolve issues and problems. The teacher can also help students begin to think about specific components of the meaning of the material and resources. Through the discussion of value and meaning, students are helped in crafting and making tentative statements and hypotheses about what they have learned. Interacting, sharing, and conferencing needs careful teacher preparation and planning as well as active student involvement in the planning of organization and sequencing activities.

Conditions and parameters need to be set for this strategy. The teacher and the students should work these out together. Timing is important, and both students and teachers need to be aware of time constraints and focused on the purpose of the strategy and the projected outcomes. Students tend to become intensely involved during this strategy and their interaction enhances the investigative level of the interactive learning process. The outcomes from this strategy lead the students toward building provisional assumptions and even tentative hypotheses about the information and the data they share with each other in this interacting/sharing/conferencing process. They are beginning to gain insight into the issues and areas of need they have identified. The students, as they become more involved in this process, begin to assume organizational leadership and to take charge of directions toward achieving successfully the projected outcomes of the learning experience. Students are also identifying with the learning sequence, the objectives, and the goals of the process. The teacher, as an arranger, as stage setter, as moderator, and as resolver, senses needs and arranges opportunities for interaction, discussion, sharing, and conferencing. The teacher also continues to ask probing questions to generate new perspectives and direction for students. Although this strategy is presented here, variations of it may occur later in the taxonomy of interactive learning. As each of the strategies in this investigation level of interaction emerges, students assume more responsibility for learning. The teacher roles as moderator and resolver are absolutely essential. These roles, however, are becoming more covert than overt in terms of students taking a greater part in the planning process. The successful teacher understands the investigative instructional role and personal teaching roles. The teacher works with the students in encouraging more student leadership and in moderating the process and resolving issues. As this learning strategy progresses, the students begin to make provisional assumptions and to develop ideas and hypotheses about the material. It is at this point that the next strategy, that of hypothesizing, begins to become a part of the learning sequence.

HYPOTHESIZING

The use of this teaching–learning strategy involves students in conceiving and using provisional assumptions as a basis for reasoning. Hypothesizing also engages the students in working with those assumptions. They can use their hypotheses to predict outcomes and new activities. These directional predictions are based on their provisional assumptions and initial hypotheses. The use of this strategy is a logical and sequential outcome of the interactive sharing and conferencing strategy students have previously completed. This teaching–learning strategy emerges as the students begin to develop preliminary and provisional assumptions about the material and start to focus and assess the viability of those assumptions and how they could impact further progress. Information from the interactive and conferencing strategy is reviewed and students begin to investigate, ruminate, and study various components of the materials and make assumptions about them. They develop those assumptions into hypotheses and make the material functional for the projected outcomes of the learning experience.

Hypothesizing is usually the result of a learning setting where it is anticipated and planned. By definition, hypothesizing is the conceiving and using provisionally accepted assumptions as the basis for reasoning, testing, and actions. Hypothesizing is a logical extension for student work in reviewing data, interacting with the data, sharing and

conferencing together, and building those provisional ideas and assumptions about the data. Hypothesizing is an essential step in the process of motivation. It is through this strategy that students begin to gain real insight into what they have reviewed, studied, discussed, and learned. Here students begin to posit possible actions, directions, processes, and solutions toward projected outcomes. By the use of this strategy, students can make assumptions and develop hypotheses based on data they have examined and the information they have studied and discussed.

Hypothesizing can be as simple as a speculative "what if" or as complex as the identification, analysis, and determination of the covariance of specific variables. Hypotheses can be expressed in many ways. Hypotheses can be developed creatively in the form of a picture, a diagram, a model, or a composition. Students can work with these created items in hypothesizing about them, linking them to what they have learned, and projecting outcomes if the hypotheses are viable. They can also hypothesize about how ideas and concepts relate to the course of study and to their real life. Students can think about them and come to conclusions or consensus about them. Any expression of student work that demonstrates a hypothesis is a dimension of this teaching strategy. The teacher, in planning for this strategy, needs to be knowledgeable of the many possible variables in the process of the development of hypotheses. These variables and the concept of developing and testing hypotheses need to be discussed with the students so they understand the process and can develop their hypotheses within a learning context where they will be used.

The teacher, as moderator and resolver, needs to interact with students so that they can understand the implications of their hypotheses, the variables involved, and how they might test those hypotheses. Students, through interaction with each other and with the teacher, not only begin to understand the meaning and implications of their hypotheses, but begin to investigate them, understand the variables, and to follow the meaning and the implications as far as possible. When they have followed the implications as far as possible, students can then finalize their hypotheses in any of the forms mentioned in this section, in written form, or in other appropriate forms. When these steps are accomplished, the students have learned how to develop hypotheses, have developed some of their own, and are readied for testing their hypotheses. These are the steps leading toward the next strategy at this rapport level of motivation. When they have completed all of the processes within this strategy, they not only have developed their hypotheses, but they are thoroughly committed to the learning experience and are ready to test their developed hypotheses. They are now ready to test their hypotheses in a variety of ways. Hypothesizing is a strategy where students are making connections, experimenting with ideas and concepts, interacting with each other, and assessing ways of developing hypotheses. It is a creative and interesting time for students.

TESTING

When hypotheses are finalized and fully developed by the students, they need to be tried out in multiple situations. That is the nature and the expectation central to this teaching–learning strategy. Students have already developed hypotheses that fit within the context of the learning sequence. The testing process is designed to confirm these hypotheses, to make necessary changes within them, or to reject them when they have been tested. The first step in the testing process is to develop criteria for testing the hypotheses. Developing criteria simply means how and why to test the hypotheses, including the steps needed to complete the process. This needs to be done carefully and thoroughly. Both teacher and students should participate in the development of the criteria for testing hypotheses.

The roles of the teacher are very important as this strategy develops. The teacher, at this point in the learning process, has learned and knows well the strengths and the limitations of the students and how to work within them. The students have accepted and demonstrated real involvement in the learning experience and a stronger leadership role within the learning experience. Furthermore, they have investigated the materials, gained insight into them, and developed hypotheses. The teacher needs to work with the students through interaction and instruction to help them develop the criteria for testing. Students may need to further investigate a variety of formats and organizations for developing criteria. It is the task of the teacher to assist the students in identifying those formats and organizations. Students can then select the formats, organizations, and sequences they want to use. In addition, the students, as experimenters and investigators, can then build the criteria according to their own needs and direction based on what they have learned and what they have hypothesized.

Interactive learning, in group settings, is very important in this strategy as students and teachers establish criteria and begin the testing program. Testing hypotheses is a rigorous process that engages the students in a variety of skills. Among these skills is demonstrating good working rapport with peers, the ability to analyze material, develop syntheses, and evaluate through established criteria. Students, using these skills, can then make choices and draw conclusions about each of the hypotheses they have developed. They may confirm and accept some, make changes in some, and even reject some that fail to meet the criteria established by the students and the teacher. As noted above, testing is a very rigorous process. It is likewise a pertinent and necessary step through which students must progress to make the learning sequence even more viable for them. It is through this teaching–learning strategy that the students develop a sense of personal accomplishment so necessary for motivation and successful interaction. With this and other strategies at the rapport category, the students have come to value their learning and apply them to their lives. They begin to assess its worth to them. The students begin, through this strategy and preceding strategies, to learn and hear their own voice in the learning sequence. They students have developed and used skills necessary to the final achievement of the outcomes of the learning sequence. When this is accomplished, the students have completed the investigation level strategies of interactive learning and are ready to move to the insight category of interactive learning and use teaching–learning strategies associated with that level of interaction. They have achieved the goals of this category of the taxonomy.

> *Testing hypotheses is a rigorous process that engages the students in a variety of skills.*

SUMMARY

With the strategies in which they have participated at the investigation category of interactive learning, the students have learned through interaction with the teacher, with each other, and with a wide range of resources to value the experience in which they are involved and to which they have made a strong commitment. Experientially, students have identified with learning experience, investigated materials and resources, and gained real insights through hypothesizing and testing. Cognitively, students have used all seven levels of cognition. Application, analysis, synthesis, and evaluation have been used with application and analysis, the most apparent. Students have become much more involved in the learning process and have begun assuming more planning and leadership roles as their strong commitment motivates them toward achieving the outcomes and objectives of the learning sequence. Student skills as learner and leader have greatly improved.

The teacher, through interaction, challenge, and support, has helped students come to value what has engaged them in their learning activities and what they have accomplished through working together. Each of the strategies used within this category of interactive learning has helped students develop a strong interactive working rapport with each other, with the teacher, and with the learning experience. At this investigation level of interactive learning, students have become deeply and strongly committed to the experience and have a vested personal, emotional, intellectual, and group interest in achieving the projected and now more clearly defined outcomes of the learning sequence.

Through the five strategies at this investigation level of interaction, a cooperative and comfortable rapport has been established; both students and teacher have found that they can work together to accomplish what needs to be done. They have made connections and they have communicated well. Students have been experimenters. They have organized materials and have written in detail. In testing hypotheses they have tried options and have accepted some. From field activities through the development of hypotheses and the testing of those hypotheses, there has been consistent interaction by the students in a variety of interactive settings including cooperative groups. Although interaction remains necessary throughout the learning sequence, it is of great importance in this category of the taxonomy. That is why one learning strategy has been specifically identified as interacting/sharing/conferencing. Once rapport has been established through the use of all of these strategies and the teaching–learning activities associated with them, the students have achieved the goals for them at the investigation category. They have functionalized the information and have totally identified with the learning experience. When all these things come together, students are ready for the next category of interactive learning, that of insight.

Activities

Activities here focus on the learning process at investigation. Each activity should be done in small groups and reported to the total class. Written and oral reports can be expected. Again, the students need to use this book as a resource for developing their responses to designated activities. Other references can also be used. All activities should be discussed within the small group and then presented to the whole group.

1. Discourse is important at every category of the taxonomy of interactive learning. How is it manifested at investigation? How has discourse changed from invitation through involvement to investigation?

2. Identification is the experiential level at investigation. Through what process do students identify with the learning experience? Interact with your group about this process and develop a report on how it happens.

3. How do students connect with each other through a working rapport? What would you see in a classroom where students demonstrate strong working rapport with each other? What teaching–learning strategies are most compatible with rapport at the investigation category? Explain.

4. What group formats would you use during the interacting/sharing/conferencing teaching–learning strategy? Why would you use these group structures and how would they be evidenced? Discuss this in your group and prepare a report for your peers.

5. At the investigation category "students are experimenters." How is this student role fulfilled in each of the teaching–learning strategies at investigation?

6. Identify at least four learning activities that could be used with the teaching–learning strategies at this category of interactive learning. How would you evaluate these activities? What evidence of success with each learning activity would you look for in each of the teaching–learning strategies? Prepare a report of your findings.

Insight Teaching–Learning Strategies

Insight is a category of interactive learning that emerges from a continuum that begins with invitation, continues through involvement, and develops into investigation. When students have established a strong working rapport with each other, the teacher, and the resources, and they have identified with the learning sequence, they have completed the investigation level of interactive learning. They are ready for the insight category of interactive learning. When students have completed the rapport category of teaching–learning strategies and activities, they are ready for the next category of interactive learning. They have demonstrated a felt need to continue through the process to the next category, that of insight. Insight means internalization and thus becomes the emergent evidence of achievement and internalization. Through the teaching–learning strategies and the activities that students use in this category of interactive learning, students and teacher demonstrate growing respect for each other. Students have learned to work well with each other; there is a growing mutual respect among them. There is also an emerging respect for the teacher and for what they have accomplished in their studies a well as in their work together and with the teacher.

At the insight category of motivation, the roles of the teacher become those of a sustainer and adviser. The roles and the very words denote respect and support the gaining of insight. The student roles at this level of motivation are those of an extender and creator. These two roles imply the extension of learned skills and activities into additional contexts of meaning and function and the creation of products consistent with the learning experience. The instructional role in this category of the taxonomy is applicative; again, this connotes student appreciation for the learning sequence and its application in the learning context as well as in the real world. There is a focused emphasis on valuing in this category of the taxonomy of motivation. Valuing, in this context, means valuing classmates, valuing the materials being learned, and valuing the contributions of the teacher and other human resources. Teaching is valuing what is being learned; in this category of interactive learning, teaching and learning become the applicative roles of not only the teacher but of the students themselves as they learn from each other, applying what they have learned to new conditions and new settings. The subcategories within this level of interactive learning are continuity, caring, and creating. These subcategories themselves are clearly and directly related to the strategies and activities associated with respect. The subcategories also connote valuing. The

Creative Expressions of Respect

Writing
Art
Music
Self-expression

affective, experiential, and attitudinal dimensions of learning are very important at this level of interactive learning.

At this category of interactive learning, the goals demonstrate increasing respect for students, teacher, and resources. They include both affective and cognitive respect. Cognitively, students use synthesis and evaluation. Synthesis is the prime level of cognition used. Students will demonstrate esteem for each other, the teacher, and themselves. Students demonstrate a sense of confidence and personal self-esteem. Students achieve most or all of the objectives of the course of study. Students conceptualize the roles of the teacher as sustainer and advisor, working closely with the teacher. Students create products and summarize what they have learned. Students realize how they have changed through the course of study and how those changes have come about. Students assume a very strong leadership and planning role. These goals are encapsulated by the teaching–learning strategies and activities at this insight category of the taxonomy. Students at this category of interactive learning are able to begin selecting solutions to problems.

There are a number of activities associated with this level of interactive learning. The core purpose of the activities here is to build and demonstrate respect. Among the many activities associated with respect are having students describe, clarify, and analyze situations and systems. Students determine and evaluate similarities and differences. There is discussion and group work as well as questioning and thinking at all levels of cognition, including analysis, synthesis, and evaluation levels of thinking. Students use data and learning in a whole spectrum of practical situations. There are creative expressions where students demonstrate personal styles through writing, art, music, and self-expression. At this level of motivation, there are activities in content areas such as mathematics, writing, poetry, science, and manipulative materials (construction). Students become involved in interactive studies and discussions for advanced learning and to solve problems. At this category of interactive learning, they select solutions and internalize what they have learned. They also can develop simulations and other activities requiring originality and synthesizing.

During this category of insight, students have internalized the learning experience. Their activities and learning experiences have impacted them in terms of their attitudes, skills, and behaviors. Because of this, they can be encouraged to become actively involved in individual and group exercises and activities to develop new uses for products and for techniques that employ data and information learned. At this category of interactive learning there is almost always a review of the learning process and some effort toward determining future directions, needs, and trends. Panel discussions to present ideas and perspectives are used. Students do probing activities, in-depth studies, "behind the scenes" investigation, and research. Activities are recreated using new learning and new experiences. Students engage in media development, point-in-time activities, and simulation and role-playing activities. Various methods and activities are used to provide opportunities to display and express new learning, skills, and behaviors. The development of games or simulations in which the emphasis is on strategy and learning are other possible activities. Use of these and other activities will enhance the building of respect for each other, for the teacher, and for what students have learned. These teaching–learning activities promote the use of ideas, feelings, behaviors, and skills that result in the building of respect among the students. Throughout the use of these teaching–learning activities, there comes a recognizable sense of continuity, caring, and creating. These are demonstrated by the students through the building of respect for each other, for the teacher, and for the concepts and materials learned. Students begin to modify their thinking. Once respect and insight have been established, students are ready to move to the final level of interactive learning. These teaching–learning activities are associated with the five teaching strategies for this level of motivation. Many of them can be used with all the teaching strategies, some with two or three and some with only one or two. The teaching strategies at this level of motivation are skill reinforcement, re-creation, simulation and role-playing, analysis through comparing and contrasting, and summarization.

SKILL REINFORCEMENT

Students have already learned much about the materials studied and have learned skills associated with them. They have come to the point where they are beginning to apply and internalize what they have learned. This teaching–learning strategy is an important step in that application and internalization process. At this category of the taxonomy of interactive learning, and through this strategy, the students are reinforcing learned skills through a series of teaching–learning activities, some of which have been mentioned earlier. Skill reinforcement is an important strategy for students at the insight category of interactive learning. Hypotheses have been tested and students have accepted those that have particular meaning to them in terms of the learning process and course of study. They have acquired identified skills related to the focus of the study. Skill reinforcement involves a deepening understanding and internalizing of those acquired skills, concepts, and attitudes. Students, using this strategy, need to know those skills, concepts, and attitudes so well that they can use them in a variety of contexts and in many different ways. They need to internalize them. The use of this strategy will help that internalization to happen. Students are enabled to apply and reinforce their newly acquired behaviors and skills through different sets of activities, thus broadening the context of their skills and honing them through their use in many contexts. Sometimes these skills and behaviors are expressed creatively, sometimes through problem solving, and sometimes in terms of critical thinking. Individual skill reinforcement can be done, but more frequently skill reinforcement is accomplished through interactive group work.

> *Students are enabled to apply and reinforce their newly acquired behaviors and skills through different sets of activities, thus broadening the context of their skills and honing them through their use in many contexts.*

The teacher, as sustainer and adviser, has an important role during this strategy. The students have accepted their greater role in the leadership and management of the learning experience, and it is the teacher who sustains the students in their activities and becomes their adviser during this and other strategies at this category of the taxonomy. This is essential to student learning. As adviser and sustainer, the teacher keeps the students focused and ensures creativity and direction. The student roles as extender and creator fit well with the teacher roles as sustainer and adviser. Extender equates with transfer. Creator equates with doing and building something new. Both roles correlate well with the respect level of motivation. The instructional role is applicative and this role also correlates closely with the activities and expectations of this insight level of interaction. Students, in terms of discourse, are considering and choosing ideas for change. They are completing products and are able to generalize about what they are learning.

The teacher understands the need of the students to transfer learning from one context to another and sustains, supports, and guides the students in extending their learning and insights to new contexts and to new levels of application, analysis, synthesis, and evaluation. Skill reinforcement and transfer require higher level thinking skills; this teaching–learning strategy accentuates that requirement. The teacher needs to help the students discover and use creative ways to apply and extend their learning. It is not always enough to simply do the activity only once. Students need to be involved in different creative activities, frequently more than once, to ensure that the reinforcement of skills is accomplished. When this is done, students can express those internalized skills in different applications and in new contexts. The ability of the students to express and use skills they have learned increases their motivation and insight. They want to use them and to continue to apply them wherever appropriate. Students, when using this strategy, demonstrate a felt need to extend their learning and skills in different ways and in different settings and contexts. Students can take pride in what they have done and what they have learned; they show it through this teaching–learning strategy.

The reinforcement of skills is a teaching–learning strategy that can improve student self-esteem. Reinforcement can help them recognize what they have accomplished and what yet remains to have done. Through this strategy and others at the insight category of interactive learning, students begin to value even more what they have learned and how they and others can use those learning and skills. Recognition of the utility of what they have learned is important to all strategies at the insight level of interaction. Students can develop values and meanings and begin to internalize how these values and meanings relate to them and to other contexts. Skill reinforcement, as used by students and teachers, can clearly demonstrate the roles of teacher as sustainer and adviser and the student roles as extenders and creators. Skill reinforcement can help students to come to consensus and conclusions about the content they have studied and the ways it can be used. The teacher does two things during this strategy. The teacher provides, in conjunction with the students, an opportunity for them to extend their skills and learning in a wide array of contexts. The teacher makes suggestions, identifies possible contexts, and discusses with students some of the conditions and issues in the various contexts. Students then make the choices about application and contexts based on their own learning and what the teacher has discussed with them. The teacher then supports, sustains, and advises the students on their decisions about the extension of skills and about the contexts to be applied. The teacher may advise changes or bring new ideas for students to consider.

Both students and teacher will recognize this as an important and viable strategy at this category of interactive learning. The use of this strategy emphasizes the three subcategories of continuity, caring, and creativity. The student use of many contexts for reinforcement emphasizes both creativity and continuity. The interactive component and the student sense of success emphasize the valuing and caring dimension of the strategy. When these have been accomplished, another teaching–learning strategy can be used.

RE-CREATION

This teaching–learning strategy, although in some ways similar to skill reinforcement, has a specific role in the interactive taxonomy at this level of insight. Through the use of this strategy, students assume a stronger and more evident leadership role in the direction of their learning experience. They have identified new contexts for their learned skills and have tried them out. Now they are ready to review and study the processes for the meaning, value, and development. Students are doing this by their own choices based on prior learning experiences and strategies. They have assumed major leadership responsibility during this strategy. Through this strategy the students are expected to re-create the learning experience in thought, verbal expression, written communication, or media expressions. Students individually, or in a number of group formats, construct and re-create the components of the learning experience. In many instances, students can do this without the specific direction of the teacher, who acts only as sustainer and adviser. This strategy both enhances the student's appreciation and valuing of the learning experience as well as provides leadership opportunities and a reflective re-creation of what they have done. This reflective re-creation, a looking back and a looking forward, is an essential component of process assessment and evaluation. It is during this strategy that students assess the process for effectiveness and efficiency. They talk about changes they could make and successes they experienced. The teacher role as leader, while much less overt than in previous strategies, is to advise and help create a climate in which the students can express creatively their own re-creation of the process they have experienced and project it toward dissemination.

This reflective re-creation, a looking back and a looking forward, is an essential component of process assessment and evaluation.

Art, music, PowerPoint presentations, and creative writing are some of the formats students can use in re-creation and thus be enabled to critically examine their learning process. This is a time for the teacher to encourage creative expression as well as critical analysis. Some inventive ways to re-create the experience could be a mural, a collage, or a multimedia program. Some other ways to re-create the experience could be in a thoughtful written analysis of what they have achieved, or a focused discussion about the process along with a review of the issues and problems they dealt with along the way. These are but some of the ways students can effectively re-create their experience. The use of this strategy expands the meaning and value of the learned skills and strongly motivates the student's sense of success and accomplishment. Re-creation provides for the students an evaluative, reflective, and process review of their efforts and their achievement. Re-creating and reviewing processes are very important to students.

Demonstrating their learned skills in new ways and in creative exercises is also a very positive experience for students. Sharing, discussing, and interaction are important during the use of this strategy. The teacher, as sustainer and adviser, can work with some students who may not be at the level of other students in reviewing the learning experience or in creatively expressing their learned skills. Students can also help each other attain the level of analysis and expression needed within this learning strategy. The cooperative, positive interaction of students with each other and with the teacher can greatly enhance the valuing of the experience and the creative expression of the learned skills. Valuing is an intrinsic component of this strategy. Although there is much interaction and cooperative grouping for creative expression, there is also a personal dimension to this strategy. Each student needs to feel confident in what has been learned and in the review and re-creation of the experience, as well as in the creative expression of that learning. Each student becomes involved in this strategy in a unique personal way as well as in working with other students and the teacher. The role of the student as extender and creator is particularly apparent at this level of interaction. Re-creation, although interactive in nature, is also a demonstration of student internalization of learned behaviors, attitudes, or skills. The strategy can emerge from testing hypotheses or from the activities used at the skill reinforcement category of interactive learning. Re-creation is a strategy that is effective for the individual student as well as for the whole group. It is a strong step in the process of interaction and it provides the basis for student acceptance of more leadership in planning and direction for the skills learned.

Although we have emphasized the reflective dimension of re-creation, there is also a projective dimension. Every activity in this strategy both reflects and projects. Through reflection, students realize they have not yet completed the entirety of the learning experience and there is yet more to do. Students not only reflect, they project activities to be implemented for dissemination. This is the spirit of reflective re-creation and should be integral to all the activities of this learning strategy.

SIMULATION AND ROLE-PLAYING

This teaching–learning strategy is one that students need to experience as they internalize the learning and skills they have achieved and demonstrate more and stronger ownership of the instructional process and sequence. This strategy involves structured role-playing and the overt demonstration of learned skills and the interpretation of roles. Earlier in the learning experience students were involved in unstructured role-playing. At this level of interactive learning, students are involved in structured role-playing and simulation. In consultation with the teacher, the learning context for role-playing and simulation is creatively and interactively developed by the students. At this point in motivation, the students have demonstrated readiness, developed relationships, established rapport, and earned respect. In these steps through interaction, they have developed confidence in themselves and confidence in each other. The use of this simulation and role-playing strategy can enhance their confidence even more.

Simulation vs. Role-Playing

Simulation: job- or task-oriented
Role-Playing: relationship- and behavior-oriented

The development of the simulations and the role-playing formats requires creativity as well as the cognitive skills of application, analysis, synthesis, and evaluation. The development of simulation and role-playing also requires consistency in effort as well as support and advice from the teacher. By now in the learning experience a level of trust and respect has been built so that students are prepared cohesively and cooperatively to create these simulations and role-playing scenarios. The development of these formats demands consistent and cooperative interaction among students, with the teacher involved as sustainer and adviser. Once students have developed the formats, roles are selected, tasks are defined, and students are ready to become involved, the simulation or role-playing scenario is complete. Although higher levels of cognition are essential to this strategy, students also need to use affective and experiential skills. Attitudes have been changed and learning has become internalized. Role-playing is primarily affective in its orientation while simulation has a stronger cognitive skill orientation. Role-playing has a stronger focus on human relationships and interaction. Situations in role-playing tend to be more open-ended.

Simulation references a focus on interaction and roles in a specific setting with more defined skill parameters. Simulation is more job or task oriented, while role-playing is more relationship and behaviorally oriented. Role-playing and simulation can become important activities through the interactive process. Students develop them, use them, and cherish them. Through the use of this strategy, students overtly demonstrate their understanding and internalization of the skills they have learned. The use of the strategy allows them to creatively, and in a public context, demonstrate what they have learned and how they value it. Its use allows students to also become much more comfortable and self-assured with what they have learned and accomplished. Simulation and role-playing are much more sophisticated than the unstructured role-playing used at the insight category of interaction. The purpose for simulation and role-playing differs from the unstructured role-playing strategy. The earlier strategy was used as a basis for beginning the process of reviewing and studying data and identifying learning needs. At this level of interactive learning, role-playing and simulation are designed so that students can demonstrate to each other and even to others what they have learned and how well they understand and have internalized the learning. Unstructured role-playing is an exploration for furthering the learning process. Simulation and structured role-playing are demonstrations of what has been learned and how well the skills, attitudes, or behaviors have been learned. Students usually enjoy these activities both in terms of the creative expression from preparing them and from participation in the activities. They allow for a wide variety of personal and role expression. This strategy, like others at this level of interactive learning, is also projective. Students become aware both reflectively and consciously of the need for completing the learning process through dissemination.

The teacher roles as sustainer and adviser are integral here, not only in the planning but also in the creation and preparation of the simulations and the role-playing. The teacher roles are also important in the evaluating of the simulations and the role-playing. The teacher advises, supports, and suggests, but it is the students who create, develop, and express the simulations and roles. The teacher sustains their efforts and helps them through the creative development, sometimes with strong advice where necessary. The teacher also has a key role in working with the students in evaluating the roles. The teacher can help enable the students to assess and evaluate their work. Students will carry much of the burden for assessment and evaluation, but the teacher is key to successful assessment and evaluation. Evaluations can involve discussion and continuing interaction between teacher and students, but the primary role belongs to the students. The teacher can suggest direction and follow-up activities, but again, the students make the final choices. Through role-playing, students can simulate particular roles, sequences of activities, and problem situations. They can, using simulation, demonstrate identified behaviors related to a particular role, a set of activities, or problem resolution.

Games and gaming may well be involved in simulations. Students usually enjoy these activities. Whether it is role-playing, simulation, or a gaming situation, students know the roles and what is needed to express those roles. The teacher roles are not only to support the students, but also to ensure that the role-playing and simulation are consistent with the learning experience and with this category of interactive learning. The teacher must observe the role-play and the simulation very carefully to make sure that the students have expressed in their role-playing and simulation a consistency with the skills learned. The simulations and role-playing also need to demonstrate that the students have definitely internalized the skills, attitudes, and learning they have completed. Successful simulation and role-playing are key activities in the continuity of building respect. Continuity, caring, and creating are also essential elements in this strategy. The interaction following the role-playing is critical for the students and teacher as they assess and evaluate what they have created and how it reflects what they have learned. Assessment and evaluation also provide assurance that objectives and expectations have been met and that direction for the next steps and for the next teaching–learning strategies in the interactive instructional sequence is being developed. When direction occurs, the next teaching–learning strategy becomes a part of the learning process.

COMPARATIVE–CONTRASTIVE ANALYSIS

This teaching–learning strategy involves analysis of similarities and of differences in systems, situations, contexts, and learned skills. Using this strategy requires interaction, higher thinking skills, and an interrogative modality within the activities used. It is important in the progress of the learning sequence and in the interactive process that students have not only an opportunity to compare, to contrast, and to analyze what they have done, but also to configure different contexts into their analyses. This strategy provides that opportunity. Involved in this strategy are critical thinking, problem solving, and higher levels of cognition including analysis, synthesis, and evaluation. In terms of critical thinking, the students need to identify an issue or variable to be reviewed, define it in specific terms, organize and structure meaning, and make a generalization. They then need to repeat this process in terms of all of the issues, ideas, and variables they have dealt with during the learning experience. This strategy is designed to help them cross-check, compare, contrast, and develop some internalized generalizations about what they have done. They need to also identify problems and issues, explore them, try solutions, select particular solutions, and affirm those solutions. Thus students use critical thinking and problem solving to compare and contrast ideas, issues, and behaviors. These are the processes and sequences that the teacher and the students need to work through as they become more intrinsically and integrally involved in the activities related to this teaching–learning strategy. It is during this strategy that the students are required, in effect, to justify and affirm the efficacy of the new learning, the new skills, and the new behaviors and attitudes they have acquired. Through the use of comparative–contrastive analyses, this can happen. When this and other strategies at the insight category of interactive learning have been used, students are ready for the final strategy at this level of interaction. They need to review and summarize the whole of the learning experience.

> *This strategy is designed to help them cross-check, compare, contrast, and develop some internalized generalizations about what they have done.*

SUMMARIZATION

When students have come to this point in their learning and interactive experience, they need to do one more and final reflective review and summary of all the experiences they have had within the learning experience and the course of study. They need to summarize what they have done, accomplished, and learned. Although re-creation had some elements of reflection within it, the specific focus in this strategy is on reviewing and summarizing the entire learning experience. This is both the formative and the summative assessment of the learning experience. This is also the time when students bring things together in a final summary of what they have done. That is the purpose of this teaching–learning strategy. The student has by now totally identified with the learning experience and has internalized specified skills, concepts, behaviors, and attitudes. Now the question arises as to how has it been done and what it means. This brings forth a reflective summary of the sequence and process of the learning experience. Both process and product reflective summaries are included in this strategy.

There emerges, through this strategy, a need to order and organize the experience, to value it, and to establish personal and group meaning for it. The context, the value, and the meaning of the experience are central to this strategy. They are also central to this teaching–learning strategy and provide for a felt student need to determine the meaning and substance of the experience. Through this strategy, students review the totality of what they have been a part of and the process through which they have gone. Students and the teacher have kept records, journals, and notes on the process as well as lesson plans, student reports, student sharing, and other records. These may be in writing, through pictures, from by-products, and through aesthetic expression. The sequence followed along with problems and issues along the way are reviewed and discussed.

This strategy also embodies a celebration of success. This celebration of success is an important culminating activity for the whole learning experience. Through this strategy students can genuinely realize what they have been through, recognize the process, and celebrate the success. Students have demonstrated that they have achieved the objectives and goals and have stayed the course in terms of the parameters and limitations of the study. Recognition becomes a matter of pride and a rationale for celebration of what has been accomplished.

> *Through this strategy students can genuinely realize what they have been through, recognize the process, and celebrate the success.*

Summarization can take many forms. Some have already been done through other strategies at this category of interaction, but through this strategy the final review and summation is accomplished. The summary, whatever its form, emerges through interaction and discussion and through personal review of materials, records, and notes. Summarization is both an individual strategy and a group strategy. The final format for summarization, however, is done by group consensus and group decision. The purpose of summarization is threefold. First, summarization is a thorough review and the bringing together of sound perspectives on what has been achieved and how it was achieved. Second, summarization is a strategy from which plans for disseminating the learning takes place. Third, summarization allows for finalization and celebration. Students, when they have completed this strategy, should also have some ideas about how they can assume the responsibility for sharing and disseminating to others what has been learned and achieved. Learning does not take place in the classroom only. Learning is shared and disseminated through additional strategies and a final category of interactive learning. When this need emerges through the summarization process, a new level of interaction becomes apparent. That level of motivation is responsibility, when students assume a final dimension of motivation through dissemination.

SUMMARY

Through the use of strategies at the insight category of interaction, students gain and demonstrate respect for each other. They have extended their learning to new contexts and have fully internalized and used what they have learned. The strategies at this level of interaction are designed to allow students to do that. Skill reinforcement helps them apply what they have learned to new contexts and extend it to new areas of interest and focus. The use of re-creation, through creativity and higher levels of cognition, allows students an avenue to demonstrate what they have learned. Simulation and role-playing are overt demonstrations of skills, concepts, and behaviors learned. Analysis of what they have learned through comparing and contrasting is thought-provoking and essential to the process of motivation. Finally, the use of summarization brings the learning experience all together; it allows the students to explore and choose ways of sharing and disseminating what they have learned and to celebrate what they have done and learned. The insight category of interaction is just that. Through a variety of activities and through the implementation of the teaching strategies, students first begin to know what they have learned, then apply that, and finally summarize what they have done, how it was accomplished, what they have learned, and what they have produced. They have then become ready to assume full responsibility for disseminating the learning experience. Students know what has happened to them, and how they have been impacted by what they have done. They are ready to share and disseminate all of these things. These strategies are also designed to project the need for dissemination; this happens when the strategies are used well. The respect level activities fully demonstrate the teacher roles as sustainer and adviser and the student roles as extender and creator. These roles are apparent in all the strategies; through these roles the students know what they have learned and value that. The subcategories of respect are important. Continuity, caring, and creativity are intrinsic to the insight category. They are demonstrated through the teaching–learning strategies, group structures, and learning activities at insight. These strategies and activities are designed to firmly establish internalization of learning and to point toward activities and strategies that are part of the insight category of interactive learning. When these strategies and activities are completed, the students are able and ready to assume full responsibility for dissemination.

Activities

Insight category teaching–learning strategies show that major goals and objectives have been achieved. As you work on these activities in your small groups, keep this in mind. Make sure that you provide evidence for your responses to the activities on which you work as you share them with your peers.

1. "Insight means internalization" (Chap. 12, p. 153). What does this mean and how is it evidenced through the teaching–learning strategies at this category of interactive learning? Discuss this in your small group and prepare a report for your peers.

2. "Students demonstrate a sense of confidence and personal self-esteem" (Chap. 12, p. 154). Comment on this statement. What would you see in a classroom that would evidence this? How would respect relate to this statement? Would you see evidence of this in every teaching–learning strategy at insight? Share your responses with the total group.

3. How do the strands of thinking, learning, and teaching relate to cognition during the teaching–learning activities at insight?

4. Identify learning activities and group structures students use to "describe, clarify, and analyze situations and systems" (Chap. 12, p. 154). Detail your responses and share them with peers.

5. Note the kinds of group structures and learning activities that foster creativity at insight.

6. Discuss "continuity, caring, and creativity" (Chap. 12, p. 161) as they relate to the teaching–learning strategies at the insight category of interactive learning. Prepare a brief on this statement and how it is demonstrated through the teaching–learning strategies at this category.

Implementation Teaching–Learning Strategies

Implementation is the final category in the taxonomy of interactive learning. Within this culminating category of interaction students disseminate what they have learned, created, and experienced. Students, at this final category of the taxonomy, assume the role of influencer and disseminator; the teacher fulfills the roles of critiquor and consultant. The instructional role is disseminative. There are broad goals at this final category of interaction for the students. These goals extend beyond the specifics of celebration and success: students will take full leadership responsibility for dissemination; students plan, develop, and rehearse dissemination formats; students share their experiences with others as well as how they have learned and changed; students work closely with the teacher, who acts as a critiquor and consultant; and students, working with the teacher, focus on new learning experiences.

The activities and strategies at this final level of interactive learning are focused on the dissemination of student success. These activities and strategies are exemplified through the three subcategories of motivation at this implementation category of interactive learning. They are affirmation, aspiration, and action. Among the teaching–learning activities are simulations, skits, or plays in which students present what they have learned to various audiences. Students can also present written summaries and reports on their work to peers, parents, and other audiences. They can campaign for an issue or point of view and conduct debates on differing points of view. Students can show or demonstrate a product they have designed or created. They can organize seminars and presentations for other students and for families. They can do cross-age and peer teaching and counseling, emphasizing their learning experience. Students can develop and share multimedia presentations, dramatization, poetry reading, scriptwriting, publishing, and arts and crafts. Students can plan activities that involve overtly influencing others to accept and use the information, ideas, attitudes, and skills they have learned. They can distribute or sell developed products, productions, and services. They can become involved in advertising and recruiting activities in terms of their products and services. They can design their own learning packages, learning activities, minicourses, and other learning and instructional materials related to their own experience and success in learning. Students can write to influence, including letters, essays, instructions, and narratives. These can be sent to identified audiences and to other interested people.

In essence, students can be involved in sets of activities in which they will disseminate what they have learned, what they have achieved, and the process through which

Implementation is the culmination of interaction and the learning experience.

they have achieved their goals and objectives. The whole rhythm of their learning experience can be disseminated and shared with others. Implementation is the final category of interactive learning. Responsibility for leadership rests with the students. Implementation is the culmination of interaction and the learning experience. It is the communication and sharing dimension of the process where students are affirmed through what they have done, aspire to develop and implement a series of dissemination activities, and become personally involved in all the actions pertaining to the dissemination process.

The student roles as influencer and disseminator and the teacher's roles as critiquor and consultant come together through affirmation, aspiration, and action activities. The ultimate role in teaching and learning is to act on what has been learned and internalized. This final level of personal motivation and group interaction culminates the process with action through dissemination. The teaching–learning strategies in which all these activities are used are reporting, oral and visual presentation, dramatization, group dynamics, and seminar.

REPORTING

Through the use of this strategy the students prepare a written, graphic, or multimedia report in which students share, show, or explain the learning process, their experiences, and what those experiences mean to them. These reports can be developed based on some of the strategies and activities of the respect level, with special emphasis on teaching–learning strategies and the products developed there. Students can expand these to meet the needs of dissemination, but they can also develop new reports. The students, using this teaching–learning strategy, now present, post, display, or make available for review a summary statement report, a graphic representation, or a multimedia report on what they have done, how it happened, and what it means to them. These can be orally presented or they can be reviewed by other students and disseminated to other audiences. Teaching and learning involve valuing and the students are sharing not only information, but the meaning and the personal value of that meaning to others. Intrinsic to this strategy as well as to all other strategies at dissemination is meaning and value. The process of reporting must include both. Reporting must also be substantive and not superficial. Students must report with thoroughness and a rigor that demonstrates a clear understanding of process, of personal growth, of problems, and of their meaning and value to them. The students

are the influencers of others during this and other strategies at the implementation category of interactive learning. Students are the ones who take the lead in reporting and sharing. They are the ones who assume and demonstrate ownership of the learning experiences. Although this may sound difficult for all levels of student learning, it can be done from primary grades through graduate school.

The teacher's roles as critiquor and consultant, however, continue to be important to students during this strategy and others at this level of learning and sharing. As critiquor and consultant, the teacher's roles are to ensure that students demonstrate a depth of understanding, have real insight into the meaning of the learning experience, and can demonstrate its value and meaning to them. Students do this, with the teacher as consultant and critiquor, through well-prepared and rigorous dissemination. Through interaction with students and a critical response to their work, the teacher can work in a collegial and consultative manner to ensure that meaning and value are intrinsic to the reporting process. When the teaching–learning process has been carefully and sequentially developed and followed, the activities of dissemination and responsibility follow naturally. The students must plan for and prepare for their dissemination. The reports must be critiqued and the teacher consults with and helps the students create the best report they can. For the students, activities at this level are an affirmation of what they have done, an aspiration for others to know about it, and the completion of an action plan that reflects both the affirmation and the aspiration.

Reporting is a written, graphic, or multimedia response to the implementation category of interaction. Students make the decision as to which of these responses they will use, as a part of their dissemination strategies, to report to others. Student writing, at this level of interactive learning, shows all five of the levels of writing: define, describe, detail, discuss, and determine. Choices through this strategy become the student's responsibility, but the teacher can critique their choices and assist and consult with them in the preparation and presentation of their reports. Interaction with others is not the primary focus of this strategy; rather, it is informing and sharing with others. Some questions from audiences may be asked and they should be encouraged. Discussions could even take place. When interaction becomes central to the dissemination process, it is, however, usually the result of other strategies at this level of responsibility. Additional interaction is more intrinsic within oral and visual presentation, the next strategy, and through succeeding strategies, including group dynamics and seminars.

ORAL AND VISUAL PRESENTATIONS

Using this strategy, students begin a process of additional interaction with their audiences. They make the choices relating to the format for the presentation and how it is to be presented. Through oral and visual presentation, they demonstrate and present, in their own format and in their own words, what they have learned and what they have accomplished. They do this through oral or visual presentations. Included in this strategy are preparation, practice, editing, presentation, and responding to their audiences. In all these, the teacher as critiquor and consultant is available to work with the students. There also needs to be an assessment component where teacher and students can reflect on what they have done and how it was received. Students know that people will be listening and watching what they do, what they show, and what they say. Students must assume the responsibility for careful preparation, presentation, and response to any questions.

In all the tasks from preparation through presentation and evaluation of the presentation, the roles of the teacher are as a critiquor and consultant. The teacher's roles

Role of Critiquor and Adviser

Critiques:
content of what they will present
editing process in terms of writing, multimedia programs, presentation
Advises:
preparation of materials
assessment of what has been done
responding to audience questions and comments

are essential to optimum success in dissemination. This is true of the process even though students have assumed responsibility for content, preparation, and presentation. The role of critiquor and adviser describes what the teacher does; how the teacher uses those roles is central to the quality of the student presentations. The teacher critiques the students on the content of what they will present and advises them on the preparation. The teacher critiques and consults with the students about the editing process, coaches and advises in terms of presentations, and collegially participates in the assessment of what has been done. The editing process requires certain skills in writing, using multimedia programs, and presentation in front of other groups. Editing also entails consideration of responding to audience questions and comments. The teacher may well need to consult with students, advise them, and assist them in developing and using these skills.

Responsibility as well as affirmation, aspiration, and action are operant in this teaching–learning strategy. The student roles as influencer and disseminator are apparent as they work through this activity—in particular, how they present their material. Their roles are evident as they assess and evaluate how well they presented. Their presentation can be informational or can be designed to influence others. Student presentations can also be focused on changing the audience's attitudes about the experience and trying to ensure that people in the audience have the same feelings about the experience that the presenters have. Through this, and the other strategies of interaction, students have achieved the ultimate levels of experience, motivation, discourse, creativity, critical thinking, and problem solving.

Assessment and evaluation activities should address issues concerning the effectiveness of the presentation. The assessment and evaluation of the product and the presentation are also useful in helping students gain insights into the next learning experience. Their experience as presenters can help them focus on how they can transition from this learning experience to another course of study or area of focus. Presenting helps build self-confidence and makes success apparent if it is done well. The teacher's roles as critiquor and consultant are essential in this context. The teacher's roles are reflective, evaluative, and projective. The focus of the teacher in the consulting role is to help the students reflect, as objectively as possible, on how they presented, the content of what they presented, and how the audience responded. In the projective sense the teacher needs to consult with students about valuing the learning and the skills and how they can transfer to new learning experiences. Thus one of the purposes of this strategy is to build a bridge between what they have done and a whole spectrum of possible new learning experiences. Students, through this strategy, as well as others in this category of interaction, sense not only the process through which they have gone, but they also strongly sense their role as influencers of others. They have developed their voice and are using it to influence others. In addition, students also need to ruminate on how this learning experience can lead to new learning experiences and other areas of focus for them. This strategy, along with all others in this category of interactive learning, is a clear example of students accepting responsibility and thoroughly valuing what they have done. Dissemination, as shown in this strategy, is the fruition and culmination of a learning process, of careful planning, of effective interaction, and of thoughtful progress through the daily and long-term objectives and goals of the experience. This strategy, as with all other strategies at this category of interaction, is a reward and recognition of a job well done both for the students and for the teacher.

DRAMATIZATION

This teaching–learning strategy is another important one for students, but has a more formal context than does oral and visual presentation. It differs from reporting in that the audiences both see and hear what the students have to say, rather than just hearing about it. Like all other strategies at this level of interactive learning, dramatization requires choices, planning, preparation, practice, editing, presenting, and evaluation.

Again, the teacher roles as critiquor and consultant are important through all the processes and activities of this strategy. The teacher consults with the students and works with the students in making choices for content, format, and organization as well as in the preparation, practice, editing, presenting, and evaluation of their dramatization. Dramatization involves acting and the teacher may need to help coach and direct the presentation. When involved in this strategy, students are presenting for others. They want their audiences to understand and to see those skills, behaviors, concepts, and actions that they have accomplished through this learning experience—in particular, the ones they emphasize in their dramatization. Students are formalizing what they have learned and achieved for others to see and to experience.

Dramatization can range from skits and pantomimes to a formal play. They are written, produced, and acted by the students. They can be informational or they can be both informational and persuasive. They could also be homiletic if the students feel strongly that others need to internalize the same skills, behaviors, concepts, and actions. Students need to decide, with the teacher's support and consultation, what the purpose of the dramatization is and to whom it will be presented. The teacher again must be the critiquor, the consultant, and sometimes the coach. It is the teacher as consultant who encourages, assists, and focuses the students on the process in which they are involved. Again, however, part of that role as critiquor and consultant is to establish links between what the students have accomplished and possible new learning experiences. Culminating activities, such as this one, both reflect and project. The teacher's role is to project from this setting and this presentation toward new options for learning.

> *Dramatization can range from skits and pantomimes to a formal play. They are written, produced, and acted by the students.*

Dramatization, like all other strategies at implementation, needs to have an assessment and evaluation component. Students need to review their presentations and talk about how the audience reacted, the pluses and minuses of what they have done, and the influence they have had on their audience. They need to think about how the audience responded because they may not have had much interaction with the audience. The teacher, here, is important to the process and can really help the students through the consulting role. The teacher also must generate within the students a "where do we go now" thinking modality so students will be ready to use what they have achieved and be ready to move on to new learning experiences. Students have been extenders and creators in this category of interaction. During implementation, they are influencers and disseminators. Through their extending and creative activities and through the influencing and dissemination activities, they have become ready for new dimensions of learning and experience.

GROUP DYNAMICS

This is a strategy specifically designed for interaction and discussion with a number of audiences inside and outside of the classroom. This is an interactive strategy that, if well planned and executed, can be of great interest and satisfaction to students and to the teacher as well as to the participating audiences. The strategies at the responsibility level, and in particular this one, are extrinsic expressions of internalized motivation. Group dynamics is a social dimension of responsibility and dissemination. The basic expectation for this strategy is interaction with others. This interaction may take the form of telling, sharing, discussing, questioning, selling, reporting, answering, and debating. Students need to think on their feet and respond to any questions or issues brought up by the audience. With younger students this strategy is done with peers. It can be used with peers at almost any level of learning. Usually in this strategy, a combination of these forms is used. Group dynamics is an alive, appropriate, and interesting strategy that can be used by all levels of students from kindergarten through graduate level.

To use this strategy, careful planning on the part of the students is necessary. In addition, students must ascertain how they are going to respond to questions, comments, and opinions expressed by their colleagues in this interactive process. Planning, practice, editing, and evaluation are important to the success of this strategy. How to be involved in this interactive process in a positive way is also a skill that the students need to practice and learn.

> *Group dynamics is an alive, appropriate, and interesting strategy that can be used by all levels of students from kindergarten through graduate level.*

The teacher, as critiquor and consultant, is vital to this process. To the students, the teacher has become a respected colleague and an honored and caring authority. The teacher is a consultant who can advise, assist, and help students through their issues and concerns as they work on this strategy. The teacher needs to consult and work with students to develop the plan, to identify how the dynamics will work, to set time frames, to cover all their points in the presentation, and to respond to any questions or issues brought up by the audience. The teacher needs to work with students to help them understand how to react to all kinds of comments and questions, and consult with them in learning how to summarize what has happened following their interaction with others.

Group dynamics takes much planning and effort if this strategy is to be put in motion. Students may additionally need to learn the skill of leading and participating in presentations. If they have been interactively learning throughout the experience, this may not be a problem. But if it is, there must be a learning process set up for students to get this skill. It is usually better for students to first use this strategy with peers. Once they have done it with peers, they can then plan to use it with other audiences. In the evaluation process, students and teacher need to realize that the experience they have completed can lead to a harvest of new opportunities to learn. They need get involved in a whole new series of skills and concepts. The teacher as critiquor and consultant needs to ensure that the students are aware of these opportunities.

SEMINAR

The use of the seminar is a strategy where the students present information to a group of peers or other audiences. The seminar participants are the ones who are the learners. The students who have had the experience are the presenters and the coordinators of the seminar. The purpose of the seminar is to inform, influence, or persuade. A seminar is a small group of students who have completed the learning experience and present information and share their experiences with other students and other audiences. A seminar is set up so that there is the opportunity for the audience to ask questions, respond to the information, and participate in discussions about it. All of the seminar presenters share in providing the information and experiences to the listeners. Seminar presenters should expect audience and participant interaction as the audience reacts to the presentation. A seminar is designed so that the audience can be co-participants in the exercise

Seminar Needs for Success

Lesson plan with objectives and goals
Plan for questions and prepare responses
Contingency plans; learn to adapt
Understand the process they need to go through with co-participants

of the seminar. In short, participants are both the students who have been involved in the learning experience and who assume the role of teacher, and other people (usually peers), who are the learning participants. This can be done as a large group or can be done in smaller groups. Seminars are usually most effective when there are groups of no more than fifteen to eighteen, so that all can participate.

The seminar should have about a two-to-one ratio, at least, of coparticipants to a smaller number of students who, as presenters and teachers, have been through the experience. Because of this ratio, several seminars can be held with coparticipants so that most or all students can participate as teachers. Again planning, preparation, and specific understanding of the process and the projected outcomes are necessary. In the seminar. the students are doing the presenting and teaching. They need, in effect, to have a lesson plan with objectives and goals. They need to plan for questions and prepare responses. They need to have contingencies in case something unusual happens. They need to learn to adapt and think on their feet. Students need to understand the process they have to go through with the coparticipants so they can know that their seminar has been successful. Students who participate in seminar activities are usually strongly motivated to do so, and this strategy for motivational responsibility is an effective one for students who feel this way. It is often difficult to do and students become more effective as they repeat the process. Very often the coparticipants or other students who are part of the seminar also have an interest in the content and outcomes of the seminar. This way there is a pairing of interest and a willingness on the part of the presenters and the coparticipants to go through the process together. The teacher, as critiquor and consultant, works with the students to ensure that the planning has been thorough, that the process is clear and understood, that the goals and objectives are well designed, and that there is an opportunity within the seminar for all participants to assess and evaluate what has been done and its importance to them. Assessment and evaluation also need to be built into a postseminar session where the activity is discussed and students and coparticipants ascertain the meaning of the seminar experience. In this context, both students and teacher need to discuss their next steps and new learning opportunities so that this strategy along with any others used at this level of motivation can indicate possible new learning opportunities. Intrinsic to the purpose of all strategies at this level of motivation is that they are designed to be the link, the bridge, the direction setter, pointing toward the ultimate choice of new opportunities for learning.

SUMMARY

Implementation is the final category in the taxonomy of interactive learning. The teaching strategies represented in this category have major areas of focus. The first area of focus is to provide for the students with a methodology for sharing and disseminating their learning experiences. The second area of focus is to provide opportunities for students to assume leadership roles in dissemination. The third area of focus is the preparation and the creative effort the students must demonstrate before they actually disseminate. The fourth area of focus is to improve student self-evaluation and have them become active and informed participants in the assessment and evaluation process. The fifth area of focus is to use these strategies as a bridge to new areas of learning.

When this level of interactive learning has been achieved and becomes operant, students assume the responsibility for dissemination through those strategies and activities noted. They carry the burden of doing most of the planning, preparation, and presentation. The teacher's role, however, is essential to the success of the strategies at this level of interaction. The teacher critiques, sustains, moderates, acts as a catalyst, and motivates. The teacher also acts as a consultant and adviser in all the strategies. In essence, all the roles of the teacher throughout the whole learning process are reprised in order to reinforce successful outcomes of these dissemination strategies. The primary roles of the teacher are, of course, those of a critiquor and a consultant, but the other roles are necessary as the planning, practice, and presentation take place.

As has been noted, evaluation has an important place in this level of interaction. Evaluation focuses on both what the students did and how they did it. Evaluation focuses on the efficiency and effectiveness of the learning process and on the quality and functionality of the products developed. Evaluation focuses on the level of achievement of identified objectives, outcomes, and goals. Evaluation is the final determiner of success for the students in their dissemination activities. Evaluation also focuses on the direction and the next steps in the learning sequence. Through the evaluation process, and the focus on direction, the roles of the teacher become more apparent and more proactive than in the other dimensions of assessment and evaluation. The teacher is responsible for making suggestions, getting student response, and then together with students making a decision for the next steps in the learning sequence. The question of whether all strategies should be used during this level of responsibility is pertinent. It is obvious that it takes time to do the job well at the responsibility level. Because of this, the teacher and the students should be selective in what strategies they choose. The use of one strategy is very acceptable. The use of more than one can give students more opportunity to creatively express to others the success they have experienced and the pride they take in what they have done. All of the strategies at this level of interaction affirm learning and self-image. They are also used as a part of the celebration of success that began with the strategies of the rapport and respect levels. They are designed to involve students in aspirations both for the dissemination of their work and for the direction they will take in new learning experiences. These strategies also involve actions in which the students frame what they have learned. This last subcategory of action is very important to ensure that students understand both the complexities of dissemination and the responsibilities they have to others. Students must be able to disseminate honestly, sequentially, contextually, meaningfully, and persuasively. It is these framing actions that create substantive meaning to students, to their audiences, and to the teacher.

In these past five chapters we have presented twenty-five teaching–learning strategies along with a representative sample of a wide spectrum of activities related directly to the process of teaching, learning, and establishing meaning. The strategies and activities are arranged sequentially within the five sequential categories of interaction so that they may be followed and used in an orderly progression. It is, however, important to understand that these five strategies are not definitive. Many others, familiar to teachers, can and need to be used in any category. Teachers should only make sure that they are consistent with the category of the taxonomy in which the students are learning. Teachers and students can select those that most clearly represent the needs of the particular study in which they are involved. There are, of course, other strategies and activities that could be used. The categories of interactive learning, however, need to be followed sequentially. Students learn throughout all the levels of interaction from invitation through involvement and investigation to insight and implementation. Teachers also need to plan to follow these sequential categories as they plan lessons and ensure that students become involved in those lessons and committed to the learning experience.

Before we leave these chapters on teaching–learning strategies, we need to reiterate that the basic focus of teaching is valuing what students are learning and discovering the personal meaning involved in that valuing. Valuing is what teaching is all about. Certainly there are skills to be learned, objectives to be achieved, concepts to be internalized, and achievements to be shared. All of these, however, are done within the context of valuing both the process of how the students have learned and the outcomes of what they have achieved and internalized. If the students do not value what they have learned and what they have internalized, it is of little use to them. If the teacher does not value what the students have done, the teacher will gain neither rapport nor respect from the students. Valuing is central to the whole teaching–learning process and it should not be forgotten in the description and explanation of the strategies presented.

In continuing this work there are three other components that need to be addressed: the planning component, the change process, and the implementation of the taxonomy. Throughout the sequence of teaching–learning strategies we have presented an interactive sequence where students could work together in a wide spectrum of settings, a series of teaching–learning strategies, and many activities. Following this chapter is one on planning the instructional program. We present the chapter on planning because we feel that teachers need to clearly understand how to plan for the sequence and the constructs of the taxonomy. The penultimate chapter deals with interaction and the change process, where we discuss the change process and how it relates to interaction. We have, in earlier chapters, presented the sequence of change and discussed how it fit into learning activities, group structures, and teaching–learning strategies. We felt, however, that we needed to augment what we have already presented. In this chapter on change we discuss what we term *ethical transformative learning*. For us, this is a positive discussion of critical pedagogy. We define ethical transformative learning and relate it to the taxonomy. We look at learning and instruction through this process. In the last chapter we talk about how this method of lesson analysis has been implemented in learning settings and posit that these strands of interactive learning can be used at any level of teaching and learning from kindergarten through graduate school.

Activities

This is the culminating chapter on teaching–learning activities or instruction. In these activities the instructional process comes together at implementation. They are designed not only to illuminate this chapter, but to provide you with the opportunity to reflect on the total instructional process and link it to theory and classroom organization. Prepare a report on the activity you are assigned.

1. Disseminating student success is intrinsic to the process of implementation. Show how it is important for the students and to their audiences. Provide a rationale for this dimension of implementation.

2. Discuss the leadership roles of the students and the teacher at implementation. How have these roles changed from invitation to implementation?

3. How do the teacher and the students make a decision to move to a new learning experience? Discuss this in your small group and detail the process for the total group.

4. Trace the writing process through all five categories of interactive learning. How is writing demonstrated in the teaching–learning strategies at implementation?

5. Identify a teaching–learning strategy and decide on three learning activities and group structures that could be used. Provide for the total group a rationale for choosing the learning activities and group structures.

Planning for Student Learning

A major dimension to any successful learning experiences for students and for the teacher is careful and thoughtful planning both by the teacher and by the students. Planning is a process that starts before the experience is introduced and continues through the experience. Initially, the teacher must do the planning and the preparation, but as students become involved in the learning experience and progress through the categories in the motivational sequence, they can and should participate more in planning. When responsibility emerges as the final step in motivation, students should, and usually do, assume almost total responsibility for planning, with the teacher acting as consultant and critiquor. From almost the very beginning of a lesson sequence or unit of study, planning becomes an interactive task with the teacher and students participating together in assessing what has been achieved and thinking through the next steps. Interaction and cooperative groupings are conducive to the learning experience and also require careful planning. The teacher may initially plan and organize group structures, but students should participate in the process as the learning experience deepens and moves to higher levels of interaction. Students need to learn to work in groups, and plan for learning. Students must be included in the planning process and in the instructional delivery.

Planning a lesson is an essential professional activity. Careful and thorough planning for optimal student learning demands from the teacher an understanding of how students learn, what they have already learned and experienced, and what they need to learn within the planned learning experience. Planning is a process that is simple in mechanics, structure, and organization, but more complex in terms of how students learn, of delivery, and of ensuring that students learn, internalize, and are able to use what has been planned (Reeves 2002). Planning, when students are involved, remains equally straightforward and simple, but also requires that students think through their needs and expectations and plan very carefully along with the teacher their next steps, including what needs to be learned and the scope and sequence of the learning experience. As they are included in planning, students identify with the experience and become stakeholders in the success of the learning process. Students, personally and as a group, seek to achieve the outcomes of the learning experience. They feel a need for the learning to go well and to be successful.

Careful and thorough planning for optimal student learning demands from the teacher an understanding of how students learn, what they have already learned and experienced, and what they need to learn within the planned learning experience.

Lesson plans, and the process of planning from the very beginning, should be open to the students. As students progress through the interactive learning categories, they should become more involved in planning. Finally, at the implementation level, they are managing their learning program and are taking a leadership role in lesson planning. After the initial teacher planning, students should be included in the planning process at every step in the motivational taxonomy. They should become more completely involved as the sequence of the lessons builds toward responsibility where they assume the role of principal planners.

Planning, as has been stated, is a simple process. It is a straightforward process that is clear and needs to be followed specifically. There are, however, some essential steps that go into planning. Each of these steps is important and cannot be left out. The first of these steps in planning is taken by the teacher. Later, the students will begin to become part of the planning process. Planning begins by identifying the standard that the students are working toward (Reeves 2002). Expected outcomes, goals, and/or objectives are planned first by the teacher, who then can help students become participants in planning.

One must know the destination before the journey can begin and before the plan can take shape. The outcomes and expected behaviors and skills should be stated, wherever possible, in demonstrable and measurable objectives. You should also identify the standard that you are addressing with the students (Reeves 2002). Johnson et al. (2008) stated, "If standards are to have any real effect on schools and student achievement, they need to be supported by other elements in the school structure" (369). We concur, but we reiterate the need for specific and careful planning. The teacher initially, and later the students and teacher together, should determine what standards, behavioral outcomes, and identified products will be the end result of the lesson or learning experience. What the students are able to do, to demonstrate, or to create by the end of the specific lesson or learning experience must be answered. These are basic questions. The teacher should know the students' background and what they have previously learned. This information helps for planning purposes. Behavioral or demonstrable outcomes, the proposed products, and the objective should be written as clearly and succinctly as possible. They should be clearly understood by the students. Students need to be cognizant of all objectives and outcomes of lessons, including those that the teacher has planned. They need to know the objectives and outcomes so that they can understand what is expected from them. Students need to be aware of direction and the steps in the learning sequence from the very beginning, as well as the nature of the long-term objectives and outcomes toward which they are working. Students need to know what is expected of them in terms of the learning expected and the series of outcomes, objectives, and goals toward which they will be working. They also need to know the affective or behavioral outcomes. As students work through the learning experiences, and through the levels of the interactive learning sequence, they will become more involved in the planning. It is therefore incumbent that they be exposed to planning and have a participatory involvement from the very beginning. Outcomes or objectives should always be discussed with students so that they are clear on expectations, on behaviors, and on demonstrable learning and changes to be shown at the end of the lesson, or even at the end of the learning experience. Adjustments, based on student commentary and involvement, should be made as the learning experience develops and as the students become more committed to the experience.

Once the standard is selected and the objectives or outcomes are clearly and concisely written, the teacher and the students, as they become more involved in planning, should develop a sequence of steps that need to be accomplished to ensure that the objectives are met. The development of steps needs to be done for daily lessons as well as for long-term outcomes. In a sense, this kind of sequencing is a task analysis on how to achieve the objectives. The planned steps and activities associated with the steps should be keyed to the levels of interaction to be achieved through the course of the lesson or series of lessons. A series of teaching–learning activities for each level of the taxonomy of motivation is included in an earlier chapter on teaching–learning activities. Teachers

Categories of Interactive Learning

Science of teaching and learning
Levels of the sequence of motivation
Cognitive thinking sequences
Purposes of classroom and group structures
Processes involved in the learning experience

and students should select activities from these lists of activities, or select other activities that would be specific to the lesson or lessons the teacher and the students will be working on together. The teacher and students should sequence the selected activities and correlate them with the categories of interaction. If the teacher and the students are involved in a series of lessons, a unit, or a course of study, both the teacher and the students should be aware of short-term objectives and outcomes as well as long-range end-of-unit/course-of-study goals, objectives, and outcomes. Planners include those in lesson or unit structures. A sequence of activities for each daily lesson should be prepared as a regular part of the planning process. As the instructional plans and processes develop through the lesson sequence, the students should become partners with the teacher in planning lessons and in the total planning process. Under no circumstances should students not be part of the process. Even very young students should participate in planning for groups and for the class.

Students should be aware of the categories of interactive learning. The science of teaching and learning should be known and understood by the students. They should know the levels of the sequence of motivation, the cognitive thinking sequences, the purposes of classroom and group structures, and processes involved in the learning experience. This means that the students need to learn these components of the science of learning. The age and maturity of students is a factor in how the components are learned and how they are taught. All students should know and demonstrate awareness of the components of motivation, experience, cognition, evaluation, and the other strands of the lessons as they develop more skill in their own lesson planning. The teacher and the students should address these components early in the year or course of study and make sure that all students clearly understand them and can use these components in planning and preparing for learning. They should be revisited, as needed, throughout the learning and planning processes. With young students discussion should be centered on "why we are doing this" and "why we are doing these things in this order." Young students can understand this and from their initial learning set they can begin to use the vocabulary of planning and learning.

Teaching and learning become more exciting and involving when everyone is participating in planning and preparing for continuing learning. Next, the teacher and the students should consider the roles they will be taking in the learning sequence. These roles are listed and discussed in chapter 1 of this work. They are also noted throughout the text as different categories and different content emphases of interaction are discussed. Students should know their roles at each level of interaction and they should also know about the teacher roles. They should not only be aware of the roles, they should understand what they mean and how they are demonstrated in class. Both the teacher and the students should clearly understand the changing instructional roles and how they function through the levels of the interactive learning taxonomy. Students should understand leadership roles. Students should also understand the process involved in evaluation and planning. Again, student understanding of the processes is important for optimum achievement of the objectives. Nothing should be mysterious or unexplained in the teaching–learning process. From time to time during the lesson sequence the teacher and the students should focus on where they are in the process, on how well they are fulfilling their roles, and how effectively the process is developing. This kind of focus helps both the students and the teacher be aware of both progress and process. This is time well spent. It is also an informal evaluation of the effectiveness and efficiency of the learning process. Time for this kind of discussion and learning should be built into the planning process. This kind of attention and review is consistently helpful for both teacher and students and helps move the process along more efficiently and more rapidly. Do not fail to do this regularly during a lesson sequence.

After these steps have been accomplished, the next focus in the planning process is to decide on the materials and resources that will be needed to accomplish the outcomes and the objectives of each lesson, and of the whole learning experience. Materials and resources need to be gathered and readied for use before they are available for the lesson itself. Both teacher and students need to work on ensuring that the resources and materials are ready when they are needed. There is, of course, a wide range of materials and resources. Paper, pens and pencils, print materials, realia, human resources, media resources, and technology all comprise the wide spectrum of resources. Technology and its use in the classroom must be part of the planning process. Picciano (2006) notes that to use technology to enhance learning "refers to incorporating technology in classroom presentations and other teaching activities" (33). All of these resources need to be considered and selected if they will correlate with, and be pertinent to, the lesson or the lesson sequence. Resources should be selected for use and should be consistent with the activity sequence. For each activity in which students and teachers are involved, there should always be a review and consideration of the materials and resources needed for learning and instruction. Both teacher and students should be aware of the learning needs in terms of resources and materials and should participate in ensuring that they are ready when needed. Students, as the learning sequence develops, become very aware of the kinds of resources they will need. Their ideas should be strongly considered when materials and resources are selected. The teacher, initially, will assume more responsibility, but as the levels of motivation develop and change, students will become more responsible for gathering and organizing resources and materials.

Following the identification of materials and resources needed, there should be thoughtful decisions on the teaching strategies appropriate for optimum student involvement in the learning process and the achievement of the planned objectives and outcomes. In this work we have identified twenty-five teaching strategies keyed to the levels of the taxonomy of motivation. They are identified and discussed in this work through five chapters beginning with chapter 9 and ending with chapter 23. We encourage you to use these strategies or identify and use other learning strategies with which you may be familiar and which would be compatible with and equivalent to the level in the sequence of the motivational taxonomy on which you are working.

Each teacher needs to identify the strategies that are pertinent to the activities that they have selected and utilize them appropriately in the lesson sequence, ensuring that they are consistent with the level of taxonomy on which students are functioning. The strategies should be written into the lesson plan at the appropriate motivational level. Again, students can and should participate in the planning of strategies to be used. They need to be aware of and clearly understand not only the strategies, but their

role in ensuring that those strategies are successful. When a teaching strategy is introduced, students and teacher should talk about it and make sure the students understand what it is and how it is to be used. If both the teacher and the students are aware of the strategies and use them appropriately, success in learning is greatly enhanced. Some may worry about the time expended, but in the final analysis this kind of discussion will make the learning experience go more smoothly and will decrease the total time spent on the unit of study. The teacher and students are not limited to the strategies listed in this work. Other strategies that will fit with the class, with the lessons, and with the activities that have been chosen for the level of motivation on which the teacher and the students are working can be used. They can fit well into the interactive category with which they are correlated.

Next, classroom structures, group formats, and interactive learning processes should be a part of the planning process (Steinaker 2007). Consideration needs to be given to the kinds of interactive groups and classroom structures that will be used. Interactive learning, especially through appropriate group formats, can ensure that students learn effectively and optimally. Interactive group structures in the classroom are an important organizational format through which augmented learning outcomes can be accomplished. Again, students should be a part of the process of identifying and selecting group structures. They should understand and be keenly aware of the importance of interaction. They should also learn how it can be done effectively and efficiently.

Time needs to be taken to ensure that they know how to do group work. Once they have learned the process, and they do at the readiness and relationship levels, students thrive in the interactive group learning settings. The kinds of group structures that could be used at different levels of the taxonomy are presented and discussed in two chapters of this work. These are only suggestions for groups. There are, of course, many other kinds of group structures and formats appropriate at different levels of the taxonomy. Use those structures if they are pertinent to the learning process. These group structures and formats are matched with teaching strategies in an earlier chapter.

Finally, there must be a consideration of the evaluation process. Evaluation and its correlation with the taxonomy of motivation is discussed in the chapter on evaluation. In that chapter, identified roles in evaluation were presented along with how to implement and use them. These defined roles in terms of evaluation are directly related to the categories of taxonomy of motivation. These roles and associated strategies of evaluation and assessment protocols should be included in any planning process. Some can be used at any level of the taxonomy. Students and the teacher should be aware of these evaluation roles and discuss them as the lesson sequence progresses through the levels of interactive learning and through the learning experience.

Evaluation has three major areas of focus. The first area of focus is process, next is product, and the third is performance. Process evaluation is very important (Steinaker 2005). Indeed, process evaluation is a major key to learning. Process evaluation was touched on earlier in this chapter, with both teacher and students focusing at various times on how they were doing and why they were following the process in a particular way. This needs to be done throughout the learning experience and the process of interaction. The teacher and the students should participate in the focus on process

The Areas of Focus in Evaluation

1. **Process:** focusing at various times on how they were doing and why they were following the process in a particular way.
2. **Product:** includes a review of achievement at any level of motivation.
3. **Performance:** has to do with attitudes, feelings, and changes.

evaluation and on the quality and effectiveness of interaction. Product evaluation, while it becomes a major focus toward the end of the learning sequence, needs to be considered as the lesson sequence develops and different levels of interaction emerge. Product evaluation includes a review of achievement at any level of motivation. Performance evaluation is needed at all levels of interactive learning. The question of "how well did we do?" is always needed to help students reflect on and think about performance. Through this, students link it to further learning. Performance evaluation also has to do with attitudes, feelings, and changes. Again, these evaluation areas can, and should, be discussed and considered by students from the beginning of the sequence, with some focus on whether this activity or what is being done will ensure achievement of the outcome or objective. Be sure that the students use the teacher and student roles during the focus on both process and product evaluation. This will help in terms of clarity and sequence as the focus is on evaluation and outcomes. Evaluation begins at the initial activity in the lesson sequence and continues throughout the sequence to the very last activity. Process, product, and performance need to be considered. Product evaluation is emphasized as the conclusion of the learning sequence becomes apparent. Even then, however, students and teacher should consider any changes they would make if the sequence, or one similar to it, were to be done again. Evaluation should be interactive when possible, although written evaluation responses can also be used when appropriate and needed. It should be noted that students participate in the evaluation process from the very beginning of the learning experience and take stronger roles as they progress through the taxonomy of interactive learning.

Once all these elements in lesson planning are completed, the plan can be put in motion. With both teacher and student participation in the process, success and optimum learning can be expected in terms of achievement of outcome and objectives. As new levels of interaction emerge, particularly from investigation, insight, and implementation, student participation in planning becomes more and more important. Student involvement in planning at these levels of motivation is essential. Planning should become an integral part of the lesson closure, which also includes daily assessment and evaluation of the process, the product, the performance, and the progress toward achievement of the outcomes and objectives. Lesson closure, sometimes called "cloze," should consistently include an interactive review of what was done, how it was done, and the next steps in the process. Planning the next steps in the learning process is the final area for decision in the closure of the lesson. Both teacher and students should have good ideas about what comes next, what is to be accomplished, and how it is to be done. These should be discussed; consensus should be developed and included in the planning process. The teacher in concert with the students may wish to formalize the planning in writing so students have it the next day to begin their learning sequence thoroughly cognizant of the process they will follow. Careful and thorough planning is essential to student learning, and students must partner with the teacher in that planning as they assume a more active leadership and planning role in the learning experience. Planning and assessment logs should be kept by teacher and students so that they can review and reflect on the process as needed and have it available for the next steps. A format for lesson planning and a planning log are necessary components for both teacher and students. A lesson-planning format is included in an Appendix.

One component of lesson planning and instruction that is not included in the format is discourse. Discourse is the conversation, the communication, the dialogue, the consideration, and the consensus in the interactive context of learning (Steinaker 2003b). Through dialogue and discourse, the teacher and the students define the expectations for outcomes and products expected at the end of the lesson. Discourse can also set the lesson or lessons into the perspective of previous learning as well as into the context of current study and the context of long-range goals and outcomes. Initial dialogue and discourse prepares both the students and the teacher for discussion and group activity that will be the heart of the lesson. Discourse takes place in dyads, triads, and small groups as well as in class discussions. The format for discourse needs to be determined by the teacher and the students in the context of specific lesson focus as well as in the context of the planned lesson outcomes. Any of the kinds of groups noted in the chapter on group structure can be used as formats for dialogue and discourse. Students and the teacher need to negotiate the kinds of groups to be used to best serve the expected outcomes of the lesson or learning sequence. The students should be aware of the sequence of the taxonomy of interactive learning as well as the correlation of discourse with the taxonomy. This is more thoroughly discussed in the following chapter. In the planning process discourse and dialogue should be integral and evident. Again, although discourse is not included in the lesson plan format, it should be thoughtfully and specifically included in every lesson and in every activity in which the students and the teachers are involved. A planning format for the components of the lesson plan is included in Appendix A. In Appendix B, directions for completing the interactive lesson plan are provided. Appendix C contains descriptors of sixteen SDAIE strategies.

Activities

The activities here focus on planning. All students will do at least one lesson as noted in the fifth activity. Students will complete other activities as assigned. Reports and presentations will be made for all activities.

1. "Planning a lesson is an essential professional activity" (Chap. 14, p. 173). What does this mean for a teacher? What components need to be included in a professional lesson plan? Why include them and why is each component important?

2. "Students should be aware of the categories of interactive learning" (Chap.14, p. 175). Do you agree with this statement? Why or why not? Justify your answer.

3. Detail the role of the students in the planning process. How does it change from category to category? Discuss this in your small group and report your perspectives to the total group.

4. How should students participate in evaluating what they have learned? How does their participation relate to planning?

5. Plan a lesson or series of lessons using the planning format in the Appendix. Share your plans with your peers.

Interaction and the Change Process

The purpose of the instructional and learning process is to bring about change. Change is manifested through the internalization and dissemination of identified skills and attitudes. Change is a process. The change process can be correlated with the taxonomy of interactive learning. Indeed, it takes place within the interactive process. Like the taxonomy of interaction, there are five steps in the sequence of change. They are condition, communication, consideration, consensus, and change. The change process is expedited within an interactive context. Interaction is generally with people, but change can come about through interaction with intellectual material and resources that are integral to the taxonomy of interactive learning. Change is accomplished through discourse, discussion, and direction. It is effectively accomplished through interactive learning and group processes. Human discourse is a process of change. Discourse begins with identifying a condition. In terms of the taxonomy of interaction, the teacher, at the invitation category, presents the condition through defining the parameters of the study and the vision for its completion, including the process through which the students will become active participants. The next step is communication about a vision that relates to the condition, but provides perspectives on new outcomes, goals, and objectives. It is at the relationship category that students and teacher look at and discuss variables, see where different ideas come together, and resolve any conflict of ideas. Creating a vision for students is essential to the change process. The creation of the vision through communication is best done interactively. Communication correlates with the involvement category of interaction. It is through communication that the students and the teacher work out the details of the vision and any issues or problems that may have come up. It is at this communication/involvement level that the student voice begins to emerge. It is here that the students and the teacher come together and begin to value the vision and to understand its meaning to them. Here students explore the vision, discuss it, begin to value it, and make a decision to commit to the vision.

The next step is consideration, where various ideas and points of view are investigated. Investigation is the category of interaction to which this level of change is correlated. Here the students investigate and identify with the vision. It is through investigation and insight that students make the process and the implicit change their own. They work together with rapport and goodwill; with cogency, they find their voice through their emerging ownership of the learning process. The students identify with the vision and it becomes operant for both themselves and the teacher. The fourth step is consensus, where there is agreement on

> *There are five steps in the sequence of change. They are condition, communication, consideration, consensus, and change.*

basic issues and the group accepts and internalizes the consensus. This step, which is the equivalent of the insight category of the taxonomy, correlates with the teaching strategies and activities of insight category of interaction. During this level of change and interaction, students internalize the vision and achieve the goals and objectives of the process. They have made it their own and through the process they have come to value what they have learned, understood and internalized the meaning of the learning experience, and accomplished the goals and objectives they planned and worked to achieve. Change is vindicated when the group disseminates and shares with others the results of their process of change. This is where their voice and internalization of how they have changed is disseminated to others. This final level in the change process correlates with responsibility in the taxonomy of interaction. Students are the disseminators of what they have done. They are disseminators of the change process and disseminators of how they have been impacted by change and how others should experience the same changes. Change is twofold. It is intrinsic because it changes the students. It is extrinsic because, as the students disseminate, they can influence and change others.

One can immediately see the correlation with the taxonomy of interactive learning. Change and interaction are two ways of defining the same process. In the taxonomy of interactive learning, the correlation is as follows:

Interaction	Change
Invitation	Condition
Involvement	Communication
Investigation	Consideration
Insight	Consensus
Implementation	Change

In this chapter we will discuss each category of change and correlate the categories with the taxonomy of interactive learning. We will also correlate change with the roles of students, teacher, instruction, and leadership. We will further correlate change and interaction with the process of thinking and organization, critical thinking, creativity, and problem solving. When change occurs, all these processes are involved and should be understood as students become transformed by change. These are the elements of the transformative nature of education. It is our contention that this must be done within an ethical transformative process.

CONDITION

Initially, at the invitation level of interaction, the teacher presents the condition. *Condition* can be defined as the focus and parameters of the course of study or lessons and the sequences needed to achieve the vision implicit within the condition. In essence, the vision is presented and the students are brought into the process through discourse in small groups, interactive questioning, dialogue among each other, and review and discussion of materials presented. Within this context of condition, students need to challenge the condition as well as to determine what it means to them. Students do this through questioning and interaction. They also need to make connections. As they make connections, new ideas and new perspectives about the course of study can be made clear. It is as connections are made that the parameters and sequence of the learning experience are defined and new levels of discourse can

Condition can be defined as the focus and parameters of the course of study or lessons and the sequences needed to achieve the vision implicit within the condition.

become evident. In terms of critical thinking, this is the recognition level from which the student will begin the critical response to the lesson sequence. Creativity begins with readiness, condition, and connection. Here the need for creatively pursuing the learning experience is developed through discourse, dialogue, group work, and interactive questioning. Problem solving begins here, and this is where the problem is identified. These three, critical thinking, creativity, and problem solving, correlate closely with the taxonomy of interaction and the change process. The correlations are shown in the chart that follows.

Interaction	Change	Critical Thinking	Creativity	Problem Solving
Invitation	Condition	Recognizing	Need	Identifying
Involvement	Communication	Interacting	Visualizing	Discovering
Investigation	Consideration	Organizing	Making	Trying options
Insight	Consensus	Generalizing	Completing	Selecting solution
Implementation	Change	Utilizing	Sharing	Implementing

These are the correlations at the invitation category of interaction and the condition step in the change process. These components are a part of the interactive learning so critical to the interactional process. The teacher and the students should be cognizant of these as the learning sequence moves from category to category of interactive learning and progresses through the other steps in each of these taxonomies. Students can learn that they are involved in critical thinking, creativity, and problem solving. Students can also know what they are involved with during the steps of each of those ways of thinking and doing. The subcategories of the readiness level of motivation fit well into this first step in change. They are parameters, presentation, and preparation. The teacher roles of presenter and preparer along with the student roles as attender, questioner, and participant all relate closely to condition and readiness. These subcategories also fit well into critical thinking, creativity, and problem solving. During the teaching–learning act, both teachers and students should be aware of the multiple contexts of learning that are involved during instruction. Before we leave condition as the first step in change, it should be noted that there are other correlations with the cognitive taxonomy and the experiential taxonomy. We present them here at the beginning of this chapter as a point of reference.

Interaction	Change	Cognition	Experience	Writing
Invitation	Condition	Memory	Exposure	Define translation
Involvement	Communication	Interpretation	Participation	Describe
Investigation	Consideration	Application	Identification	Detail
Insight	Consensus	Analysis	Internalization	Discuss synthesis
Implementation	Change	Evaluation	Dissemination	Determine

Again, one can observe the correlations. It is not our purpose here to go into detail and explain each one of these, but we want them to be available for teachers who can in turn relate them to the students. See the appendices for additional information on the taxonomies of experience, critical thinking, creativity, and problem solving. As we move on to the next categories of interaction and change, teachers need to keep these in mind. These are not overt expectations or requirements, but are points of reference and designed to help teachers understand the full context and multilayered meaning of the instructional and learning process.

Aspects of Communication during the Change Process

Describing
Interpreting
Participating
Exploring
Interacting
Visualizing
Discovering

COMMUNICATION

At the communication level of change and the involvement category of interaction, the dialogue continues. Here students are exploring the course of study. They are interactively involved in finding out more about what they are expected to be a part of in the learning process. They are describing for each other and for the teacher what they are thinking and how they are reacting to this new learning sequence. They begin to reflect on and think about the process. Communication allows each student or groups of students to explore issues and to discuss them through a variety of discourse structures and group formats. Ideas, reactions, and points of view are further defined and described. The teacher as catalyst and coordinator fosters the discourse and dialogue. Students are interpreting what they are learning and can begin to categorize it. Describing, interpreting, participating, exploring, interacting, visualizing, and discovering are all part of the process at this level of motivation and change. They become cooperative participants in the process. It is an exciting time for both the teacher and the students (Steinaker 2003b). To ensure communication at the relationship level of interaction is important. The teacher role as catalyst and the student role as explorer relate strongly to communication. Likewise, the leadership role of the teacher as coordinator and the student leadership role of cooperator are closely related to communication. Through communication, coordination, and cooperation, students are moving through this level of change and this category of interactive learning. The subcategories of direction, discussion, and decision fit well with communication. It should be noted that discussion in the subcategory of relationship is not the same as discussion in the writing/organization sequence. Discussion is an interactive process that leads to decision making and helps the students move to the next category of interactive learning. The meaning of discussion in the writing sequence will be presented at the insight level of the taxonomy of interactive learning.

CONSIDERATION

Consideration is the next step in the change process. It is at this step in change that students seriously consider the whole of the course of study or learning sequence. They are able to reflect on what they have done. They can look forward to outcomes that have substance and meaning to them. Experientially, they have identified with the learning process and activities. They use all the cognitive skills but with emphasis on application, or how to apply what they have learned and what they will continue to learn. With consideration, students go into detail about what they have done and the development of the course of study. The teacher roles as moderator and resolver and the student roles as experimenter and investigator are demonstrative of the excitement, candor, and interaction involved at this step in change. It is at this step in change that rapport is truly achieved. This is a time of organizing in terms of critical thinking. At investigation, consideration of what students are doing and making needs to be an area of focus. Consideration of what they need to do and create should be done. Students have identified with the vision and in terms of problem solving they are trying out many optional solutions. Investigation and consideration reflect both a strong working relationship among the students and teachers and a serious and detailed retrospective and projective assessment of the learning experience. The teacher as moderator and resolver is a key to this kind of assessment. Students as experimenters and investigators are actually the doers and the makers and are assuming more of the leadership role in the learning experience.

Investigation and consideration reflect both a strong working relationship among the students and teachers and a serious and detailed retrospective and projective assessment of the learning experience.

Investigation and considerations are where they begin to mold their ideas and establish their own way toward completion of the learning experience.

CONSENSUS

Insight and consensus are very compatible. They are linked closely together. To arrive at group consensus and complete goals and objectives, there must be insight, respect, and a consensus of ideas, achievement, and completion. This is a time of felt achievement and gives the students and the teacher a sense of pride in what has been done. Students also recognize that they have, at the close of this step, achieved what they set out to do. In terms of cognition, they need to analyze and synthesize what they have done. Students have to be creative and complete what they set out to do. At consensus, they have internalized the vision and it has truly become theirs.

> *This is a time of felt achievement and gives the students and the teacher a sense of pride in what has been done.*

Students and teachers are measuring what they have done and are evaluating their process, their progress, and their products. Here they discuss the totality of their experience and are able to record it in a variety of ways, ranging from written summaries to completed projects, realia, and products. They can generalize about what they have done and share it with one another. They have completed what they set out to do and selected solutions for the issues and problems they had to address in the learning sequence. The teacher roles as sustainer and adviser are consummately correlated with the insight and consensus levels of interaction and change. Student roles as extender and confident creators also are concomitant to consensus and respect. The motivation subcategories of continuity, caring, and creating are a close fit with insight and consensus. This is a time of celebration and pride—and justly so, because the students and the teacher have achieved what they set out to do. It is at the consensus step and the respect category that the vision is internalized and becomes part of the student's lifestyle.

CHANGE

Change is the ultimate goal of any lesson or learning experience. Change is what instruction is all about. Change is the consummation of thinking, learning, and valuing. We need to remember that teaching is, at its core, valuing the learning that is taking place in the students. The vision is not complete until it is shared; at this step in the change process and the responsibility category of motivation, this change does occur. Cognitively, the students are evaluating what they have done in terms of dissemination. They may also use any other levels of cognition necessary for disseminating the changes that have occurred in them through the learning experience. Experientially, this is a time of dissemination, of sharing, and of homiletically suggesting changes in their audiences. In terms of the organizational/writing sequence, they make determinations about what they have done and record it in appropriate dissemination formats. The teacher as critiquor and consultant plays a vital role in the process of change and the assumption of responsibility by the students. The students as influencers and disseminators have the major responsibility in the sharing of their work and their success. In terms of evaluation, the role is determiner. Critical thinking is exhibited as students use what they have developed as well as the products they have created. In terms of creativity, it is a time of showing and sharing. Problem solving results in implementing both what students have done and what they have chosen to disseminate. Part of their dissemination is sharing and part of it is a homiletic suggestion for change within their audiences. Dissemination is a time where students are true leaders and are disseminating and sharing what they really care about. The motivational subcategories of affirmation, application, and action are clearly a strong and integral part of the dissemination process. Dissemination is a time of celebration, sharing, and looking ahead. Part of the teacher role as critiquor is to bring closure to this learning experience and prepare with the students a new and challenging learning experience. The students have been involved in a process of learning and with this experience they will be ready and willing to move to new dimensions of learning.

In this chapter we have summarized what the taxonomy is all about and have brought in other sequences and taxonomies. We feel strongly that this taxonomy of interactive learning and all the other sequences and taxonomies associated with it make a professional and practical approach to the teaching–learning act. We know that if teachers apply all or parts of it to their own planning and instructional program that the students will learn effectively and strongly. The key to learning is interactive instruction where students are coparticipants in the process and learn roles of leadership and responsibility. This work is designed to help teachers and educators come to a better understanding of the teaching–learning process and assume the professionalism they so richly deserve.

Before we leave this discussion of change, we need to revisit the concept of ethical transformative learning. We believe in change and change must be a part of the content of every learning experience. We further believe that change is needed in society. Slattery (1995) notes that "democracy is an ideal that is filled with possibilities but also an ideal that is part of the ongoing struggle for equality, freedom, and human dignity" (192). Freire (2006) puts change in the context of dialogue. He says that "only dialogue, which requires critical thinking, is also capable of generating critical thinking. Without dialogue there is no communication, and without communication there can be no true education" (92–93). Freire (2004) believed in change and that education was a key to making changes. His view and that of other critical pedagogues was that schools and teachers should be the catalyst for societal change (McLaren 2003).

We have a different view of critical pedagogy. For us, critical pedagogy is about change. It allows us to connect with people and be involved in communication. Critical pedagogy is challenging who we are and who we need to become. Critical pedagogy helps us gain the confidence we need to confront and critique the issues we face. Critical pedagogy is about understanding a concept and analyzing its characteristics. Through critical pedagogy, we can build community. Critical pedagogy helps us better comprehend our world. Critical pedagogy helps us create a curriculum that will work in the classroom. Critical pedagogy allows us to choose our own path in an accepting environment. Critical pedagogy is about comprehension within a competitive spirit that

Critical Pedagogy

Challenging who we are and who we need to become.

Helps us gain the confidence we need to confront and critique the issues we face.

About understanding a concept and analyzing its characteristics.

Aids in building our community.

Helps us better comprehend our world.

Creates a curriculum that will work in the classroom.

Allows us to choose our own path in an accepting environment.

About comprehension within a competitive spirit that lifts us to a connectedness we could not have imagined.

Helps build a class culture where all feel welcome.

Becomes most effective when there is a cooperative spirit of learning and all voices are heard.

lifts us to a connectedness we could not have imagined. Critical pedagogy helps build a class culture where all feel welcome. It can be concluded that critical pedagogy becomes most effective when there is a cooperative spirit of learning and all voices are heard. This is how we define critical pedagogy and it is in this sense that we are indeed critical pedagogues. Change comes from the interaction and the dialogue that is built within the classroom through this approach to critical pedagogy.

We believe in change. We believe that changes can and should come within an ethical context in which changes can be articulated and negotiated. Ethical transformative education takes place within a community of learning and in a process of dissemination that brings the concept of change to others in the larger community. Ethical transformative learning means that the students have a voice. Through interactive learning, that voice is clear and cogent. Students are deeply involved, through interactive learning, in the process of change. They can understand it, take control of it, and know how it has impacted them. Through interactive learning, students learn how to arrive at consensus, make decisions, listen to each other, and to make sound judgments. They learn what needs to be changed and how to change it within the context of ethical imperatives. They bring about change through intellectual and interactive learning experiences that have substance and direction. Change requires students to demonstrate courage in making ethical sense of what they are learning. Wink (2005) captures the idea of courage and change. She notes that "courage promotes change and democracy provides all learners equal access to power" (61). Voices heard and listened to in a context of ethical empowerment moves students toward fresh goals and a self-confidence to accept new challenges, finally becoming positive and productive adults.

This means that the dissemination and focus on change happens, consistent with ethics, mores, and customs of the community. With the new perspective that students share, change becomes evolutionary, not revolutionary. Change, to be positive, needs to be evolutionary. Change needs to be part of the instructional vision. This process of evolutionary change can transform students, provide them with a strong voice, and impact the community with which they have disseminated what they have learned and how it has affected their lives. Change comes through the legal processes as well as through a strong and thorough presentation of the need for change and a format for what those changes mean. The ethical dimension of proposed changes should be understood through the religions, customs, mores, and legal systems of the culture.

Students may not understand the implications of change in this way. They can learn the meaning of change and how to accomplish it through the use of the taxonomy. Teachers, however, must be aware of the meaning of ethical transformative education from the very beginning of a learning experience and work with students through the taxonomy so that they can understand and use an ethical dimension to their learning processes and to their dissemination efforts. In this way, change becomes compatible with the community and can be negotiated and become a reality. As we implement the taxonomy of interactive learning, both students and teacher need to keep this in mind. Students need to consider change as a negotiated and evolutionary process. They need to learn and understand that, in terms of change, they are part of a process and are not the sparks of negative interaction and negative confrontation.

Activities

Change, as has been shown, is a process. In these activities you will review the change process and show how it fits into the taxonomy of interactive learning. Discuss your responses to each activity in your small group, develop a report, and share it with the total group.

1. "The change process is expedited within an interactive process" (Chapter 15, p. 181). Connect the change process with the interactive learning process. Detail your responses to the statement.

2. Show how the change process relates to critical thinking, creativity, and problem solving. Provide evidence for your perspectives.

3. How does writing develop in each category of the change process?

4. What evidence of the consideration level of change would you observe in a classroom? Provide a report on your ideas of what you would see in the classroom.

5. Relate dissemination (insight) with the change process. Why is the dissemination of change important? Justify your response.

6. Ruminate about critical pedagogy. Compare our perspective on critical pedagogy with other critical pedagogues and then write your own perspective. Share your ideas and perspective with your peers.

Implementing the Taxonomy

The taxonomy of interactive learning, although new in theory and fresh in approach to thinking, teaching, and learning, has a history. When the taxonomy on interaction was first disseminated, there was an immediate interest by the staff of Corona School of which Norm Steinaker was principal. The categories of the experiential taxonomy (Steinaker and Bell 1979) correlate closely with the taxonomy of interaction. Invitation equated to exposure. Involvement and participation were similar. Investigation related to identification. Insight and internalization were closely related, as were implementation and dissemination. There was a clear and coherent relationship, but the motivational taxonomy was not the focus. The taxonomy of motivation was conceived later and augmented the experiential taxonomy.

One of the most exciting programs at Corona School was what we called the "electronic classroom." Through state and federal funding and with a one-year window of a room without students, we set up a lab school with two purposes. The purposes were to train staff in the use of technology and to provide students in all grade levels from kindergarten through sixth grade with a learning experience dependent on technology and a sequence of learning that would require the students to focus on units of work based on technology. There were no tables or desks in the classroom. It was set up with what we termed *workstations*. No books, pencils, pens, or other print materials were allowed. Every class was scheduled into the room every week. The program was planned and coordinated by Scott Turnbull, a teacher on the school staff. He had two kindergarten teachers, Gladys Duke and Diane Juaregui, as colleagues. They shared a kindergarten class half-time, but also served half-time in the electronic classroom. In addition, teachers were to be in the electronic classroom with their students.

The session with each class always began with readiness/invitation. The students gathered on the rug, whether kindergarten or sixth grade, and were introduced to the plan for their session. This exemplified the invitation category of interactive learning. Next, groups of students were assigned to workstations and organized in groups ranging from pairs and triads to cooperative groups. Each group had a task to complete during their time in the electronic classroom. Sometimes these tasks would cover several sessions, sometimes only a few sessions. Students had access to the Internet. Students from third through six grade had personal keyboards on which they took notes or wrote the information they needed, which could then be downloaded and printed. They could also take the keyboards home for homework and other regular class work. In the groups and through the cooperative learning that was the focus of the session, students and staff reacted very positively. Relationships were developed at the involvement level, rapport was established at investigation, and respect for each other was earned during the insight category. There were many moments of optimum student learning. One of the most touching moments was in the spring of the year when a kindergarten student who came to school with a home language other than English was able to write on the computer "my name is Maria," then draw a picture of herself on the computer and read it aloud to her peers. She was delighted—this was a real triumph for her.

For implementation, there were numerous avenues for dissemination. Each student from kindergarten through sixth grade developed, with the teacher, an electronic report card for parent conferences. This report card consisted of pre- and postrecorded reading passages demonstrating fluency and learning. The students had writing samples, pre- and post-mathematics tests, as well as a portfolio of projects they had completed in the electronic classroom or in their regular classroom. This was done in a barrio school where seventy-five percent of the students came to school with a home language other than English. There was a transiency rate one year of more than one hundred sixty percent. That year we had a larger turnout for parent conferences than we had ever had in the years before. Students participated with their parents because they had assumed responsibility for sharing their learning. Student scores on normative tests improved dramatically.

> *Students participated with their parents because they had assumed responsibility for sharing their learning.*

Videoconferencing equipment was purchased. This provided a new window to the world for the students and there were numerous opportunities to really learn through these. Sixth-grade students participated in videoconferences with two members of Congress. They had to review issues within the congressional district and the nation and write cogent questions for these congressional members. They were able to ask pertinent questions about issues and concerns in the area and to hear the responses of the Congress member. The students shared their views and asked questions. The Congress members responded with their positions on the subject. After the videoconferences the students, at the implementation level of the taxonomy, then disseminated information about the conferences throughout the school by the local area network within the school.

Another series of videoconferences was a course of study on British colonial and early independence art and life. This was done in cooperation with the Philadelphia Museum of Art and with a middle-school class from New York. This was a rich learning experience. Interaction occurred between our students and the docents. Students at our school also interacted with students in New York. Students learned a great deal about art in historic America. They also had to develop and share their own project relating to the course of study. Students from fourth through sixth grades participated in this project. They followed the taxonomy. They were invited, involved, investigated, and gained insight as the process developed. They also implemented their achievement through their projects and disseminating their projects with the docents, with the students in New York, with their classmates in school, and with the community. They received local coverage in the newspaper.

There were other videoconferences, uses of the Internet, and e-mail. Kindergartners were able send pictures and poetry they had developed to a kindergarten class in Texas and share what they had learned. Third-grade classes and, indeed, other classes from fourth through sixth grade had videoconferences with other classes in the United States as well as with a class in Japan. In every case, students had to prepare for these conferences. One student who had reading problems spent more than three hours preparing and writing questions for the conference with the Japanese students. His class stayed after school to participate in the conference. This was responsibility in action. We called it dissemination then, but the students saw it as a personal and group responsibility.

Another strategy that was used for middle-grade students was to develop personal objectives for themselves to achieve during the year. Students conferenced with the teacher and sometimes with the principal, then were expected to achieve their personally developed objectives. This worked very well. In the spring, school staff and students were invited to make a presentation of what we had done for the school board. The students led the presentation after an introduction by the principal and staff members. The students did an excellent job and when they were asked "Can you manage your own learning program?" they unanimously responded with "You bet we can." They had demonstrated this and had demonstrated responsibility for personal learning as well as classroom learning. They did this through a year of focus, staff development, the use of technology as a tool for learning, and a dedicated staff who worked wonderfully well with the students. They did it through readiness, relationships, rapport, respect, and responsibility.

Staff development was important. We had a strong focus on the instructional process as well as on technology. One of the staff goals for the year was to take responsibility for disseminating what had been done at the school. Together that commitment was made. That year and the next, twenty-three out of a staff of twenty-seven made presentations to other schools, to district meetings, to regional meetings, and to national conferences about what had happened at the school. It is necessary to work with staff through a focused professional development program. That focus must be on the how of teaching. In the case of this fine staff, invitation was established, and involvement through relationships was developed. This happened in grade-level teams and during staff development programs. In terms of the investigation level of interaction, rapport was established as the staff worked together on the total school program. Mutual respect was developed during insight and the staff assumed responsibility for disseminating what was done. In these ways, insight and implementation were exercised. It should also be noted that test scores for the school improved dramatically. In addition, every classroom had computers available to the students. Records of usage were kept and they were in use in the classroom most of each school day.

This school experience was the precursor to the taxonomy of interactive learning, but the context and sequence followed the categories of the taxonomy. Once the taxonomy was developed, it was implemented by Marvin Holm in all his highschool classes. He organized his teaching around the taxonomy. He developed his instructional program around the taxonomy and identified expectations for each category of the taxonomy. These were noted earlier in this work. He established activities for invitation, involvement, investigation, insight, and implementation. He also brought into the taxonomy what he called his seven *p* words: *purpose, partnership, planning, priorities, principles, passion,* and *perseverance.* His use of the taxonomy was exceptionally successful; he was asked to share the taxonomy and his use of it with all district beginning teachers. The use of the taxonomy at the highschool level has been a success and is expanding.

At the graduate level, Norm Steinaker, Lorraine Leavitt, and James Mbuva have implemented the taxonomy in their classrooms where they worked with adult graduate students. At National University they have nine lengthy sessions for each class. There are two major areas of focus for each class. One is to master the content and to demonstrate it in a variety of ways. The second is to write a review of literature paper, a research proposal, or a project. We do this through readiness and invitation in the first session through the syllabus and by outlining how the course will be organized. We also do this through group work. During the first session, groups are established. Students group themselves and work begins. In each session there is an agenda or lesson plan that is specifically followed. This is invitation. Involvement and investigation are established through the group structure. Each group has a specific content assignment that must be shared with the total class. Students must establish good rapport at the investigation level to accomplish their tasks and in the process develop insight into the content and respect for each other. Their joint responsibility for implementation is to make presentations on content areas and to report to the class what they have done in their review of literature paper, in their research proposal, or in their project. We meet each session with every group to ensure that they are on task, that they understand the process, and to clear up any questions students may have about content or their paper or project. The process of writing is outlined in *A Handbook for Writing Formal Papers* (Steinaker and Bustillos 2007). This *Handbook* is correlated with the American Psychological Association style and format and has been very helpful to students writing graduate papers.

Meeting with groups is essential and the instructor has an obligation to meet with each group to keep interest and motivation high, to help resolve any issues and problems, and to get to know the students personally. In every session groups have an increasing involvement in the content. These are outlined in the agenda or lesson plan. Students have a copy of that agenda or plan. Students do a group presentation on their area of content and an individual presentation on their paper or project. We as the instructors respond to the presentation, fill in the gaps, and ensure that the content has been effectively and efficiently presented. We usually do this interactively, but may use direct instruction with graphic organizers as needed. We seldom lecture or present material except in the early sessions of the course or when needed. There is, however, built into every session a time for us to comment on group work, to bring out additional content illustrations, and to present information that students may need in terms of the content of the course or assistance with their paper or project.

The taxonomy works at the graduate level. The taxonomy works at the high-school level. The taxonomy is effective from kindergarten through sixth grade and in middle school. The taxonomy can be used by any teacher at any grade level and in every content area. It is a sound instructional process, has been field tested at all levels, and can be used in any setting. The key to success in using the taxonomy—indeed, using any instructional format—is careful planning. A format for planning is included in the Appendix. Trusting the students is another key to teaching and learning. Students want to learn and they want to succeed. With the establishment of readiness, any teacher is on the way to further implementation of the taxonomy. Holm's (2003) outline of affective and cognitive steps and demonstrated behaviors at each category of the taxonomy helps focus the sequence of student and teacher roles as the learning sequence develops. His formulations can be used in any classroom setting. He also used the words *purpose, partnership, planning, priorities, principles, passion,* and *perseverance* to illustrate those behaviors. These words, coupled with the categories of the taxonomy, provide a strong focus for both teacher and students.

We wish you well in your use of the taxonomy. We have found that it has made us better teachers and more effective in working with our students. Likewise, students, when they take responsibility for their own learning at implementation, will come through with strong academic results and outstanding creative products. Interactive learning as a process within the instructional program is a powerful learning tool. Leadership, intrinsic to motivation, provides for both teachers and students an opportunity to lead and become leaders. Leadership fosters thinking, learning, and valuing. Teachers who value what they teach and use the interactive learning can help their students achieve much as they work together with purpose, focus, and strong motivation.

Activities

This is the final chapter in this work. The focus is on implementation of interactive learning. We showed how it has been implemented at all levels of learning. In view of the focus of this chapter, we are suggesting only one activity: Develop a plan to implement interactive learning at a grade level of your choice. Go into specific detail about your implementation plan. Document how you would use all the strands of interactive learning and how you would engage students in learning. Write an overview of a learning sequence and its implementation.

End Note

The focus of this work has been on education. We are all teachers and this has been our primary emphasis in writing this work. Our purpose in this work has been to help colleagues in the field gain a more holistic and broader view of interactive learning as well as a basis for an analytic approach to the teaching–learning and instructional process. Indeed, this is a work that can be used by individual teachers for action research in the classroom and by researchers studying teaching and learning. This, we feel, has been accomplished. We know that when teachers and personnel in the field of education review this work carefully and initiate the process in their planning and in their work with students, they will have improved their professionalism, their skill as teachers, and their ability to help students work at an optimum level of learning. Students using these processes will grow in their achievement and involvement in the process of learning. We call ourselves, and justly so, critical pedagogues and seek to help students develop their own voice and become empowered to take an active role in the dialogue of learning. We believe that students are to be valued and the curriculum must be valued both by the teacher and the students. This was our purpose and this is what we have done.

We need to make it clear, however, that interaction, motivation, leadership, and their utilization in all areas and levels of education will make a difference both to the teacher and to the students. Furthermore, each of these seventeen components of interactive learning is meant for all teachers and students. Interactive learning can be useful for all professions where training and learning are needed. Positive interaction and leadership are also important within family relationships, within group memberships, and in dimensions of social interactions. We say again that the process of interaction that we have outlined and detailed in this work is viable in any professional, occupational, or organizational context as well as being for social and personal relationships. It is our hope that people in all fields will review this work and be able to associate the theory and the practice with their own areas of concern and interaction. When they are successful in doing so, then they can more effectively motivate and lead those with whom they are associated. This is not only our hope but also our goal beyond our commitment to teachers and to our colleagues in education. Finally, we must remember that learning is valuing relationships and learning is part of the change process through which we make the intangible tangible.

References

Alfasi, D. M. 1998. "Reading for Meaning: The Efficacy of Reciprocal Teaching in Fostering Reading Comprehension in High School in Remedial Reading Classes." *American Educational Research Journal* 35(2): 309–332.

Anderson, L. W., and D. R. Kathwohl, eds. 2001. *A Taxonomy for Learning, Teaching, and Assessing: A Revision of Bloom's Taxonomy of Educational Objectives.* New York: Longman.

Ausubel, D. P. 1968. *Educational Psychology: A Cognitive View.* New York: Holt, Rinehart & Winston.

Bloom, B. S., M. B. Englehart, E. J. Furst, W. H. Hill, and D. R. Krathwohl. 1956. *Taxonomy of Educational Objectives: The Classification of Educational Goals. Handbook I: The Cognitive Domain.* New York: Longman.

Bloom, B. S., J. T. Hastings, and G. F. Madaus. 1971. *Handbook on Formative and Summative Evaluation of Student Learning.* New York: McGraw-Hill.

Brown, A., and A. Palinscar. 1989. "Guided, Cooperative Learning Individual Knowledge Acquisition." Pp. 393–451 in *Knowing, Learning, and Instruction*, ed. L. Resnick. Hillsdale, NJ: Erlbaum.

Forehand, M. 2005. "Bloom's Taxonomy: Original and Revised." In *Emerging Perspectives on Learning, Teaching and Technology*, ed. M. Orey. Retrieved September 5, 2007, from http://projects.coe.uga.edu/epltt/.

Freire, P. 2004. *Pedagogy of the Oppressed: 30th Anniversary Edition.* New York: The Continuum International Publishing Group.

Giffi, L. C., and N. H. Deane. 1974. "Questioning our Questions." *College Composition and Communication* 25(4): 284–291.

Holm, M. L. (2003). Teacher professional development workshop: Motivating students through positive motivation. (Available from Lakewood High School, 4400 Briercrest Ave. Lakewood, CA 90713).

Holm, M. L. 2003. *Teacher Professional Development Workshop: Motivating Students Through Positive Motivation.* Long Beach, CA: Long Beach Unified School District.

Hunter, M., and D. Russell. 1981. *Increasing Your Teaching Effectiveness.* Palo Alto, CA: Learning Institute.

Johnson, J. A., D. Musial, G. E. Hall, D. M. Gollnick, and V. L. Dupuis. 2008. *Foundations of American Education: Perspectives on Education in a Changing World.* 14th ed. Boston: Pearson Education.

Joyce, B., M. Weil, and E. Calhoun. 2004. *Models of Teaching.* 7th ed. Boston: Pearson Education.

Kaleidoscope. 2002. Ontario, CA: Ontario–Montclair School District.

Lessow-Hurley, J. 2005. *The Foundation of Dual Language Instruction.* 4th ed. Boston: Pearson Education.

McLaren, P. 2003. *Life in Schools: An Introduction to Critical Pedagogy in the Foundations of Education.* 4th ed. Boston: Pearson Education.

Ornstein, A. C., and F. P. Hunkins. 2004. *Curriculum: Foundations, Principles, and Issues.* 4th ed. Boston: Pearson Education.

Ovando, C. J., M. C. Combs, and V. P. Collier. 2006. *Bilingual and ESL Classrooms: Teaching Multicultural Contexts*. 4th ed. Boston: McGraw-Hill Higher Education.

Picciano, A. G. 2006. *Educational Leadership and Planning for Technology*. 4th ed. Boston: Pearson Education.

Reeves, D. B. 2002. *Making Standards Work*. 3rd ed. Denver, CO: Advanced Learning Press.

Sample, S. B. 2002. *The Contrarian's Guide to Leadership*. San Francisco: Jossey-Bass.

Sanders, N. M. 1961. *Classroom Questions What Kinds*. New York: Harper & Row.

Schwab, J. 1965. *Biological Sciences Curriculum Study: Biology Teachers' Handbook*. New York: Wiley.

Serdyuko, P., and M. Ryan. 2008. *Writing Effective Lesson Plans: A 5 Star Approach*. Boston: Pearson Education.

Slattery, P. 1995. *Curriculum Development in the Postmodern Era*. New York: Garland Publishing.

Slavin, R. E. 2006. *Educational Psychology: Theory and Practice*. Boston: Pearson Education.

Steinaker, N. W. 2002. "Experientialism." Unpublished manuscript, National University at Costa Mesa.

Steinaker, N. W. 2003a. "Bridging the Gap: Experientialism: A Philosophy for the Postmodern Era." Unpublished manuscript, National University at Costa Mesa.

Steinaker, N. W. 2003b. "The Dialectic of Discourse: A Process of Change." Unpublished manuscript, National University at Costa Mesa.

Steinaker, N. W. 2005. "Process Assessment: Toward More Efficient and Effective Teaching." Unpublished manuscript, National University at Costa Mesa.

Steinaker, N. W. 2007. *Heuristic Electronic Lesson Planner*. Trabuco Canyon, CA: Communications Ltd.

Steinaker, N. W., and M. R. Bell. 1979. *The Experiential Taxonomy: A New Approach to Teaching and Learning*. New York: Academic Press.

Steinaker, N. W., and M. R. Bell. 1981. *The Master Teacher and the Experiential Taxonomy*. Claremont, CA: Expanding Leadership Associates.

Steinaker, N. W., and T. A. Bustillos. 2007. *A Handbook for Writing Formal Papers: From Concept to Conclusion*. 3rd ed. Boston: Pearson Custom Publishing.

Whitehead, A. N. 1929. *Process and Reality: An Essay in Cosmology*. New York: Macmillan.

Wink, J. 2005. *Critical Pedagogy: Notes from the Real World*. Boston: Pearson Education.

Interactive Lesson Planner

On the next two pages you will find a format for planning ILPs. This format is easy to use. In the pages following the format, you will find directions for each category of the ILP. Be sure to read them carefully and then plan your lessons, completing each item in the format. An excellent background for lesson planning can be found in Serdyukov and Ryan (2008). They define a lesson plan as

> a model of organized learning events within a standard time period. . . .A lesson plan is a projection of a real lesson, a structure filled with concrete processes, assignments, and learning tools. . . .A lesson plan is a blueprint on which to construct a learning process. (5)

We concur with this definition. We would add only that lessons should be interactive and involve small-group activities. That is why we call our lesson plan format the "interactive lesson planner." We believe that in every lesson there should be a major interactive component. This component should consist of group work and should reflect designated activities that require student interaction and cooperative learning.

Although each lesson has an integrity, a sequence, and identified outcomes, it is usually part of a theme or a unit. We believe that each lesson is self-contained. At the same time, every lesson is linked to past lessons and to future lessons. When you plan a lesson you should ponder how it fits with what has been learned and where it fits into short- and long-term goals. Keep this in mind as you plan your lessons.

Lesson planning is continuous for teachers. It needs to be done daily. Teachers are always responsible for planning, even when students take part in the planning process. It is the teacher who makes the overall plan. Ideas and specific sequences can be planned co-operatively with students, but it is the teacher who has the final responsibility for planning. The practice of using the ILP will be helpful to you. Plan several lessons either individually or in groups. Share them with each other. You will soon learn that the process is more quickly completed and the plans have become more thorough and easier to use. Lesson planning can also be seen as an exercise in creativity. You, as teacher, are creating learning experiences that students should enjoy and during which they should be engaged.

Create your lesson plan so that you are thoroughly aware of the sequence, the activities, and the interactive group work that are included in the lesson plan. Have all the materials and resources you need immediately available to you and to the students. Before the lesson is taught, be sure to go over it and be able to envision the steps in the sequence, the nature of the activities, and the group structures you will use. Careful planning is the most important part of instructional success and student learning. Always remember that whenever you teach, you spend time planning and evaluating the outcomes of the plans so that the next lessons will even more completely engage the students.

Finally, study the ILP. Know the categories. Know what they are and what they mean. Follow the categories and fill them out one at a time. Be sure that you write the actual plan as you envision it. Know what you must do to complete the plan. After you have reviewed the plan, print the form and begin filling it out. Follow the instructions that begin on the page following the ILP. As you complete one lesson and teach that lesson, put your plans in a binder so you will have a copy for future reference. It is important that you keep a professional log of your plans. You have, with the saved series of lessons, an instructional resource that can be very important to you. After each lesson, write some reflective comment so you have a self-reflection and self-evaluation of each lesson. This, too, can be very valuable for your professional development.

Keep on planning. Make it a personal responsibility and a personal task to be completed for every instruction period and day. You are on your way to becoming a more effective professional through careful and thorough planning.

Interactive Lesson Planner (ILP)

Lesson Goal(s)

Standard:	Goal:

Lesson objective:

Lesson Data

Lesson Date:	/ /	Group Structures:	
Start/End Time:	: to :	Cognitive Level:	
Primary Programs or Mat'l		Technology:	
Primary Classroom Structure:			

Classroom Activities

Invitation	Insight
Involvement	Implementation
Investigation	Cooperative

Teaching Strategies

☐ Goal Setting	☐ Modeling-Recall	☐ Selection of Data	☐ Using Acquired Skills	☐ Reporting
☐ Data Presentation	☐ Generating/Using Data	☐ Using/Interpreting Data	☐ Observing/Sharing	☐ Presenting
☐ Demonstration	☐ Unstructured Role Playing	☐ Discussion/Interaction	☐ Role-Playing/Simulation	☐ Dramatizing
☐ Directed Observation	☐ Use of Manipulatives/Realia	☐ Hypothesizing	☐ Comparing/Contrasting	☐ Disseminating
☐ Data Exploration	☐ Ordering	☐ Testing Hypotheses	☐ Summarizing	☐ Evaluating

SDAIE Strategies

☐ Writer's Workshop   ☐ KWL   ☐ Selective Listening/Cloze   ☐ Print Rich Environment

☐ Think-Pair-Share   ☐ Interactive Writing   ☐ Shared Writing   ☐ DRTA

☐ Shared Reading   ☐ Guided Reading   ☐ Reader's Theater   ☐ Language Experience

☐ Graphic Organizers   ☐ Found Poem   ☐ Oral Patterned Responses   ☐ Clustering

Assessments

☐ Normative test   ☐ End of Chapter/Unit Test   ☐ Teacher Made Test   Other Assessments:

☐ CRT   ☐ Demonstrations   ☐ Written Response

☐ Running Records   ☐ Oral Reading Rubric   ☐ Skill Test

☐ Writing Sample   ☐ Multi-Media Presentation   ☐ Observation

Instructional Processes/Sequence

Reflective Revision Date & Time:

Completing the Interactive Lesson Planner

The ILP is a format that is straightforward and easy to complete. In the following pages, we will provide specific instructions for planning lessons as a step-by-step process. When planning the first few lessons, more time may need to be taken. After developing a few plans, your time for developing lesson plans will dramatically decrease. Let's get started.

Standard: Your state or district has identified standards in each content area and for every grade level. Select one standard that you want to use and place it in the space marked "standard."

Objective: Write an objective in the space noted as "Lesson objective." Your objective should be written so that the outcomes are clearly stated. This should be what we call a *behavioral objective*. You may have more than one objective for your lesson.

Lesson date: Fill in the date of when you plan to teach the lesson.

Start/end time: Note the time you plan to start and the time you plan to finish the lesson.

Primary programs or materials: Note the resources you will use for your lesson. Those materials could be textbooks, teacher-prepared materials, supplementary books or materials, audiovisual materials, a computer program, newspapers, magazines, or any other kind of resources you plan to use.

Primary classroom structure: Here you name the primary structure. Among the classroom structures you can use are cooperative groups, cross-age/peer tutoring, individualized partners, small-group instruction, triads, and whole-group instruction. You may use a number of structures in a lesson. We encourage you to use group structures as often as possible in your instructional program. You may use whole-group instruction, then do your group work, and then come back to the whole group for discussion and closure. If so, put both classroom structures in the space.

Group structures: A list of group formats and structures is found in chapter 8. Refer to that chapter and select the group structures that would work effectively with your lesson.

Cognitive level: The teaching strategies are keyed to the identified strategies you selected to be used in the classroom. See the section on strategies for the cognitive level you can expect from the teaching strategies you use.

Technology: Note the technologies you use in the lesson. They can be computers, overhead projector, films or CDs, calculators, television, smartboards, or any other technology you use in the lesson.

Classroom activities: Classroom activities at every level of the taxonomy are listed in chapter 7. You need to select one or more activities using ones from chapter 7 or using ones you have developed. Most activities listed should be done in groups. Use at least one activity for each category of the taxonomy you use in your lesson.

Teaching strategies: You will use a number of teaching strategies in any lesson. As you have learned, there are five teaching strategies at each category of the taxonomy. Each is keyed to the highest level of cognition you could expect to achieve using that teaching strategy. Sometimes the level of cognition could be higher than the one listed in some of the earlier teaching strategies. Teaching strategies with cognitive levels follow.

Teaching Strategy	Cognitive Level
Goal setting	Translation
Data presentation	Translation
Demonstration	Interpretation
Directed observation	Interpretation
Data exploration	Interpretation
Reflective modeling	Interpretation
Generating/using data	Interpretation
Unstructured role-playing	Application/analysis
Use of manipulatives/realia	Application/analysis
Ordering	Application/analysis
Selection of data	Application
Using/interpreting data	Application
Discussion/interaction	Application
Hypothesizing	Application/analysis
Testing hypotheses	Analysis
Using acquired skills	Analysis
Observing/sharing	Analysis
Role-playing/simulation	Synthesis
Comparing/contrasting	Synthesis
Summarizing	Analysis/synthesis
Reporting	Synthesis
Presenting	Synthesis/evaluation
Dramatizing	Synthesis/evaluation
Instructing/teaching	Evaluation
Evaluating	Evaluation

These are the correlations between the teaching strategies and the cognitive taxonomy. You will note that both the strategies and the cognitive taxonomy are sequential. If you expect to achieve synthesis or evaluation in a well-planned lesson, you will need to use one teaching strategy for each level of cognition you pass through to get to synthesis or evaluation.

SDAIE strategies: SDAIE strategies are listed on the ILP. Select the strategies you plan to use and check them off. Brief descriptors of the SDAIE strategies listed are given in appendix C.

Assessments: Possible assessment strategies are provided on the format. Check the ones you plan to use. If you use other assessment strategies, write them in the block provided for you.

Instructional processes/sequence: This is perhaps the most important category in the format. Here you write in sequence the steps you will follow in delivering your lesson. Be very specific and note each step. Add any information about the steps in terms of materials, activities, group structures, teaching strategies, SDAIE strategies, and assessments that you may need to ensure that you are totally prepared for instruction. It is important that you go into as much detail as needed for this category. When it is completed, the plan will be a summary and guide for you and your students in creating and delivering strong instruction that will result in optimal student learning. As you work closely with your students and as the learning experience deepens from invitation to involvement, investigation, insight, and implementation, be sure to include students in the planning process so that they can assist in the planning process. Even then, however, you will need a fully detailed sequence to ensure that you are ready for instruction.

Reflective revision date and time: You complete this category after the lesson has been delivered. Write in how the lesson went and put in some ideas for follow-up on the next lesson or lessons. This is your self-evaluation of the lesson and a projection of next steps.

You have now completed the ILP. You have done a professional job in preparing a strong lesson for your students. Use the additional formats provided in this text for more lesson planning.

SDAIE Strategies

There are sixteen SDAIE strategies listed on the ILP. Review these before you fill out the ILP. There are other SDAIE strategies that you can use. If you use additional strategies, indicate those in the lesson sequence. Check off the SDAIE strategies you use on the ILP. The cognitive level of each strategy is listed in parentheses at the end of the definitional statement.

Clustering/semantic mapping: Accessing prior knowledge, reviewing lessons or unit, using as a prereading (clustering) activity. Reviewing a lesson, assessing comprehension (semantic mapping) of a postreading activity. (Clustering: memory, translation; semantic mapping: interpretation, application, analysis)

Cooperative learning: Cooperative learning is a generic term for a variety of group structures. For a more complete discussion of cooperative learning, review it in chapter 8 on group structures. (All levels of cognition)

Directed reading–thinking activity (DRTA): This is a prereading activity involving an interactive dialogue about the story including predicting, examining, illustrations, reading, discussion, review of predictions. [Memory, translation, interpretation (prereading) application and analysis (postreading)]

Found poem: Using a work of literature, document an original work to help students develop and define personal meaning and interpretation. Remembering main points of the work. (All levels through analysis)

Graphic organizers: Organizing information visually. Used in all areas of the curriculum, including vocabulary developing, processing information in content areas. Visually organize and contextualize language. (All levels to analysis)

Guided reading: Introduction of reading material including new vocabulary. Discussing story and making predictions. (Memory, translation, interpretation, and application)

Interactive writing: Focusing on particular skills in writing, phonics, spelling, grammar, punctuation, editing, revising. (All levels up to and including synthesis)

KWL: Focuses students on what they are learning. Students list what they *know*, what they *want* to learn, and what they have *learned*. (Analysis primarily, but some synthesis)

Language experience approach: "If you can say it, it can be written. If it is written, it can be read." A student-centered method that uses student language as a basis for reading and writing. Can be individual writing and group writing. (All levels up to and through synthesis)

Oral patterned responses: Students respond or generate dialogue by using a particular pattern. (All levels up to application)

Print-rich environment: Meaningful text posted around the room that students use for information. (Memory, translation, interpretation, and some application)

Reader's theater: Teacher (or student) narrates story as students act out story. Choral reading and student-developed skits can also be used. (Application, analysis, and synthesis)

Role-playing: Students dramatize situations or stories. For more information, see chapter 12 of this work.

Selective listening and "cloze" procedure: Uses "cloze" procedures to check on comprehension and vocabulary. Used to reinforce writing skills at intermediate proficiency levels. Includes partnering and small-group activities. (Application and analysis)

Shared reading: Teacher and students share reading a story, poem, chant, rhyme, usually in a large-print context so that all may see. Can focus on skills such as rhyming words or use of quotations. (Memory, translation, interpretation, application)

Shared writing: All students contribute to the writing of a story. Individual students write their own sentences or words in different colored markers or chalk. (All levels up to synthesis and evaluation)

Think–pair–share: Used in all content areas. Students are to *think* about the question, *pair* up with a partner, and *share* their answers with partner and class. (All levels up to analysis)

Writer's workshop: Collaborative approach to the use of the writing process. Students spend time (after teacher discusses areas of emphasis) writing and conferencing. Teacher comments on student writing (selected students, not necessarily all) and provides encouragement. Writing is shared and teacher works with students to bring writing to publishing stage. (All levels of cognition including evaluation)

These are the SDAIE strategies that are noted on the ILP. Please know also that these SDAIE strategies are not sequential. These are brief descriptors and not a full explanation of each SDAIE strategy.

Index